P9-CWE-867

A Guide to Personal Happiness

Albert Ellis, Ph.D.
and
Irving M. Becker, Ed.D.

Foreword by Melvin Powers

Thomas & Sarah Clerkin
9416 Pendergast Rd
Phoenix, NY 13135-9501

WILSHIRE BOOK COMPANY
9731 VARIEL AVENUE
CHATSWORTH, CALIFORNIA 91311

Copyright 1982 by Institute for Rational-Emotive Therapy

Printed in the United States of America
Library of Congress Catalog Card No: 82-050850
ISBN 0-87980-395-9

Contents

About the Authors

Albert Ellis was born in Pittsburg and reared in New York City. He holds a bachelor's degree from the City College of New York and M.A. and Ph.D. degrees in clinical psychology from Columbia University. He has been chief psychologist of the New Jersey State Diagnostic Center and of the New Jersey Department of Institutions and Agencies, and is now adjunct professor of psychology at Rutgers University, the United States International University and Pittsburg State University. He has practiced psychotherapy, marriage and family therapy, and sex therapy for more than 38 years and continues this practice at the Institute for Rational-Emotive Therapy in New York City, where he also serves as executive director.

A fellow of many professional societies, Dr. Ellis has been president of the Division of Consulting Psychology of the American Psychological Association; president of the Society for the Scientific Study of Sex; vice-president of the American Academy of Psychotherapists; and a member of the board of directors of the American Association of Marriage and Family therapists, the New York Society of Clinical Psychologists, and the American Association of Sex Educators, Counselors and Therapists. Several societies have honored him with special awards, including the American Humanist Association, the Society for the Scientific Study of Sex, the Academy of Psychologists in Marital and Family Therapy, and the Division of Psychotherapy of the American Psychological Association.

Dr. Ellis has served as associate editor of many professional journals, including the *Journal of Contemporary Psychotherapy,* the *Journal of*

Individual Psychology, the *Journal of Marriage and Family Therapy,* the *Journal of Sex Research, Rational Living,* and *Cognitive and Behavior Therapy.* He has published over 550 papers in psychological, psychiatric, and sociological journals and anthologies and has authored or edited 45 books and monographs, including *Sex Without Guilt, How to Live with a "Neurotic," The Art and Science of Love, Reason and Emotion in Psychotherapy. Growth Through Reason, Humanistic Psychotherapy: The Rational-Emotive Approach, A New Guide to Rational Living, A Guide to Successful Marriage, Handbook of Rational-Emotive Therapy, Brief Psychotherapy in Medical and Health Practice, Overcoming Procrastination,* and *Rational-Emotive Therapy and Cognitive Behavior Therapy.*

Irving Becker was born and reared in Brooklyn, New York. Dr. Becker holds a bachelor's degree from Brooklyn College, a master's degree in psychology from City College of New York, and a doctorate in psychology from Temple University in Philadelphia. Dr. Becker has worked as a psychologist for the Trenton, New Jersey board of education and currently works for the New York City board of education. He is in the private practice of psychotherapy, also in New York City.

This is the first book published by Dr. Becker. He has studied rational-emotive therapy at the Institute for Rational-Emotive Therapy in New York, has written his doctoral dissertation about RET, and published an article on RET in the *Journal of Clinical Psychology.*

Foreword

It is a pleasure to present another book by the famous Dr. Albert Ellis. His *A New Guide to Rational Living* co-authored with Robert A. Harper has already sold over a million copies, and I look forward to *A Guide to Personal Happiness* doing even better.

In the first chapter of this amazing book, Drs. Ellis and Becker state that if *you* don't search for personal happiness, no one else is going to do it for you. Their approach is tough and straightforward, though cantankerously likeable all the way.

It is these authors' contention that you have a *right* to personal happiness, *and* you have a *right* to fight, if necessary (and it usually is), to get it!—even if it means putting yourself first, before significant others. (Putting self before family members has long been considered immoral by many, but not Drs. Ellis and Becker.)

Morality consists of two rules which form the basis of rational-emotive therapy (RET): (1) Be kind to yourself and (2) don't hurt others. But beyond that, the authors have a brilliant unorthodoxy in their approach to the world. They make it jarringly clear how many of our accepted beliefs and rules of life actually go against us.

For example, they state, "If I were a *rotten person,* this would mean that I have some *essence,* some *soul* that is completely rotten." However, they argue, what you call *I* is an ongoing, everchanging process. Sometimes the product is good and sometimes it is not so good. But to hold the Western orthodox view that one bad act damns you forever, does, in fact, via the self-fulfilling prophecy, do this very thing. Believing that an act makes you a rotten person destined for hell leaves little motivation for doing better in the future. There are no fatal mistakes in Ellis' and Becker's system, only the ever-present possibility of going "back to the drawing board." What a relief!

Life is viewed in problem-solving terms. Problems are conceived as caused by basic irrational beliefs that are to be actively disputed until you come up with a new effect and feel better. Then you realize that problems are simply problems, not horrors.

Ellis and Becker show how thinking in terms of what you desire or prefer rather than *must* have increases the probability of achieving your goal. Again, their approach is unorthodox. It goes against most of our conditioning that to get anything you really want, it is necessary to give it your total attention and refuse to settle for anything less. It is this refusal that leads to nervous breakdowns and deep depression. Getting rid of *musts* leads to many more alternatives than you would think!

I admire their approach not only because it works, but because they really make you sit up and re-examine *everything* you've been taught throughout your lifetime. All the lessons and platitudes that seemed so patently right at the time suddenly appear ridiculous. You find yourself hitting your head in disbelief, saying, "No wonder I never got what I wanted. How could I have been so stupid all these years?" Cheer up! We're all victims of faulty programming. It won't kill us. Obviously. It's simply time for a change.

Many behavioral exercises are given to produce this change. Nothing is shameful, embarrassing or humiliating unless you think it is. Unless you *tell yourself* that it is. If other people erroneously think you're a nut, that's *their* problem.

The authors continually and incisively illustrate how much reality is a function of the way you *decide* to react to it. Exercises are presented to help modify and control this reaction. It is a wonderfully here-and-now approach without spending years dredging up garbage from the past with which psychoanalysis concerns itself.

Action is at the core of the methods outlined in this book. Unlike other therapies that hope insight and motivation to change will do the job, RET believes this is not enough. Conditioning and background alone are not sufficient to account for maladaptive behavior. People "seem to have strong innate tendencies to think crookedly, emote inappropriately, and to behave self-sabotagingly." Definite techniques must therefore be implemented in order to effect change. You learn by doing.

I personally found the most beneficial technique to be rational-emotive *Disputing* to rip up irrational beliefs that something is *too* hard; *shouldn't*

be that hard; *can't* be *stood* and is *awful.* Gain almost always necessi-
tates pain; things are what they are; you can stand anything or you'd be
dead; and something may be displeasing but it's not intolerable. The
world can still be a nice place to live.

While many therapies work at attempting to discover why a particular
problem exists or at eliminating a piece of behavior such as smoking or
drinking, RET is remarkable in that it teaches a whole new way of living.
Not only does it help alleviate the problems brought on by past irrational
thinking, but it prepares you to enter a brighter future. Irrational beliefs
are described that lead to low frustration tolerance (LFT). LFT blocks the
way to long-range pleasure and to achieving personal happiness.

Changing a belief system to a more rational one can even serve to
prevent depression if and when an unpleasant event occurs. This is truly
the mental health model of the future. With all our research and endless
volumes of psychological theory, wouldn't you think that we would by
now know something about how to keep some of mankind's problems
from happening? *A Guide to Personal Happiness* does just that. If you're
unhappy, Ellis and Becker will tell you how to end your unhappiness. And
if you're happy you'll learn how to stay that way!

May you experience the same enthusiasm as I did in reading a book I
believe will lay the foundation for a new era in psychology. Good luck.

Melvin Powers

CHAPTER 1

Why Search for Personal Happiness?

Why search for personal happiness? Because you'd damned well better! If you don't achieve some measure of *your* desires, *your* goals, *your* values, who will get them for you?

If you put others first and greatly sacrifice yourself to help them achieve their personal goals, you do so on the assumption that they will do the same for you. But you can bet your life that they usually won't!

Many people object to this fact of life; they say it's immoral. But actually it may be immoral to put yourself last and not to strive for your personal satisfaction.

Morality, when it is sensible (which it often isn't!), consists of two basic rules that form the basis of rational-emotive therapy (RET): (1) To thine own self be true; or be kind to yourself. (2) Do not commit any deed that needlessly, definitely, and deliberately harms others—because you, in being true to yourself, normally live in a social group or community that may not continue to exist, or to exist in the manner in which you would prefer, if you do harm to others. Unless, of course, you choose to live as a hermit!

Social interest, in other words, fuses with self-interest. No one asks you whether you want to be brought into this world; but once you are here, and once you realize that you have a choice of staying alive or letting yourself die, you almost always decide to remain alive for a reasonably long time. For biological as well as social reasons, you *choose* life over death; and you *choose* to try to be reasonably happy and relatively free from severe pain or frustration. This second choice—to make yourself as happy as is feasible—is almost a direct corollary of your first choice: to stay alive. For if you choose to live and be miserable, life will hardly seem worth living and you will probably tend to neglect and ultimately to kill yourself.

Because humans are gregarious or social animals, you tend to find happiness when you are relating, both generally and intimately, to others; and although you have the ability to be happy when you are completely alone, you would rarely choose to be for any considerable length of time. You naturally *enjoy* talking to, being with, encountering, concerning yourself about, affecting, and having love-sex relations with other humans. Why? Largely because that is your nature: your innate tendency to commune and share.

Once you decide to cater to your gregarious desires, you subscribe to a social contract which we call morality or responsibility to others, or rule number two. For group life entails some restrictions and rules of conduct. As a hermit, you can fearlessly make all the noise you want or defecate wherever you wish. But not as a member of a family, a clan, or a community! Nor, when you decide to live with others, are you perfectly free to grab all the food you want, appropriate all the available land, steal anything in sight, or physically harm or kill your intimates and associates—at least nor for very long!

These moral rules are especially desirable in today's complicated, socially and economically interdependent world. In the past, people could live in a cave with just a few other people. A small group could take care of itself even if it remained fairly isolated from and hostile to the rest of the world. However, in today's technological society we rarely grow our own food or spin our own yarn. Instead we are dependent on other workers and on a well-established division of labor. And we frequently live in sizable towns or cities, where we have to hobnob with literally hundreds of people in the neighborhood, at school, at work, and in our social lives.

Social morality, therefore, becomes more important almost every day; and unless we heed its rules, the human race may well kill itself off. Individuality and personal freedom have come to be thought of as noble virtues in the past few decades. But if we neglect to place these virtues squarely within a social context, they may actually stultify and maim our happy—or even continued—living.

Quite a dilemna, isn't it? On the one hand, we'd better be socially conscious, have sincere interest in other humans and make our own lives better thereby. On the other hand, we'd damned well better put ourselves first. A nice balance—if we can achieve it!

Why, again, put your personal happiness in the forefront? For several reasons:

1. On the surface, it might seem more sensible to put others—especially others you love—first, and yourself a close second. For wouldn't you help create a better, more loving, finer society if you lovingly sacrificed yourself for others thereby insuring that they will treat you equally well? Wouldn't you get better results if you loved others first, practically guaranteeing that they would love you back?

No, you wouldn't unless you happen to live as exceptionally few of us do—among a group of angels. For angels, in all probability, would be the kind of creatures who, when you loved and made sacrifices for them, would invariably return love with love and kindness with kindness. In such an angelic society, sacrificial morality would surely beget return sacrificing.

Angels, alas, are exceptionally scarce in our present-day world. Consequently, what would almost certainly happen if you did decide to be self-sacrificing, expecting to reap moral rewards from others as a result? Some of these others would love you and sacrifice themselves for your interests—but many more would not. A good many of the people to whom you were most considerate, in fact, and for whom you went out of your way and put yourself second, would quite probably be nasty, knife you in the back, and exploit your kindness in various nefarious ways. For, like it or not, many people are relatively exploitative and would delight in taking advantage of you. Many more are quite moral, but because of their stupidity, ignorance, or emotional disturbance cannot be relied upon to behave morally to you or to the rest of humanity.

Therefore, when you make self-sacrificing the first law of morality and of your personal conduct, you assume that those to whom you sacrifice your own interests will almost invariably sacrifice theirs for you. Quite an assumption!—with little or no evidence to confirm it.

2. Self-sacrificing or putting yourself second actually often encourages others to keep exploiting you and to look upon you as something of a ninny. Instead of leading to fair, transactional morality among humans, it tends to encourage dependence, emotional disturbance, and an increase in people's inhumanity to people.

3. Putting yourself second usually stems, as we shall see in some detail later, from having a dire need for others' approval and of needing (or thinking you need) their love so badly that you are practically willing to

sell your soul to get it. Out of dire need for love, you make yourself into a patsy, refuse to assert your own thoughts and feelings—and then wind up hating yourself for being that way, as well as hating the people who "forced" you to act in this manner.

4. Planning your personal happiness is an enormous, challenging task that pits you against some of the most powerful forces in the universe. For as Voltaire sagely noted, this is *not* the best of all possible worlds. Life is filled with a constant series of muddles and puddles. It is not, we teach in rational-emotive therapy (RET), horrible or awful; but it frequently is a royal pain in the ass. And if you actively seek happiness, you mean that you will fully accept the challenge of this difficult existence and will be utterly determined to make it less difficult for you personally—and, in fact, damned exciting and enjoyable.

Not that you run the universe. But if your basic philosophy is that of running your own life as well as you can and being happy in spite of innumerable troubles that are likely to beset you, you then have an excellent chance of being spirited and joyful even in this reasonably crummy world. What is more, you also have a much better chance of being able to make some significant contribution toward improving that world.

5. By striving for personal happiness, you will almost inevitably become a person with whom others can more lovingly and beneficially relate. When you really go after what you want in life and are determined to get something good going for yourself (and possibly for others), you have something special and unique to offer others—particularly those who would share love with you. Your very self-interested activity gives them some resources to sink their teeth into: either in your doings, in your work, or in your substantive self. The more you offer yourself, the more you will have to offer others; and, paradoxically, by enhancing your own life you can often help these others and make the world, or at least your immediate environs, a better place in which to live.

6. Working for your personal goals and ideals is open and honest. Many of those who ostensibly wear hair shirts and sacrifice themselves for others are actually intent on gaining the Kingdom of Heaven—for, of course, themselves! Many of those who humble themselves and devote themselves to helping the sick, the tired, and the poor, are firmly hooked on becoming holier than thou, thereby achieving their *own* nobility. Behind virtually every goal or desire that we can imagine, no matter how selfless and sacrificing it seems to be, there is usually a hidden agenda: that of quite selfishly pleasing the goal-maker. Perhaps some incredible

saint somewhere or sometime actually worked way beyond the call of duty *only* for others and for no personal satisfaction whatever. Perhaps! But if you are a fallible human instead of an infallible saint, it seems far more honest to acknowledge your goal of self-interest than to "nobly" deny it. If, as Carl Rogers pointed out, emotional health largely consists of openness, honesty, and self-congruence, it would seem much healthier for you to follow the uncorrupted path of acknowledging yourself first than the one of simulated self-sacrifice.

For reasons such as these, consider vying for personal happiness. Not *against* other people. Not *against* all institutions, indiscriminately. Not in order to show that you are a *better person* than other humans nor that you deserve to sit on the right hand side of God, while you know perfectly well where they deserve to sit! Not even, in an egotistical way, to prove that you *can* best all others at the happiness game. No; your main purpose had better be the same purpose for which you tend to do practically everything else in life: to live longer and more pleasurably.

Are there disadvantages to striving for personal happiness? Indeed there are. Virtually everything you do has disadvantages. If you really look out for yourself, certain unfortunate things will probably happen. Other people, for example, will often conclude that you're cold and heartless—even if you aren't. They will sometimes be afraid of you, or so dependent on your strength that they will try to exploit you. Or they may worship you so much that they become pains in the neck.

Satisfying yourself also takes time and trouble: for planning and scheming about what you really want and how you can go about getting it; for being assertive and resisting the demands of others; for experimenting with things that you later discover you don't truly want; for consciously, albeit efficiently, striving for the long-range pleasures of tomorrow as well as the short-range satisfactions of today. You rarely get something for nothing, and self-interest has its hassles and limitations. But it's usually worth it!

Let us briefly outline the main blocks to seeking personal happiness as a preview to what you will discover in the discussions in this volume. The main blocks to almost all kinds of happiness and emotional health are various forms of needs, demands, commands, insistances, absolutes— or what in rational-emotive therapy we call *must*urbation. This was discovered thousands of years ago by Western philosophers such as Zeno, Epictetus, Marcus Aurelius, and other Stoics, and by Eastern thinkers such as Gautama Buddha. Modern philosophers, including Baruch Spinoza, John Dewey, and Bertrand Russell, rediscovered this ancient teaching; as did some of the pioneering psychotherapists of this century. No, not Sigmund Freud—who got sidetracked into people's early-childhood history, their lusting after their parents, and their deeply unconscious hatreds and guilts (none of which seems to have much to do with causing their emotional upsets), but therapists like Alfred Adler, Paul Dubois, Alexander Herzberg, and George Kelly, who much more clearly realized what the philosophic causes of disturbance really were, began to develop practical means of dealing with emotional difficulties.

I (I.B.) began to see how these blocks—my *shoulds, oughts,* and *musts*—stood in the way of my getting along academically and of my love life when I read about rational-emotive therapy a number of years ago and began to use some of its principles on myself. Within several months of applying aspects of its antimusturbational and antiawfulizing philosophy, I lost the greatest part of my academic and social anxiety and began to do much better in both these important areas of my life.

I (A.E.) believed in the Freudian view of emotional disturbance and cure and consequently went through psychoanalysis myself, was supervised in this method by a training analyst of one of the leading schools, and practiced classical analysis and psychoanalytically oriented psychotherapy for several years before I realized that it was exceptionally inefficient and was helping my clients to only a small degree. Having something of a gene for efficiency, and also having a background in philosophy (which had been one of my main interests since my college days), I sought for nonpsychoanalytic methods of helping people overcome their problems and soon observed that just about all so-called emotional disturbances were closely linked to *irrational ideas,* and that if I could help people clearly see and strongly dispute these self-defeating notions, they could successfully overcome their disturbances.

In experimenting with these new conceptions of neurotic behavior and exploring techniques for helping my clients overcome their feelings of anxiety, depression, hostility, and worthlessness, I developed the system of rational-emotive therapy (RET) or cognitive-behavior therapy (CBT), which has now become exceptionally popular. But it was hardly so in the beginning! In the 1950's, when I created RET, practically all the other therapists screamed and yelled about my arrogance—including the Freudians, Jungians, Rogerians, and classical behaviorists. How could I have the arrogance, the consummate gall, they asked, to claim that emotional disorders are largely problems of crooked thinking, and that by changing one's thinking, one can overcome serious neurotic states? And how could I have the audacity to confront people directly with their crazy thoughts, to work intensively and forcefully with their feelings, and to give them homework assignments that would help them practice new ways of behaving and feeling?

Well, I could! Against the opposition of the vast majority of schools of therapy, I continued experimenting and developing RET. At first I had only a handful of followers. Then the encounter movement came along and greatly added to the number of therapists who used *active* exercises and urged people to express their real feelings, no matter how uncomfortable they felt about doing so—which is one of the emotive techniques of RET. Finally, the behavior-therapy got well under way and, in a revolutionary manner, began to become the cognitive-behavior movement—with RET (or cognitive restructuring) at its very core. Many outstanding people in psychology and psychiatry—such as Drs. Aaron T. Beck, Gerald Davison, Marvin Goldfried, Arnold Lazarus, Richard Lazarus, Cyril Franks, Michael Mahoney, and Donald Meichanbaum—have joined the cognitive-behavior-therapy bandwagon; and this kind of therapy now seems to be the hottest in town.

The public has recently been almost overwhelmed with literature, talks, courses, and workshops that, whether the authors and speakers acknowledge it or not, are clearly RET-oriented. A host of popular books have appeared which frankly and honestly espouse rational-emotive therapy. Ironically enough, however, some of the writings that clearly derive from RET but that give little or no acknowledgement to it are among today's most influential publications, including works by Wayne Dyer, William Glasser, Haim Ginott, Ken Keyes, Werner Erhard, and Manuel Smith.

We find it exceptionally gratifying that RET has become one of the most influential therapies of the twentieth century and that it specializes in a self-help approach. For one of its outstanding tenets is that people create their own basic emotional difficulties and are not merely conditioned or made the way they are by outside influences. Because they largely invent self-defeating ideas and behaviors, and because they go through an endless process of *self*-conditioning to make self-sabotaging thoughts and feelings semiautomatic and easily maintained, they also have the power to significantly change themselves.

As RET has pointed out for a good many years, with just about any thought that you choose to believe and to follow, you can also *dis*believe and *refuse* to follow. If the psychoanalysts were right and your mother and father made you what you are today, you might well have relatively little ability to change yourself for the better. Fortunately, they are largely wrong; and because *you* mainly created your own thoughts and feelings, *you* have considerable power to change them or, as Carl Jung, Abe Maslow, and others have said, to actualize yourself and to grow and develop emotionally. RET, in the course of individual and group psychotherapy, tries to show you exactly how to do so. Being an educational as well as a therapeutic method, it tries to do this in many different ways: for example, by classroom teaching (to youngsters as well as adults), workshops, lectures, pamphlets, books, articles, audio recordings, and TV and film presentations. For, although this may seem a bit grandiose, the goal of rational-emotive training is to help all humans, not merely those who are seriously disturbed and who acknowledge that they could use specialized psychotherapy. Even more important than its aim of helping people who are already disturbed is its preventive aspect: that of showing men, women, and children how to *ward off* serious emotional problems rather than trying to cure them after they have arisen.

In this book, we shall attempt to show you the main sources of everyday emotional and behavioral difficulties that you and your friends and associates are likely to encounter; to demonstrate precisely how you and they creatively fabricate or "invent" most of these problems; and, in particular, to indicate precisely what you can do to stave them off before they arise or to minimize (and preferably eliminate) them after you feel plagued with them. Not that we expect to succeed completely in this regard. As noted in the most popular of all the RET self-help books, *A New Guide to Rational Living*—which sells over 100,000 copies a year since I wrote the first edition in 1961 with Dr. Robert A. Harper,—"To those who want to get specific personal help from this book, let us again sound a warning: No book, including this one, can cure all your emotional problems. Since you always have something unique about your individual makeup and situation, a book cannot substitute for personalized counseling. A good book, however, may nicely supplement or reinforce therapy. And it can encourage highly beneficial self-analysis."

Are you skeptical of this claim: Good. Skepticism, or the testing of its own hypotheses by calling for confirmed and repeatable results, is one of the main tenets of rational-emotive therapy. Although the scientific method is not perfect, it still stands as the best way we have of verifying whether a given procedure works. If RET—or any other system of therapy—cannot be shown to be highly effective and at least as good as other techniques of personality change, who needs it?

The same applies to your efforts to use the self-help materials that you will find in these pages. By all means try them—skeptically and experimentally. Don't take them on our say-so, just because we are respectable clinicians and researchers. As humans, we have our own prejudices. Try these methods. See how they work for you and for others with whom you use them. Then decide whether, and under what conditions, you want to keep using them. All we ask is: give them a try. We think that they will work for you, as they have helped literally thousands of our past clients and perhaps millions of our (and other RET authors') readers.

CHAPTER 2

The ABC's of Personal Happiness

Whenever we give a public talk or workshop on rational emotive therapy (RET), we find that the best way to explain it is to demonstrate to our audience that we actually do what we say we do. Telling people what we do in RET is not quite enough; unless they see it with their own eyes, they are not likely to be impressed. But with the dramatic impact of live demonstrations, the real guts of the RET method is much more likely to get across to the members of the audience.

This is what we are also going to try to do, in a somewhat different way, in this book. We will do what is attempted in a few popular books on therapy: present excerpts from actual psychotherapy sessions with real clients. These clients came to see us for various problems with which they were seriously concerned, especially problems of anxiety, depression, hostility, and self-hatred. They didn't merely *think* they had emotional difficulties; they really had them! And, using RET in a highly typical manner, we were able to help most of them quickly—in 10 or 20 minutes—zero in on their disturbed feelings and the basic philosophies that lay behind and created these feelings. This is a specialty of RET.

Ten or 20 minutes? If you are skeptical, come to some of the famous Friday night workshops in Problems of Everyday Living, which I (A.E.) give at 8:30 *P.M.* at the Institute for Rational-Emotive Therapy in New York City almost every week of the year. No matter who volunteers to raise a problem, and no matter how little I originally know about these people (which is, usually, just about nothing at all, since I have never seen most of them before), I soon get down to their major emotional upsets and start showing them what they can do to change.

Since many of these sessions are tape-recorded, and many private RET therapy sessions are also taped, we thought it would be a good idea to utilize transcripts of these recordings in the second part of this book to show you how you can employ rational-emotive procedures to tackle many of your own basic emotional problems. These transcripts are presented to help you see for yourself some of the rational-emotive techniques that we use with real-life people who have down-to-earth problems. Seeing this, and seeing exactly what clients were shown to do about the things that bothered them—or, rather, about what they were doing to make themselves upset about these things—you will be able to see some of your own self-defeating behavior more clearly and to know what to do to change it.

Not that all people are the same. But for this book we have deliberately selected some of the most common personality problems. Although probably no one suffers from all of these problems, most of us have at least several of them. And when we do, we often have little understanding of what truly caused our suffering and what remedies may best relieve it.

As a prelude to the applications of RET, let us outline some of the basic principles of rational-emotive therapy.

Most people delude themselves into thinking that they are affected by external events, especially pressures and circumstances from early childhood. To some extent, they are—because they are born *affectable.* Whenever *Activating Events* or *Activating Experiences* occur in their lives—at point A—they almost immediately react at point C—and thereby have emotional and behavioral *Consequences.* They think, wrongly, that what happens to them at A causes or creates their reactions at C; but they forget that they have innate and acquired affectability. And although this affectability—which is perhaps the largest part of the "human condition"—is quite complex, and consists of many physical tendencies, it particulary includes B—people's *Belief Systems* (what they tell themselves about what happens to them at A.)

All this, as we show in the therapy sessions, is easily provable. For if exactly the same kind of event happens to a hundred Joe Smiths at point A, and if all the Joe Smiths to whom this Activating Event happens are approximately of the same age, intelligence, social class, and station, they all tend to respond differently at point C, the emotional and behavioral Consequences of the event at A. Thus, if a hundred Joe Smiths all lose $10,000 in the stock market, a few of them would feel happy or relieved ("Good! That will teach me to stop gambling in that foolish manner again!"). Some would feel rather indifferent ("Well, I really have enough money anyway, and I don't need the amount I lost."). Most would feel unusually sad and regretful ("That was really foolish of me taking that chance! I certainly won't do such a stupid thing again!"). And a number would feel depressed and suicidal ("I must never do a stupid thing like gambling in the stock market! How awful that I did that! I am an utter idiot, and I'll never be able to forgive myself for being so irresponsible!"). It is not, then, what has happened to him that makes Joe Smith feel relieved, indifferent, sorry, or depressed—it is the way he *views* this act; his *beliefs* about it.

In RET, therefore, we assume that whenever people are really disturbed about anything, it is not the thing itself (A) which directly causes or creates their feelings of anxiety, depression, or worthlessness at C, their emotional Consequence. Rather, it is mainly (though not exclusively) their Belief System (B) *about* what is happening, has happened, or might happen at A. A, their Activating Experience, significantly *contributes* to C; but usually the more direct and important contribution comes from B.

For purposes of psychotherapy or of personality change, B tends to be more changeable than A. For A, Activating Events, are frequently out of our control. Thus, at A you may be robbed, suddenly be stricken with a heart attack, get rejected by someone you care for, or be treated quite unfairly. Unpleasantries may occur no matter *how* you behave; and some are unchangeable.

Actually, you have considerable control over the Activating Events (A) of your life; especially if you control your Beliefs (B) about them and thereby refuse to upset yourself. For even when these A's are temporarily beyond your regulation, you can frequently do something about them later and prevent them from happening again. Thus, if you are suddenly stricken with a heart attack, you can make fairly sure that you get good medical attention, do whatever you can to help your recovery, and change your eating and exercise habits to prevent a recurrence of an attack. If someone rejects you today, by refusing to desolate yourself about this Activating Event, you may get this person to care for you later—or you may be able to win the love of an equivalent person.

We emphasize in RET that even when an Activating Event (A) is uncontrollable, you can almost always influence and control B, your Belief System, that directly leads to your emotional and behavioral Consequence (C). And if you fully acknowledge this and work like hell to understand B and how you can change it for more rational and appropriate Beliefs, you practically never have to upset yourself seriously about *anything*.

RET teaches that you normally have two quite different kinds of Bs: (1) rational (rBs) which help you experience *appropriate* Consequences, and irrational Beliefs (iBs), which help you experience *inappropriate* Consequences. Beliefs are rational or irrational, sensible or foolish, in relation to your basic desires. Rational Beliefs help you get these desires fulfilled, while irrational Beliefs stop you from fulfilling your wishes.

As Alfred Adler was one of the first psychotherapists to point out, humans invariably seem to run their lives in accordance with basic goals, wishes, values, or desires. When you have a wish or desire that is thwarted, it is rational or sensible to Believe (at point B), "I don't like this! I wish it weren't so! How annoying that this has happened!" For this kind of Belief helps you get more of what you want and less of what you don't want. Thus, if you desire good health and you experience a serious heart attack, if you have the Belief, "Who cares if I have a heart attack? I really don't mind having it," this Belief will hardly help you attain your goal or purpose of remaining in good health.

In RET, then, rational Beliefs are simply those views, philosophies, and evaluations of what is happening to you at A (Activating Experiences) that help you assess whether your basic desires (goals or purposes) are being fulfilled. They also help you achieve greater or better fulfillment of your desires in the future. We do not, in RET, have any absolutistic or dogmatic view of rationality. To think rationally or sensibly merely means to evaluate what is going on in your life in such a way as to increase your happiness and decrease your unhappiness, or to get more of what you want and less of what you don't want.

The same goes for your feelings or emotions. Unlike many other schools of therapy, RET clearly distinguishes between appropriate and inappropriate emotions. You approach an A (Activating Experience) with the basic goal or purpose of remaining in good health. At A, you actually have a sudden serious heart attack. At B, you have a rational Belief (rB), "I don't like this! I wish it weren't so! How annoying that this has happened!" Then you immediately have a feeling at C, your emotional Consequence. If you actually *only* stayed with the rational Belief, your feeling would be one of strong sorrow, regret, annoyance, and displeasure. And we would call this an appropriate emotion or appropriate Consequence.

Why are feelings of annoyance and displeasure at having a heart attack appropriate? Because feelings, including negative feelings, motivate us. Without feelings, we would not *want* to live in the first place, nor to live happily in the second place. Pleasant feelings, such as joy, love, and satisfaction, inform us that we are having "good" experiences and that we had better seek for more of the same. Unpleasant feelings, such as annoyance and displeasure at having a heart attack, inform us that we are not really getting what we want, that something is interfering with our basic goals and purposes, and that we had better change our ways or change what is going on in the world, in order to more successfully achieve these goals. Both pleasant and unpleasant emotions, therefore, can abet our achieving ends that we view as important. A feeling of annoyance and displeasure at having a heart attack can quite appropriately induce us to get proper medical attention or to try to take precautions in the future. If we were happy about having the coronary problem or calm or indifferent about it, our emotions would conflict with our basic goal of having good health; hence, this feeling would be quite inappropriate. Very frequently, therefore, the most appropriate feeling we can have is one of intense or even extreme annoyance and irritation. A sensible or happiness-producing sequence of events, therefore, when we are confronted with an unpleasant or obnoxious Activating Event (A), may be outlined as follows:

(G) Goal or purposes: In general, to live happily; in particular, to win the love and approval of someone for whom you care.

(A) Activating Experience: the person for whom you care thinks that you are doing poorly in some important respects and consequently rejects you and refuses to continue to be intimate with you.

(rB) rational Belief: "I don't like being rejected like this! How unfortunate! I wish that this person I care for would act differently and accept me."

(aC) appropriate Consequence: a feeling of strong sorrow and regret, as well as frustration and annoyance; temporary withdrawal or holding back from trying to relate intimately with the rejecting person, and subsequent attempt to win the approval of this person again; or, if this seems impossible, to try to relate to another person whom you also find desirable.

This is a sensible or healthy sequence of events since, as a human, you will continually want something strongly, get frustrated, conclude that this is bad—and then presumably take steps to correct the situation and become less frustrated or more fulfilled in the future. Consequently, because this process helps you achieve your goals and purposes, we call it a rational process; and we also call the emotions of sorrow, loss, frustration, annoyance, and regret that you experience in the course of this process appropriate emotions.

When an emotionally disturbing sequence of events occurs—one that leads to needless (rather than appropriate) unhappiness—it usually takes place in the following manner:

(G) Goal or purpose: in general, to live happily; and, in particular, to win the love and approval of someone for whom you care.

(A) Activating Experience: the person for whom you care thinks you are doing poorly in some respects and consequently rejects you and refuses to continue to be intimate with you.

(iB) irrational Belief: "I *must* not be rejected by anyone for whom I really care! How awful that this has occurred! I *can't stand* it when I do poorly at something and therefore get rejected! I am a *rotten person* for acting so poorly and getting rejected!"

(iC) inappropriate Consequence: a feeling of anxiety and depression; a shocked withdrawal from trying to relate intimately with the rejecting person; or a desperate attempt to win back this person's approval; a subsequent tendency to feel anxious about and to withdraw from situations where you might become intimate again with another person who then might reject you.

In this sequence of events, you go much further than in the previous sequence of having rational beliefs. You first think rationally but you then rush on to a set of highly irrational Beliefs and these, according to RET theory, largely produce your inappropriate Consequences or disturbances.

Why are your Beliefs in the second sequence irrational? Because they will not get you what you want but will instead hinder you. For although they may be motivating, they almost always motivate you to feel exceptionally upset, to act desperately, to withdraw from trying to succeed at getting what you want in the future, and to become preoccupied with damning yourself rather than with trying to go after your basic goals again in an attempt to achieve them.

In addition, these self-defeating beliefs just do not make sense in terms of the way the world is and what kind of person you are. They are not based on factual evidence; they are overgeneralizations; they are absolutistic; they are one-sided and dogmatic; and there is no accurate way of validating them, no matter how convinced you are of their "truth."

Another way of putting this is to say that we have discovered, after using RET with thousands of clients during the last quarter of a century, that when people have irrational Beliefs that lead to inappropriate Consequences or feelings of emotional disturbance, these Beliefs stem from grandiose, unrealistic *shoulds, oughts,* and *musts.* Humans start with desires and preferences and at first *wish* to obtain their goals and purposes. But they very frequently abandon their wishes in favor of absolutistic demands, commands, and insistences; and when they do, they almost always become what we call emotionally disturbed.

Karen Horney, a noted psychotherapist, was one of the first to note this. She indicated that we tend to rule ourselves by the *tyranny of the shoulds.* With these *shoulds* we build ideal images—of the way we *should* be, others *should* be, and the world *should* be. And when we, others, or the universe are not the way we supposedly *should* be, our idealized images collapse, and we then feel and behave in a highly disturbed manner. Horney was right about our inventing *shoulds* and idealized images. But since she was committed to the psychoanalytic method and believed that insight into people's personalities is enough to change them, she never figured out exactly what to do about the human tendency to *should* on itself. Rational-emotive therapy, going far deeper than psychoanalysis and being much more concerned with personality *change* than with mere insight, tries to give answers she never arrived at.

After exploring human demands and commands for many years and discovering how they create emotional disturbance, RET views the *shoulds* as *absolutistic musts.*

Absolutistic *shoulds* can get you into real emotional difficulty. Suppose you say to yourself, for example, "I *should* marry in order to be happy." What you mean is not only that it may be preferable for you to marry and that you will in all probability be happier married than unmarried, but you may also mean, "No matter what, I *must* get married. If I don't marry, I can't be happy *at all! What* is more, if I don't marry it will probably be because I am a crummy person who isn't able to marry anybody decent. And that is *terrible!"* If this is what you mean by your *should,* you are really in trouble!

When, in other words, your *shoulds* and *oughts* are unconditional and absolutistic, you are really saying that *under all conditions,* you *should* do this or not do that; that the world will practically come to an end if you don't do what you supposedly *should;* that you will then be able to have no joy whatever in life and may even die; and that your inability to carry out what you absolutely *should* makes you a thoroughly rotten, worthless individual. This kind of unconditional *should* is really a thoroughgoing, 100 percent *must,* or a *got to, have to, need to.* And, according to the theory and practice of RET, this type of *must*urbation is the root of practically all emotional evil.

The RET rule, therefore, is this: Whenever you are emotionally disturbed—that is, feel strongly anxious, depressed, enraged, or self-hating—you can almost invariably find a *should, ought,* or *must* that lies behind, and directly and forcefully creates your disturbance.

CHAPTER 3

The Main Blocks to Personal Happiness

Although literally millions of people are rather severely disturbed—and in some ways and to some degree all humans seem to be—according to RET, there are three main kinds of emotional disturbance, and all three of them are based on implicit or explicit absolutistic *musts* or irrational ideas. *Irrational idea number one* is: "I *must* do well (or perfectly well!) in important tasks I choose to perform and *must* win the approval or love of the people whom I choose to make important to me." This *must*urbatory philosophy, which we tend to bring to almost every situation or Activating Experience has three main derivatives: (a) "Isn't it *awful* when I don't do what I *must* do to perform well and win approval!" (b) "I *can't* stand it if I don't do what I *must do* to perform well and win significant others' approval!" (c) "I am a *worthless individual,* a *rotten person* if I don't do what I *must* do to perform well and win others' approval!"

This profound, absolutistic *must* and its three major derivatives almost inevitably result in deep-seated feelings of anxiety, hypertension, and obsessive-compulsive thoughts and actions. Thinking that you may not function properly when you believe that you absolutely *must* leads to profound feelings of depression, despair, shame, guilt, and self-hatred after you have presumably functioned poorly as you think you absolutely *must* not.

The second *must*urbatory idea that causes severe emotional problems—or what we call *irrational idea number two*—is: "You (that is,

27

other people with whom I am in contact) *must* treat me considerately and kindly, in precisely the way I want you to treat me; and if you don't, society and the universe should severely blame, damn, and punish you for your inconsiderateness or injustice to me." The three major corollaries or derivatives of this irrational belief are: (a) "It is *horrible* if you treat me less than considerately and kindly, as you *must* not do!" (b) "I *can't bear* your treating me badly or unfairly, as you absolutely *must* not!" (c) "You are an utterly *bad person* for treating me less considerately and kindly than you *must* treat me."

Irrational idea number two almost always results in your feeling angry, resentful, enraged, furious, overrebellious, vindictive, or homicidal; and it also may lead to many kinds of anger-inspired actions, such as assaults, fights, feuds, violence, homicide, and genocide.

Irrational idea number three is: "The conditions under which I live *must* be arranged so that I get practically everything I want comfortably, quickly, and easily and absolutely must *not* exist so that my life is filled with hassles." The three subsidiary irrational Beliefs (iBs) that stem from this are: (a) "It is *terrible* if conditions are arranged so that I am seriously deprived or get distinctly less than what I want or have to work too hard and too long to get my desires fulfilled!" (b) "I can't *tolerate* life when it asks more of me than I want to give! It's then not only hard, but *too* hard; and it *should* not be that hard!" (c) "My life is utterly miserable when things go wrong and I don't get exactly what I want when I want it! It's so unbearable that it is not really worth living, and I might just as well kill myself to avoid its horrible circumstances!"

Irrational idea number three almost inevitably results in feelings of self-pity, resentment, depression, apathy, and alienation; and in terms of behavior it tends to lead to low frustration tolerance, inertia, procrastination, laziness, avoidance of responsibility, and withdrawal.

Each of these main irrationalities has a good many corollaries or subheadings. For example, under the heading of perfectionism, the need for achievement, and the need for love *(irrational idea number one)* you may demand that you *must* have few external pressures so that you can have a guarantee that you will do well; that you have *got* to depend on others and to bow down to authorities; and that you *should* understand the fundamental nature or secret of the universe in order to live happily in it.

Under the heading of *irrational idea number two*—that others *must* treat you considerately and kindly—you may demand that others *must* not be incompetent or stupid and thereby interfere with your happiness.

Under the heading of *irrational idea number three*—that the conditions of your life have *got* to be comfortable and easy—you may also devoutly believe that you *have* to be continually preoccupied or obsessed with any dangers that exist; that you *cannot* keep disciplining yourself, because it's *too* hard to do so; that you *must* suffer endlessly and totally because you are handicapped in certain ways; that correct and perfect solutions to your problems *ought* to exist; that you *should not* suffer from the discomforts of anxiety, depression, and other forms of emotional disturbances; and that you *have* to have utter certainty that the world *must* be fair so that you get everything you absolutely *deserve*.

Is *must*urbation, then, the essence of all disturbance? No, probably not. Some disturbances are not entirely emotional, such as epilepsy, retardation, schizophrenia, and manic-depressive states. But what we generally label emotional difficulties—feelings of severe anxiety, depression, worthlessness, hostility, self-pity, and apathy—almost invariably stem from people escalating their strong and legitimate desires and perferences into overwhelming and illegitimate demands, commands, and musts.

If you *only* desire or prefer something (such as the achievement of some task or the winning of someone's approval), you will virtually never seriously upset yourself about fulfilling this desire. For your Belief about attaining it will be: "I really do want to achieve that task and to win So-and-so's approval—but if I don't, I don't! I won't die; the world won't come to an end. I may be able to achieve the task or win So-and-so's love later; and if I never do, that's really rough, but that's all it is—rough! Too damned bad." With this kind of rational Belief (rB), you would make yourself feel sorry, disappointed, and sad—but hardly depressed and suicidal!

If, however, you slip into a single absolutistic *should* or *must*—such as, "I definitely *must* achieve that goal!" or "I undoubtedly *have to* win So-and-so's approval!"—how can you possibly *not* feel anxious, depressed, self-downing, or self-pitying when you cannot achieve that goal or win that person's approval?

Once again, then: serious emotional disturbance is *not* caused by what happened to you during your early life; nor by the rough conditions that are occurring right now; nor by the unpleasant events that may well transpire in the future. All these influences may significantly *contribute* to your feeling upset or disturbed. But it is your *reaction* to past, present, and future occurrences that much more directly and importantly upsets you! By inappropriately *reacting* to the undesired activating events that you experience, you really upset yourself. And whenever you do so, you have the ability to stop thinking and behaving in this disturbed manner.

As a child, you may have chosen to take your parents, teachers, peers, and others *too* seriously because you didn't know better. Now, as an adult, you may still have a strong tendency to take others too seriously and to think that you absolutely need their approval. You may also have another strong predisposition: to take *yourself* too seriously, and to think that even if others let you get away with a good deal and achieve less than you are able to do, *you* must not allow this kind of laxity; *you* have to achieve and to be loved outstandingly.

Fortunately, however, you have, especially as you reach maturity, other innate tendencies: the ability to perceive your own behavior and its consequences; to think about your thinking; to plan for the future; to change and actualize yourself if you wish to and are prepared to work at doing so. This is what RET encourages you to do.

What about the psychoanalytic belief that you have unconsciously tied yourself to your parents and to the standards of your culture, and that therefore you cannot possibly undo these unconscious emotions and behaviors unless you go through years of psychoanalysis, understand all the deeply hidden sources of your problems, and work them through with your analyst?

Hogwash! The truth is—and Freud saw this for a short while and then abandoned it as a hypothesis—that most of your "unconscious" or "automatic" thinking, emoting, and behaving is originated and sustained just below the level of consciousness in what Freud called the preconscious rather than the unconscious mind. Even if you have an important "unconscious" thought or feeling—such as the idea that your mother has treated you unfairly over the years and the feeling that you really hate her—you only defensively deeply repress this in few instances. For the most part, you have feelings of hostility toward her; and if someone asks you, "Come, now! Do you really love your mother as much as you say you do?" or if you ask yourself, "Do I truly love my mother *that* much?" you usually will reply: "Well, no; come to think of it, I do have some genuine feelings of love for her. But at times I hate many things she does. And, if I am honest about it, at times I really wish she were dead!"

Occasionally, of course, you may be so ashamed of some of your feelings—such as hatred for your parents—that you never acknowledge them and strongly repress them or deny that they exist. But most thoughts you don't want to face, you *consciously* suppress—as when you want to kick your boss in the teeth and you consciously force yourself not to do so. Or you may suppress your feelings of anger toward him by deliberately thinking about other things than his bad behavior.

Very often you are not thoroughly conscious of all the things you do. This is particularly true of automatic actions, like tying your shoelaces. At first, you are very conscious of how you perform these actions, and you laboriously and repetitively learn them. But after a while, your automatic thinking processes take over and you tie your laces without consciously being aware of what you are doing. We say, therefore, that you do these things automatically or semiconsciously.

In RET, we particularly take into account this kind of automatic or semiconscious thinking. For when something unpleasant or obnoxious happens to you at A (Activating Experience), when you have irrational Beliefs (iBs) about this unpleasant experience, and you then feel emotionally disturbed and act inefficiently at C (emotional and behavioral Consequence), you are usually not fully aware of your beliefs. They are not, however, deeply repressed. In order to help you discover them, we show you, in RET, how to *look* for what you are telling yourself: how to search in your heart and in your head for the sensible and not-so-sensible sentences, phrases, and paragraphs, for the *evaluations* of your Activating Experiences.

This is particularly important with regard to your irrational Beliefs. For unless you know precisely what these are, it is unlikely that you are going to be effective at Disputing and challenging them (at point D), which we shall show you how to do in the next chapter. But first, you'd better find them!

You do this, as we implied earlier in this chapter, by assuming that you have irrational Beliefs when you are feeling quite emotionally disturbed, and assuming that these include some explicit or underlying *should, ought,* or *must.* Thus, when you feel depressed after being rejected by someone, you ask yourself: "What *should* or *must* did I hook myself on to cause my feeling of depression?" Doing this, you usually come up with the answer very quickly: "I seem to have had the irrational Belief that this person *must* approve of me or else it is *awful,* I *can't stand* it, and I am a pretty *rotten individual.*"

You may be ashamed to admit that you not only desire but strongly think that you *need* the love of the person that rejected you; and you may be ashamed to admit that you disturbed *yourself,* rather than that his or her rejection upset you. So whenever you feel extremely upset, and whenever you seem to be denying that you told yourself some absolutistic *must* to make yourself disturbed, look for the possibility of your own defensiveness. Look, also, for the hidden or semi-conscious *must*.

You can say to yourself at this point, for example, "Well, if I really knew that there is *no* reason why I *must* be loved by the person who rejected me, and that it definitely *isn't* awful or terrible but only inconvenient and disappointing to be rejected, would I then really feel depressed about the rejection? I'd certainly feel disappointed and quite sorry about it, for it definitely is something that I don't want. But depressed? Angry? Obsessed with the thought of being rejected? At times thinking about suicide? Very unlikely! Maybe I really *do* think that I *must* get accepted and that it is *awful* if I don't. Let me be honest about this, now. What do I truly think about this?"

Unconscious thoughts need not be searched for endlessly through free associations and dreams. They are much more likely and quickly to be found by looking for the difference between what you *say* you think or do and what you *actually* think or do. In other words, whenever you find a discrepancy between what you think you are believing and the actual feelings you experience, look for something different: Look for the underlying ideas that seem to be more consistent and congruent with your acts and feelings.

CHAPTER 4

Disputing and Uprooting Emotional Disturbance

If you are anxious, depressed, angry, self-blaming or otherwise emotionally upset, how can you change these feelings? RET differs significantly from most other psychotherapies in that it not only reveals to people the basic irrationalities that lead to their feelings of disturbance, but it also uses several efficient methods of helping them surrender these irrationalities. These are demonstrated in the case histories in the second part of this book. The main method is that of *Disputing.*

At point A, remember, an Activating Experience occurs that works against some of your main goals or purposes: for example, you try to succeed at an important task, fail, and get rejected by some significant person whose approval you would very much like to have. At point rB (rational Belief), you tell yourself "I'd like to do well at these tasks and win the approval of the people I respect; and since I did not do what I'd like to do, that is unfortunate. How annoying! I am a person who is failing to do as well as I'd like and get the results I prefer. Too bad!" You then feel, at point C (Consequence), sorry, regretful, and frustrated.

At point iB (irrational Belief), however, you also tell yourself: "I *must* do well at these tasks and win the approval of the people I respect. And since I did not do what I *must* do, it is *awful!* I *can't stand* it! I am a *rotten person* for behaving so incompetently!" You then, also, at point C (Consequence), feel anxious and depressed.

In order to rid yourself of your anxiety and depression and to act in a determined manner that will help you do better and be more acceptable to the people you respect next time, you now can move on to D, Disputing. Disputing, in RET, is adapted from the scientific method, in the course of which you question any hypothesis or theory to see whether it is valid. The relevant questions usually are: "Where is the evidence that this idea or theory is correct?" "Show us the data on which it is based." "Does this theory give the best explanation for the observed facts?" Thus, in the example just given, you would Dispute as follows:

Disputing: "Where is the evidence that I *must* do well at these tasks and *must* win the approval of the people I respect?"

Answer: "There is no evidence for either of these *musts!* If there were really a law of the universe that I *had* to do well and *must* win the approval of the people I respect, this would be indubitably arranged and I *would* do these things. Since, in the present instance, I clearly have *not* performed that well and have *not* won the love of some people I respect, such a law of the universe does not exist. I'd better not, then, assume that it does!

"It would be *preferable,* of course, that I perform beautifully and win the favor of the people I respect, because then I would get more of the things that I want. But it does not follow that because I find something highly preferable, it, therefore, *must* exist! The rule, 'Because I *want* this I *must* have it!' is merely *my* law; and so far no evidence exists that the cosmos intends to carry it out!"

Disputing: "In what way is it *awful* when I don't perform an important task adequately and when I do not win the support of significant people?"

Answer: "In no way whatever! It is certainly bad, unfortunate, and obnoxious when I perform badly and thereby alienate others—because then I am not getting what I really want to get. But when I call something *awful* (or terrible or horrible), I really mean several things that are *more* than bad; and this is a foolish exaggeration.

"By calling my failure *awful,* I mean that not only is my performance bad and, therefore, unfortunate, but that it is awful *that* it is bad. While the first part of this statement is true, my awfulizing about its truth really means, once again, that badness *should not, must not,* exist; and that it is *awful* that it does! But if it does exist, it does; and because it actually does exist right now, it *should* exist—in the sense that it is the nature of things in the world, as this moment, that it exist. And *awfulizing* about things that actually have occurred or that might occur denies reality. I'd damned well better accept reality—whether I like it or not!

"Second, when I tell myself that it is *awful* that I fail and get rejected by significant people, I actually mean that this failure is not only bad but that in some respects it is totally bad, 100 percent bad. Well, this is most unlikely! If it were 100 percent bad that I failed, I would *only* get 'awful' results from this failure and would tend to get them *forever. No good* whatever could ever come of my failing. Actually, a considerable amount of good can arise from my failing this time: since I can learn from it and probably do better next time. And if certain people I respect completely reject me for failing, I can accept the challenge of getting them to like me later; or I can get to know others who will approve of me; or I can show myself how to accept myself in spite of the fact that significant others do not like me. So it may be 80 percent or 90 percent bad that I fail and get rejected; but it can hardly be 100 percent.

"When a thing is 100 percent bad, it is as bad as it possibly *could be.* But no matter how bad it is when I fail and get rejected, it could always, of course, be worse. Thus, if I failed 50 times in a row, I could fail 100 or more times. And if 10 of my friends rejected me for failing, 20 could reject me. No matter what happens to me, short of death itself, things could always be worse; and, therefore, although it is theoretically possible for me to experience 100 percent badness when I fail and get rejected, it is actually virtually impossible for me to experience anything except 99.9 percent. About the worst thing that could ever happen to me, at least in my imagination, would be for me to get tortured to death slowly. But even that could not exactly be 100 percent bad—for I could always get tortured to death more slowly!

"If it were 100 percent bad for me to fail and get rejected, this would mean either (1) that I would literally die because of this situation; or (2) that I could have no happiness whatever for the rest of my life. Well, it is most unlikely that failing and getting rejected is going to kill me (unless I foolishly decide to kill myself because I *think* it is *awful*) and it is even more unlikely that failing and getting rejected *this time* will utterly deprive me of all human happiness for *all time.* To think that it will is to think quite crookedly and I'd better change this kind of unrealistic thinking!

"Third, when I tell myself that it is *awful* that I fail and get rejected by significant people I really mean—if I am quite honest with myself about my meaning—that is *more than* bad; that it is at least 101 percent bad. But how can anything be *more than* obnoxious? How can it be 101 percent unpleasant or uncomfortable? Obviously, it can't be! And thinking it is *more than* bad, when at the very worst it can only be 100 percent bad, is again distorted thinking that will lead to execrable results. So I'd better revise this thinking, and believe the truth—that it is certainly undesirable when I fail and get rejected by significant people in my life. But it is *only* undesirable, and cannot possibly be *more than* that!"

Disputing: "Prove that I *can't stand* failing and getting rejected for failing."

Answer: "This is an obviously false statement. For if I truly couldn't *stand* failing and being rejected, I would literally die of these conditions, would actually fall apart at the seams and disintegrate. Well, obviously, I *am* thus far standing this failure and rejection, since I am still here and have not yet died of it.

"If I couldn't *bear* failing at these tasks and being disapproved of by significant people, I wouldn't be able to do anything else in life nor try to win anyone else's approval; and I would have to fail at everything I would ever do. But it is untrue that I can't do similar tasks—and sometimes succeed at them. For if I keep trying to succeed and to win approval I most probably will succeed to some extent.

"This means that I decidedly *can* stand what I don't like: that is, failing and being rejected. I'll never *enjoy* but I can *gracefully lump* failing. If I do so, my chances are remarkably good of succeeding later and of winning some people's approval."

Disputing: "In what way am I a *rotten person* for failing and for being disapproved?"

Answer: "In no way! Even if my *acts* are bad or rotten, these acts never equal *me* and, therefore, they cannot make *me* a bad, poor, or rotten person. My acts, deeds, performances, and traits are only *aspects* of me; they are never my totality. For I perform, during my lifetime, literally millions of actions: some of them good, some of them bad; some that win me approbation and some that win me censure. Today, for example, I may write an excellent letter or story; and tomorrow I may write a crummy one. Today, my friends and acquaintances may adore the story I write and may think I am a wonderful writer and a great person. Tomorrow, these same friends and acquaintances may abhor my writing and may think I am an abominable writer and a lousy person. Just about all my acts and deeds may be rated highly (by myself and by others) right now and rated poorly later. What I call *I* or *myself* consists of innumerable actions, all of which change from day to day, from year to year. How can *I*, therefore, *equal* any of these actions?

"What I call *I* or *myself* is an ongoing, ever-changing *process.* The products that *I* or my *process* turn out can probably all, in one way or another, be measured or evaluated—at least in terms of my goals and values. If I want to get a college degree, then it is good if I study and get high marks and it is bad if I fail to study and get low marks. But *I*, the person who studies or does not study, cannot be given a global rating. For *I* am a process that continually changes, that has a past, present, and *future,* and that, therefore, cannot be legitimately rated or measured in a global, once-and-for-all manner.

"If I were a *rotten person,* this would mean that I have some *essence,* some *soul* that is completely rotten. And this is quite unprovable. It would mean that I would *only* and *always* do quite rotten things. This, too, is unprovable. It would mean that because of my rotten acts I don't deserve any good results in the present or future—another unprovable statement! It would mean that because of my bad acts I am completely damnable, and, therefore, I *must* be boycotted and punished by every sensible and fair human as long as I live; and that if there is some kind of Hell, I probably will be damned and punished for an eternity for exhibiting the rotten acts that I have so far performed during my present existence. Another unprovable, and highly implausible, hypothesis.

"If I see myself as a *rotten* person for doing the bad acts that I have done, how will that view help me correct my behavior and do better in the future? It won't! The more I see myself as a *bad person* who is virtually doomed to behave badly in the present and future, the more will that view handicap me and serve as a nasty self-fulfilling prophecy. The alternative view—that I am neither good nor bad *as a person,* but that I am a human who does unfortunate acts and who has the power to act better in the future—will help me perform more successfully and win greater approval. So I'd better adopt that view, rather than the self-damning one of seeing *me* as a *rotten individual!*"

If you actively, strongly dispute your irrational Beliefs, you will wind up with a new set of philosophical, emotional, and behavioral *Effects* (E). You will conclude at E: "Yes, I unquestionably failed at this particular set of tasks and brought on the disapproval of certain important people. Moreover, since I tend to be the kind of human who is clearly fallible and prone to making a great many mistakes and errors, I will inevitably continue to err and to win the disapproval of certain people. Too bad!—so I will! Infallibility and archangelism will distinctly not be my lot! That is (perhaps) unfortunate. But it isn't the end of the world. I can still be fairly happy in spite of my failing and in spite of the fact that many of those I would like to approve of me often won't. Again: too bad! But if that's the way it is, that's the way it is! How can I, in spite of this set of conditions, continue to live and to enjoy myself?

"By accepting this reality and by trying to do a little better and be somewhat more approved in the future, I can gain personal happiness. So back to the drawing board! Let me try to improve and be more accepted. That is all, realistically, that I am able to do."

With this kind of a new philosophy, or cognitive Effect, at point E, you can then manage to feel (also at point E) sorry and regretful rather than anxious and depressed; and you can manage, again at point E, to act and to behave more efficiently and self-helpfully: namely, to make fewer (though never zero) mistakes and to win somewhat more (though never complete) approval from those you prefer.

Thinking homework. In RET, we give virtually all our clients and our workshop participants regular homework assignments (about which we shall go into detail in the next chapter). One of these assignments is cognitive or thinking homework, such as filling in the Rational Self-Help Form* on page 185 to 187. If you fill out this form several times a week, particularly when you are plagued with feelings of anxiety, depression, worthlessness, or hostility, you will soon get in the habit of clearly perceiving your basic irrational beliefs and actively disputing them until you come up with a new effect that will help you think and feel better.

Another form of thinking homework is *Disputing Irrational Beliefs* (DIBS), on which the Institute for Rational-Emotive Therapy puts out a pamphlet. In this procedure, you take one of your own main irrational beliefs, such as, "My boss *must not* treat me unfairly!" and you ask yourself, and write down the answers to, the following questions about this belief: "(1) What is the evidence that this belief is true? (2) What is the evidence that it is false? (3) What are the worst things that could actually happen to me if I accepted this belief as false and my boss continued to treat me unfairly? (4) What are some good things that could happen to me or that I could make happen if I accepted this belief as false and my boss continued to treat me unfairly?"

If you spend some time thoroughly answering these questions about your irrational Belief, you will soon see, first, that the Belief really is false or at least has no evidence to sustain it; second, that the worst that could happen to you if something obnoxious occurred, such as your boss continuing to treat you unfairly, would be various kinds of inconveniences and hassles—but no horrors whatever; and third, that even if your boss continued to treat you unfairly, if you gave up the belief that he *must* not treat you that way, you could find various satisfactions in life (such as doing a good job and getting paid well in spite of his unfair treatment) and could create other satisfactions (such as that of the challenge of making yourself reasonably happy in spite of his unfair treatment). As with filling in the Rational Self-Help Report Form, the more often you practice Dis-

---

*Published by the Institute for Rational-Emotive Therapy, 45 East 65th Street, New York, N.Y. 10021.

puting Irrational Beliefs (DIBS) and the more thoroughly you do it, the more firmly you will begin to see that your belief is invalid and that you can give it up.

Problem solving. When some obnoxious problem erupts in your life at A (Activating Experience), you are usually faced with two good choices: (1) solving it or (2) if it is insoluble, living with it but not unnecessarily disturbing yourself about it. If you unduly upset yourself, it will tend to be more insoluble; while if you accept a problem to be solved, and do not make yourself needlessly anxious, depressed, or self-downing about it, you have a much better chance of finding a decent solution. RET shows you how to refuse to awfulize about problems at A, and how to go back to A in an undisturbed frame of mind and do your best to ameliorate them. Compromise solutions are often best or inevitable. New problems will most likely arise soon after your existing ones are out of the way. RET helps you see life in problem-solving terms and realize that problems are simply problems, not horrors.

By emphasizing desires and preferences rather than demands and musts, RET also shows you that *you* run your own part of the universe and that you have a good measure of choice in deciding what you will and will not do in life, though, of course, your free choice or free will is not unlimited. By helping you get rid of your *musts* and other absolutes, RET shows you that you have many more alternatives than you think. If you think you *must* be a great artist, you will practically be forced to (1) work steadily in the field of art, whether or not you have any talent in it; (2) feel exceptionally anxious if you may not succeed in this field; (3) be either a compulsive worker at art or feel very guilty when you do not continue to work at it; and (4) feel like a turd when you are producing poorly. If you think, along RET lines, that it would be *desirable* to be a great artist but that this is by no means *necessary,* you are much more likely to succeed at your goal.

Moreover, when you have any difficulties, you will be in a considerably better problem-solving mood. Then, when you arrive at better solutions, you will reduce a good many of the pressures on yourself—for you will get more of what you desire and less of what you don't desire in your artistic endeavors—and you will have less of a tendency to upset yourself about the hassles of an artist's life.

Semantic precision. As Alfred Korzybski, the respected general semanticist, realized, human thinking becomes distorted partly because of our imprecise use of language; and, at the same time, the use of imprecise language often follows from distorted thinking. You can use some of the principles of general semantics to overcome emotional problems by rigorously examining and restating your overgeneralized sentences and ridding them of labeling and surplus meanings. Thus, if you say, "I *must* do well at tennis!" you can change that to, "*It would be preferable* if I do well at tennis; but if I don't, I don't!" You can change, "I *can't* consistently diet!" to "I have trouble dieting consistently, but there is no reason I can't!" When you hear yourself saying, "I always do badly every time I speak in public," you can alter this to "I often do badly when I speak in public. But there is no reason I cannot learn to do better in this respect in the future." When you hear yourself saying, "I'm *supposed* to use RET consistently because I *have to* stop my irrational thinking!" you can change this to, "I had *better* use RET to help me think more rationally, but I don't *have to* and there's no law of the universe that says I'm *supposed* to. If I don't use it, I shall merely suffer needlessly; and I am determined to try to suffer less!"

Referenting. One of the RET-oriented cognitive techniques that partly stems from the principles of general semantics is Joseph Danysh's method of referenting. When you are undisciplined and refuse to give up some pernicious, addicting habit, such as smoking, you call to mind, or referent, the good or advantageous reasons for your addiction and you ignore, or fail to referent, its evil consequences. Thus, if you are an inveterate smoker, when you think of smoking, you immediately think of something like "pleasure," "relaxation," and "tastes good." And if you think of stopping smoking, you quickly think of "pain," "terrible hassle," and "overeating." In this manner, you make it almost impossible for yourself to quit smoking.

The Danysh technique of referenting has you write down *everything* that comes to your mind when you think of smoking and of stopping smoking. Thus, in addition to the referents in the previous paragraph, you would list: for smoking: "lung cancer," "emphysema," "high blood pressure," "sore throats," "money spent on cigarettes," "offensiveness to other people," and so on. And you would list for stopping smoking such referents as: "good health," "saving a lot of money," and "being considerate of others." By forcing yourself to referent the good aspects of stopping smoking and the bad aspects of smoking, and by writing down these additional referents and reviewing them every day, you will often help yourself give up a bad habit such as smoking or acquire a good discipline such as coming to appointments on time.

Coping statements and rational philosophies. In RET, we try to induce people to look clearly at their own irrational Beliefs, to think about these many times, and to figure out for themselves why they are irrational and what better results they will get if they give them up. This technique of Disputing is highly efficacious for most bright people; and since the rational-emotive therapist teaches clients how to do Disputing for themselves, they soon become independent of the therapist and able to stand on their own feet. They develop maximum leeway to construct their own values and to achieve these values for the rest of their lives. The charge that is so often brought against psychoanalytic and other kinds of therapists—that they make their clients dependent on them for long periods of time—can not be made against the RET practitioner who teaches clients how to do their own thinking and Disputing.

As several cognitive-behavior therapists have pointed out, however, some people do not have much ability to Dispute their own irrationalities; and others, although they definitely do have this ability, won't make the effort to use it. Instead, therefore, such individuals can be taught rational philosophies or coping statements as an alternative method of giving up their irrationalities and the self-defeating emotions and behaviors that accompany them. To do this, you merely think about a number of sensible statements that will help you feel the way you want to feel and act the way you want to act; write them down, if necessary, on a set of 3 × 5 cards and firmly repeat these statements to yourself at least several times a day until you start to believe and to act on them. Such coping or rational statements can include:

Nothing is *awful* in the universe, though many things are highly inconvenient.

I never really *need* what I want, although it certainly would be nice to have it.

I distinctly *can* stand unpleasant things that I don't like.

I am not my *traits, deeds, or performances!* I am merely I!

Happiness is great! But I'd better try for long-range rather than short-range hedonism, because if I decide to "eat, drink, and be merry for tomorrow I may die," I'll probably live and have a hangover tomorrow!

Disputing attributions. A great deal of recent psychological research has shown that people significantly affect their own behavior and feelings by making all kinds of *attributions,* many of them false. Thus, if you think that your doctor has given you a marvelous new medicine and he or she has actually given you sugar pills, you may attribute considerable efficacy to the pills and may find your health distinctly improving "because" of them. Or if a friend of yours has accidentally cheated you and you stoutly believe that he has deliberately done so, you may easily attribute evil intent to him and thereby make yourself exceptionally angry at him, instead of merely displeased with some of his behavior.

Therefore, whenever you feel seriously upset about what people have done or not done, check your attributions about them. If a male friend of yours, for example, goes back on his promise to help you get a desirable job, don't cavalierly assume that he is jealous or deliberately neglectful. Consider other possible causes of his behavior, such as his merely forgetting to make an appointment for you; or his remembering his promise but being too much of a procrastinator to get going and carry it out. Whenever you think that other people have deliberately done you in, watch your attributions and look for alternative hypotheses about their behavior!

Imaging and fantasy methods. One of the main cognitive or thinking techniques people use is to imagine events and then fantasize things they would like to happen, or (in the case of anxiety and depression) to imagine the worst possible things that might happen and awfulize about these things. In fantasy, you may combine words and pictures; or you may merely see pictures—as you often do in a dream.

You can employ imagery in the form of positive thinking, by imagining that you can do something well (e.g., playing golf or the piano) when you really have serious doubts about your ability. Or you can imagine having sex with a charming and attractive partner when you have trouble getting aroused and having satisfactory sex relations (as explained in Albert Ellis' books, *The Art and Science of Love* and *Sex and the Liberated Man*).

You can also use imagery negatively, to desensitize yourself to something you fear or to overcome discipline problems. Thus, you can imagine yourself confronting a dog or a snake and can condition yourself to be able to approach this "fearsome" animal. This is discussed further on page 48. And using rational-emotive imagery (which we shall explain in more detail in the next chapter), you can imagine some of the worst things happening to you and can train yourself, while imagining these things, to have appropriate feelings (such as displeasure and annoyance) rather than inappropriate feelings (such as horror and panic). You can condition yourself in this manner to react appropriately rather than inappropriately to these obnoxious Activating Events when they actually occur.

Bibliotherapy and audiotherapy. In RET, we make considerable use of supplementary reading and audiovisual material to help people change their ideas and their disturbed emotional reactions. In our individual and group therapy sessions at the Institute for Rational-Emotive Therapy in New York and other cities, we encourage clients to bring a blank cassette to the sessions to record their portions of the therapeutic dialogue and to listen to these recordings in between sessions. This helps them learn the RET techniques of Disputing, of making appropriate rational statements to themselves, of using rational-emotive imagery, and so on. We also encourage them to listen to some of the RET audio cassettes, video recordings, and films that we distribute so that they learn the method through these audiovisual channels in addition to reading, imaging, and other techniques.

We rely heavily on clients and members of the public reading RET pamphlets and books. As supplements to the RET techniques, we find the following works useful: Ellis and Harper's *A New Guide to Rational Living* and *A Guide to Successful Marriage;* Ellis' *How to Live with a Neurotic,* and *How to Live With—and Without—Anger;* Ellis and Knaus' *Overcoming Procrastination;* Hauck's *Overcoming Depression;* Lazarus and Fay's *I Can If I Want To;* Young's *Rational Counseling Primer.* Other helpful materials are listed in the reference section at the end of this book.

Humor and paradoxical intention. Although we make sure in rational-emotive therapy, that we do not make fun of our clients (or of other people), since we are opposed to labeling humans or putting them down in any way, we frequently satirize or humorously criticize some aspects of their behavior. For, according to RET theory, emotional disturbance arises not when you take things seriously and give them importance, but when you take these same things *too* seriously and humorlessly awfulize or catastrophize about them. If you begin to see almost anything that may happen to you in a nonterribilizing light, and accept it as bad and obnoxious but not horrible, you will feel appropriately concerned but not inappropriately overconcerned about this occurrence.

You can train yourself to reduce "catastrophes" to absurdity, or focus on their humorous aspects. In RET, we often use paradoxical intention or provocative therapy: that is, urging clients to deliberately do the *wrong* thing (such as fully agreeing with their critics that they, the clients, really *are* thoroughly incompetent and wormlike) to prove to themselves that nothing horrible happens and that these extreme statements are ridiculous.

One humorous technique that we have pioneered in RET is the use of rational humorous songs, each of which includes a highly rational philosophy or satirically presents an extremely irrational view. At the Institute for Rational-Emotive therapy, we distribute a songbook and recorded cassettes of some of these songs (A. Ellis, *A Garland of Rational Songs*); and if you obtain some of these, you can sing them to yourself until their humorous messages sink into your head and your guts and you automatically start acting on them.

One of the songs that our clients find quite effective is "Whine, Whine, Whine!",* with a lyric written to the tune of the famous Yale "Whiffenpoof Song" (which was actually composed by a Harvard man in the 1890s):

I cannot have all of my wishes filled—
    Whine, whine, whine!
I cannot have every frustration stilled—
    Whine, whine, whine!
Life really owes me the things that I miss!
Fate has to grant me eternal bliss!
And if I settle for less than this—
    Whine, whine, whine!
*(Lyrics composed by Albert Ellis, copyright 1977 by Institute for Rational Living, Inc.)

Another rational humorous song you can try when you tend to belabor yourself for not being perfectly rational is "Perfect Rationality," set to the tune of Luigi Denza's *"Funiculi, Funicula."**

Some think the world must have a right direction—
    And so do I, and so do I!
Some think that with the slightest imperfection
    They can't get by—and so do I!
For I, I have to prove I'm superhuman,
    And better far than people are!
To show I have miraculous acumen—
    And always rate among the Great!
Perfect, perfect rationality
    Is, of course, the only thing for me!
How can I even think of being
    If I must live fallibly?
Rationality must be a perfect thing for me!
*(Lyrics composed by Albert Ellis, copyright 1977 by Institute for Rational Living, Inc.)

Teaching RET to others. One of the best means of learning almost any subject is to teach it to others and to be prepared to answer their questions about it. The same goes for RET. We have found that not only do therapists do better therapy as they practice it but they also use it more effectively in regard to their own emotional problems as they teach RET to others. While the use of psychoanalysis by nonprofessionals on their friends and relatives is likely to prove harmful rather than helpful, the use of RET by mothers with their children, by friends with their comrades, and by love and marital partners with each other has often proven to be exceptionally helpful.

If you would practice RET on yourself, therefore, don't hesitate to learn it thoroughly and to use it with some of your associates. Read several of the basic rational-emotive texts—which are listed in the reference section of this book. Listen to some of the RET cassettes. Have some RET therapy yourself or attend some of the workshops sponsored by the Institute for Rational-Emotive Therapy. Then use the techniques you learn on others with whom you have a close association. Not only are they likely to benefit—but, in all likelihood, so will you.

CHAPTER 5

Emotive Methods of Achieving Personal Happiness

RET, as we keep emphasizing to our clients and keep repeating throughout this book, is a comprehensive system of psychotherapy which, although it is heavily cognitive, is, at the same time, strongly emotive and behavioral. For its theory says that humans think, feel, and act simultaneously and transactionally. Whenever they think, they also desire and behave; whenever they emote, they also think and act; and whenever they engage in activity, they also reflect and feel. That is simply their natural or biological tendency.

If you want to change your inappropriate or disturbed feelings and your self-defeating or malfunctioning behavior, you had better work very hard to change some of your irrational thinking. But, at the same time, you can efficiently alter this thinking by forcefully, vigorously, and repetitively working to change your emoting and your behaving.

Almost the only way that you can tell whether you have made a real or thoroughgoing personality change is to check with your feelings and your actions. Thus, if you are extremely fearful of cockroaches and panic at the thought or sight of them, and you use various RET thinking techniques—such as Disputing, rational self-statements, and humorously reducing some of your ideas about cockroaches to absurdity—you can finally convince yourself that it is not *awful* or *terrible* but only a relatively mild pain in the neck for you to see a cockroach; and that you can live reasonably happily even in a cockroach-infested apartment if you are forced to do so. But to prove that your panic about cockroaches has vanished or significantly diminished, we would probably have to get you to face some of them and observe, in practice, how you actually react.

One of the best ways to get yourself to change your basic irrational ideas—about cockroaches or anything else—is to give you some form of emotional and behavioral *in vivo* (that is, live) desensitization. For if you really force yourself—yes, force yourself—to confront cockroaches on many occasions, and if you keep observing them and perhaps even handling them, you will very likely convince yourself that they are not *horrible* creatures, that you *can* stand coming into contact with them, and that a world that includes cockroaches is hardly a totally abominable place but one in which you can still have a good measure of happiness.

Similarly, if you remain in touch with your deep emotional reactions to cockroaches instead of running away from these emotions and making sure that you practically never experience them, you will very likely see that such emotions are not *awful,* that there is no reason why you *must* not experience them, and that you can be a happy human in spite of feeling them. By forcing yourself to put up with such feelings for a certain length of time, you will tend to become inured to them and, at the same time, you will often lose much of your original panic about cockroaches.

As we emphasize in RET, when you have severe emotional reactions to any Activating Experience, you frequently acquire a secondary neurotic disturbance *about* these reactions; and you, therefore, feel even worse than you did before. What is more, you sidetrack yourself from dealing with the original Activating Experience and defusing it. Thus, if at A (Activating Experience) you see a cockroach, and if at C (emotional Consequence) you feel panicked, you have a primary symptom—panic—that is directly caused by your irrational Belief (iB): "I *must* not come into contact with a cockroach! Such creatures are horrible! I *can't bear* seeing them! If the world provides me with such horrible things, it is a *terrible* place, and I might as well die as continue to live in it!"

Once you have this set of irrational Beliefs and once you feel panicked (at point C, Consequence) because you have them, you make your panic (C) into another A and tend to tell yourself a secondary set of irrational Beliefs, "I *must* not be panicked! How *horrible* to feel this way! I *can't tolerate* such awful feelings. What a *crummy world this* is when it provides me with feelings like these!" And you also may tell yourself, at B, "What a *stupid person* I am to allow myself to be panicked by a little thing like a cockroach!"

Moreover, because you feel so upset about your primary feelings, you tend to avoid feeling them at all cost. Thus, you avoid cockroaches, run away from even thinking about cockroaches, and stop yourself from going to therapy. But, in the course of this refusal to bring on panicked feelings, you give yourself little or no opportunity to see how nonlethal they really are, and you refuse to use almost any technique of facing them and finally overcoming them. Your low frustration tolerance (or discomfort anxiety) about your disturbed feelings sabotages your ability to face and overcome these feelings.

RET, recognizing this tendency, has developed a number of emotive methods to help you get in touch with your feelings and to change them. RET overlaps in this respect with certain other kinds of psychotherapy—such as Gestalt, encounter group, expressive, body, and cathartic-abreactive therapies. But it has a somewhat different goal than most of these forms of treatment, since it does not assume that if you merely get in touch with your feelings or express them, they will automatically go away. It assumes, rather, that expressive—emotive techniques had better be closely merged with thinking and philosophic understanding, as well as with active-directive homework assignments; else they will often do little good and may, in fact, do considerable harm.

Some of the main expressive-evocative or emotive-dramatic techniques that RET frequently employs are these:

Rational emotive imagery. Rational emotive imagery (REI) is a unique thinking-emotive-behavioral method of therapy that was originated by Dr. Maxie C. Maultsby, Jr., a rational-behavioral psychiatrist, and that has been adapted by me (A.E.) so that it can be frequently used in RET.

To use REI, take your feeling of anxiety, depression, hostility, or worthlessness, and imagine one of the worst possible things that might happen to you at A (Activating Experience) that would help produce this feeling. Thus, if you feel depressed about work, you might intensely imagine (or fantasize) that you have been doing very poorly at various jobs in recent years, have been enormously criticized by your bosses, and have lost several jobs because of your inadequate performance. As you intensely imagine this series of Activating Experiences at A, you will probably begin to feel quite depressed at point C (emotional Consequence).

Let yourself get in touch with this feeling of depression and actually experience it, deeply and acutely, for a minute or two. Then, with exactly the same imagery or fantasy in mind (you are still seeing yourself failing at work) make yourself feel *only* disappointed or sorry about what is happening to you in your imagination. *Not,* mind you, depressed or upset—only disappointed and sorry!

If you think that you cannot change your feeling in this manner, you are wrong. Don't give up! Continue to work on your depression until you have changed it, if only for a few seconds or minutes, to a feeling of disappointment and sorrow. Make yourself feel *merely* disappointed and sorrowful. You can!

When you have finally made yourself feel *only* disappointment or sorrow, ask yourself: "What did I change to make myself feel disappointed and sorrowful instead of depressed?" Get in touch with what you did. You will see that you changed some thought or philosophy. Thus, you may have told yourself, after first feeling depressed about the fantasy of losing several jobs, "It certainly is bad to behave so poorly and to suffer such unfortunate results. But it doesn't mean that I *always* have to behave this way. There is no reason I can't learn to do better in the future." Or you may have said to yourself, "Well, I just don't seem to do too well on this kind of a job. Maybe I'm not exactly suited for this sort of thing and I'd better look for another kind of employment." Or you may have told yourself, "I guess I'm just not too good at working, and I really don't like this kind of work, anyway. But since I have no other way of earning a living right now, I'd better put up with it, try to do a little better by working harder, and manage to get by until I am somehow able to retire."

Anyway, look for the new thought or philosophy that you told yourself to change your feeling and see how this thought connects with and creates a new, more appropriate feeling. Then practice rational-emotive imagery every day for a minimum of 30 days, for at least five to ten minutes a day, until you find several ways of changing your feeling from depression to disappointment. After a while you will see that you *automatically* tend to feel appropriately sad rather than inappropriately depressed, not only when you imagine yourself losing a number of jobs, but even when you actually lose one. For by using rational-emotive imagery, you will not only face your depressed feeling and allow yourself to work through it, but you will train yourself to feel sorry and disappointed rather than severely depressed when other unfortunate conditions occur.

Unconditional self-acceptance. In RET, as in several other forms of therapy, we show our clients that we can unconditionally accept them no matter how stupidly or immorally they behave. We do not, of course, always think that their behavior or their thinking is good. But we do our best to accept *them* as humans with this cruddy behavior; to follow the Christian pathway of accepting sinners, though not their sins. We do this nonverbally—by means of our tone, our movements, and our body language—as well as by verbal methods.

We also go beyond most other psychotherapies and try to actively teach our clients, philosophically and rationally, exactly how they can unconditionally accept themselves: how they can refuse to rate their essences, their totalities, or their personalities while at the same time trying to measure their deeds, performances, and traits. You can do this for yourself, as we explained in the previous chapter.

Going still further than verbal self-acceptance, you can also accept yourself emotively and dramatically. Thus, you can resolve that you will always accept yourself, no matter what; and you can work on doing so, especially when you have performed very foolishly, self-defeatingly, or antisocially. You can vigorously and repetitively tell yourself, "I am I! I am not merely my acts! I have a perfect right to be myself, no matter how imperfect some of my traits may be! I am not here to *prove* myself but to *be* myself and *enjoy* myself! The only thing I can ever really lose in life is pleasure—I can never lose *myself* if I choose to think clearly and rationally!"

Shame-attacking exercises. One of the unique techniques of RET consists of shame—attacking exercises, which are frequently given to individual as well as group therapy clients, and which you can use on your own. Shame is a common disturbed feeling. When people do something wrong, incompetent, self-defeating, or immoral, they very often make themselves feel thoroughly ashamed—or, as they often call it, guilty, anxious, depressed, or worthless.

RET specializes in helping you rid yourself of shameful feelings by showing you that you create them by insisting that you absolutely *must* do well, that you have *no right* to perform poorly, and that you are a *worm* for doing so. It then helps you Dispute (D) and surrender these irrational Beliefs; and to accept yourself *with* your failings.

Shame-attacking exercises are another RET means of helping you do this. Think first of something that you usually consider very shameful, foolish, ridiculous, asinine, embarrassing, or humiliating. Pick a "shameful" act that, if you actually do it, won't get you into serious trouble. Once you pick this act, make sure that you do it, at least once and preferably several times, in public, so that at least a few friends and relatives or strangers see you act "shamefully."

What kind of "shameful" acts shall you perform? Preferably useful ones—that is, acts that you would really like to do, as refusing to tip a waiter who has given you poor service or a cab driver who has acted in a surly fashion. Or telling someone you know that you dislike his or her behavior, when you are afraid to tell them this. Or saying something very nice or tender to someone you know, for fear that you will do so awkwardly and "shamefully."

If you can't think of anything like these useful "shameful" acts to do, you can try fairly "useless" ones as yelling out the stations in a train and staying on the train after you have yelled these out in a loud voice! Or stating the time at the top of your lungs when you are in a crowded department store or park. Or getting a bright red leash and walking a banana at the end of it down a well-trodden sunny street. Or stopping a stranger and saying, "I just got out of the looney bin. What day is it?" Or going to a crowded drugstore and, in a loud voice so that everyone can hear, asking a clerk (and preferably a female clerk), "I'd like a gross of condoms. And since I use so many of them, I think you should give me a special discount!"

Silly? Foolish? Of course—that's the purpose of this shame-attacking exercise: for you to do something that most people would think "nutty" or "crazy" and might scorn you for doing. Shameful? Embarrassing? Humiliating? Well, no. For the main purpose of this exercise is to teach you—or, rather, to help you convince yourself—that *nothing* is really shameful, embarrassing, or humiliating. Unless you *think* it is. For even if you walked down the street naked and everyone else were fully clothed and laughing uproariously at you, you don't have to feel the slightest degree of shame or self-downing.

You might feel concerned and cautious for you might, under such conditions, get arrested and suffer various inconveniences. But shame and embarrassment do not come from experiencing such hassles, only from what you *tell yourself:* what a "perfect idiot" you are for letting yourself do so. Thus, as you walk down the street naked and hear everyone laughing at you, you have it well within your power to say to yourself, "Well, I'm obviously doing the wrong thing in public; but that does not make me a foolish or rotten person!" Or: "I know why I'm walking down the street like this—to perform a shame-attacking exercise that will do me some good. And if others don't realize this and think that I'm a completely crazy person, that is their prerogative. I can agree with them that I am doing a nutty or dangerous thing. But that thing doesn't make *me* a nut, as they erroneously think I am." Or: "This is quite a challenge—to walk down the street naked as a jaybird and have everyone laugh at me, and not put myself down. I rarely dare to do things like this, but I am glad that I am doing it right now. By accepting this challenge I will zero in on my own foolish shame-creating beliefs and will be able to see them very clearly and to work on giving them up. So, actually, I am doing a good thing by acting 'shamefully' and using this exercise to work on my own self-defeating philosophies!"

If you will do shame-attacking exercises with this goal in mind—to encourage people to think you are foolish or crazy but not to make their opinions your own—you will first experience intense feelings of shame, live with them and refuse to run away from them. Then you will see what you are doing to invent or create these feelings. Then you will be able, if you persist, to successfully overcome them. And you will finally see the real purpose of the exercise—that nothing is really shameful or humiliating. In this way, your shame-attacking exercises become an excellent form of *in vivo* (in-real-life) desensitization; and they also become one of the best possible ways of revealing your embarrassment-creating irrational beliefs, of confronting them, and of giving them up.

Self-disclosure exercises. Sidney Jourard did pioneering studies showing that by disclosing some of your darkest secrets you can improve your mental health. What is more, self-disclosure frequently encourages others to disclose their own secrets and evasions; so you can use it to become more intimate with others, find out what they really are all about, and see whether they will accept you as you really are.

We use many self-disclosure exercises in RET, because they are really a shame-attacking procedure. We frequently persuade RET group members to tell something they have not told anyone before; to reveal to the group the secret they would least like to have people know; and to express themselves in some way that they consider risky. These are normally secrets or risks that the group members would consider "shameful."

When they do these exercises, the rational-emotive leader of the group asks them such questions as, "Why have you kept this thing secret up to now?" "Why is what you are now doing risky?" "How do you feel now that you have made this revelation to the group?" "How could you feel better about this?" "What could you tell yourself to make yourself more open and less secretive?" "How could you avoid feeling ashamed of the thing you have just revealed?"

Self-disclosure exercises are combined with the usual anti*must*urbating and antiawfulizing of rational-emotive therapy. You can use similar exercises by picking some people who do not have too much power over you—who cannot, for example, fire you or expel you from school—and disclose some "risky" or "secret" things about yourself. You may well see, in the process, that they react differently and more nicely than you would have imagined. But if they criticize you severely, you can convince yourself, using RET antihorribilizing methods, that the world won't come to an end; that you can bear their disapproval; that you never have to down yourself; and that some of your friends and acquaintances may well be worth having—and some may not be!

Role-playing. RET employs a considerable amount of role-playing or behavioral rehearsal procedures. Thus, if one of our clients is about to go for a job interview or wishes to learn how to approach members of the other sex, we frequently have the therapist or one of the members of a therapy group act as the interviewer or as the person this client wants to encounter. Acting her or his own role, the client then speaks to the individual she or he wants to impress; and the therapist and the other group members observe the interaction and give the client feedback on how she or he came across and what might better be done the next time this kind of encounter occurs.

Role-playing is another means of showing clients that the event they are rehearsing is not really as formidable or risky as they think it is and that if they fail, this is not the last chance they will ever have. It also shows them that even if they do poorly at the rehearsal, they never have to rate themselves as people but just had better rate their performances—so that they will have a better chance to correct them in the future.

You can often use this method yourself, by enlisting the aid of some of your friends, relatives, or associates. Although they may not have the same kind of skills that a trained psychodrama expert would have, they can nevertheless help you act out what may occur in "dangerous" or "anxiety-provoking" situations which you may encounter. The more risks you take in some of these role-playing encounters—the risk, that is, of acting poorly and having your friends and associates tell you how badly you come off—the more you will tend to benefit from psychodrama procedures. Especially if you combine them with the RET procedure of Disputing your irrational Beliefs which are very likely to be revealed during the role-playing.

Forceful and dramatic self-statements. As indicated in the previous chapter, you can make good use of rational philosophies or coping statements when you want to revise or eliminate some of your self-defeating ideas. You can also add an emotive or dramatic element to these statements by saying them in a very vigorous, highly charged, repetitive manner.

When we tell ourself irrational Beliefs—such as, "Now that I have refused to discipline myself by studying, I don't *deserve* to do well on the exam I am taking, and I really *should* fail it!"—we tend to say them to ourselves with great vigor and force; and that is why we devoutly hold to them, even when they are quite illogical. If, therefore, we merely say to ourselves in a namby-pamby manner, "Well, I guess I do deserve to pass this exam, even though I didn't do very well about studying for it," we tend to *also* say to ourselves, *sotto voce* but with great power, *"But I really don't deserve this!"* And this latter statement, because it is so very powerful, wins out over the saner, more reasonable statement that we tell ourselves.

Self-statements or rational philosophies, therefore, are effective when they are said with great emphasis. For example, you can very strongly and repeatedly say to yourself, "Damn it, I *do* deserve to do well on the exam I am taking, even though I did not discipline myself to study for it. I deserve it because I deserve any good thing that happens to me in this universe; and although it was really stupid of me to refuse to study, I still have the right to pass without studying. So I'll darned well try to do so!" Similarly, if you use rational philosophies and coping self-statements powerfully and repetitively, you will often be able to overcome some of your strongest and longest-held feelings of anxiety, depression, hostility, and personal inadequacy.

CHAPTER 6

Behavioral Methods of Achieving Personal Happiness

The basic theory of RET states that humans are not merely conditioned by childhood influences to feel upset and to act dysfunctionally but also seem to have strong innate tendencies to think crookedly, to emote inappropriately, and to behave self-sabotagingly. Once they become the victims of their own irrational thoughts and self-paralyzing feelings for any length of time, they tend to continue their neurotic behavior even when they know it is foolish and they very much want to change it.

Humans are habit-forming creatures who easily acquire and maintain good habits—eating regularly, brushing their teeth, exercising, and reading—but they also acquire many bad habits—smoking, overeating, procrastinating, worrying, and acting enraged. Insight into these habits and a strong resolution to reform isn't quite enough, in most instances, to make them disappear. Unless some definite *action* is taken to eliminate them, they frequently worsen.

Because of this, RET uses a variety of behavioral methods to supplement its cognitive and emotive techniques. You can use these techniques in dealing with your own emotional problems.

Homework assignments. RET pioneered in the use of activity homework assignments, following the lead of other active-directive therapists. This also goes back to the philosophic views of John Dewey and Maria Montessori, who stressed the fact that we learn by doing. Desensitization, discussed in the previous chapter, is an effective method that illustrates this. We tell our clients that they can overcome many of their long-held anxieties and phobias if they will do what they are most afraid of—and do it many times in a cold turkey manner. Thus, one of our clients, who had been afraid of going into elevators by himself for a period of 30 years, was shown that if he would go in at least 20 elevators a day for the next two weeks no matter how uncomfortable he felt, he would most probably overcome his extreme fear. For many weeks he resisted doing this; but when he was finally convinced that either he had better take the plunge or else suffer from his phobia for the rest of his life, he forced himself into a minimum of 20 elevators a day for the next 10 days—and almost completely got over his fear of entering elevators alone.

Similarly, you can use RET-oriented homework assignments to help yourself with your emotional problems. If you experience severe anxieties or panic states, you can make yourself do what you are afraid to do, while at the same time consistently and strongly antiawfulizing: that is, convincing yourself that nothing truly dangerous will happen to you if you do this thing, and that you will thereby overcome your fear. Or you can use another type of RET homework assignment that we frequently employ at the Institute for Rational-Emotive Therapy: that is, deliberately make yourself stay in an obnoxious and supposedly "horrible" situation until you see that it is only highly inconvenient and not in the least filled with horror. You can then leave the situation. Thus, you can stay on your job and keep working for a highly critical and loathsome supervisor or boss until you overcome your low frustration tolerance and your terribilizing about working for this individual. *Then* you can feel free to look for another job.

Don't take things to foolish extremes and truly jeopardize yourself, however. Don't, for example, keep driving around in an unsafe car that could easily get you into a serious accident; and don't keep working for an annoying boss who pays you substandard wages. But push yourself to act against your silly, groundless fears; and force yourself to stay in some "unbearable" situations where you are being roundly excoriated for your failings but not penalized in a practical way. The more you take on these kind of *in vivo* homework assignments, the more you will be able to overcome your longstanding feelings of anxiety.

Operant conditioning and self-management procedures. Although most clients seem to willingly accept activity homework assignments (see page 55) and say that they will definitely do them, the fact is that they frequently goof and fail to do their homework systematically or even fail to do it at all.

What is to be done in such cases? One of the main advantages of RET is that the therapist can then return to the ABC's of rational-emotive therapy and the Disputing technique to help the clients overcome this kind of resistance. Thus, we can ask a client: "When you thought, during the week, of filling out the Rational Self-Help Form and then you decided not to do it, what did you tell yourself just before you made this decision?" "I told myself," he will commonly say, "that I'll do it later." "But that, of course, was a lie or a rationalization! What *reason* did you give yourself for not doing it right *then,* when you first thought of doing it?" "Uh—I guess I said to myself, 'It's hard to do; I have other more enjoyable things I can do right now instead of that homework.'" "Is that *all* you told yourself—it's hard?" "Well, no. To tell the truth, I guess I also said to myself, 'It's too damned hard! I shouldn't *have* to do it! I can get better without doing that kind of work!'" "Oh! And why, may I ask, is it *too* hard? Where is the evidence that you *shouldn't* or *must not* have to do it?"

In this manner, when clients fail to do their homework assignments, we check their self-statements and almost invariably find that they consist of low frustration tolerance (LFT) philosophies: that the homework is *too* onerous; that they *shouldn't* have to do it; that they *can't stand* doing it; that the world is a pretty rotten place when it requires them to work to get better. We then show them how to actively, vigorously Dispute these irrational Beliefs and give them up. Then they almost always have a much easier time doing their homework assignments.

If this kind of procedure still doesn't work, we then often resort to operant conditioning or to self-management principles—as outlined by B. F. Skinner and other noted behavior therapists. Using this technique, we ask people what they really enjoy doing, such as reading, listening to music, eating a favorite food, having sex relations, or talking to friends. The performance of this activity is then made contingent upon their doing the RET homework assignment, such as filling out the Rational Self-Help Form, encountering new acquaintances, giving a public talk, or reading portions of rational-emotive books. If they fail to do the assignment, no performance of the enjoyable activity!

In RET, we also use penalizing tasks, in case clients do not perform their homework assignments. We don't want them, under any conditions, to *punish* or *damn* themselves; but we do want them to give themselves a stiff penalty in case they do not fulfill the self-help contracts that they have agreed to carry out. The penalties that are used for this purpose are usually set by the clients themselves and consist of things they abhor doing, such as eating unpleasant foods, engaging in boring tasks, cleaning the bathroom, or getting up earlier than usual in the morning. Every time that they do not go through with the homework assignment, they are encouraged immediately to perform one of these unpleasant tasks.

The use of immediate rewards or reinforcements for doing difficult homework assignments and the employment of strict, quickly enforced penalties for not doing them works very well with RET clients. If they select some highly obnoxious penalty—such as burning a hundred-dollar bill or contributing it to a cause that they consider highly offensive— and if they actually carry out this penalty as soon as they fail to do their homework, we find that they usually perform the assignment in short order.

For clients who say they will penalize themselves for goofing and then actually refuse to go through with the penalties, we use supervised monitoring. They select someone with whom they are in close contact—such as a mate, a lover, a relative, or a close friend—and have this person supervise and monitor their reinforcement and penalty program. Thus, if they agree to burn a hundred-dollar bill every time they do not do their homework assignment, their mate or friend will make sure that it gets burned. Or, if this is not feasible, their RET therapist or therapy group may monitor them and see that they burn the money if they do not carry out the assignment.

This kind of program, we find, usually works well if our clients agree to it. You can also arrange to use it yourself by setting yourself clear-cut and realistic homework tasks—which can be thinking, emoting, or behavioral tasks—and then immediately rewarding yourself when you carry them out and promptly penalizing yourself every time you avoid doing them. This will help with almost any kind of discipline problem. Thus, if you are having a difficult time writing a report or manuscript and you promise yourself that you will work on it every day for, say, two hours, you can reward yourself every time you carry out this plan and penalize yourself every time you fail to do so.

Skill training. RET has always espoused skill training—especially the training of clients to acquire better social, relationship, communicative, vocational, and sexual skills. This is for several reasons. First, many disturbed individuals act poorly in their everyday lives and, therefore, put themselves down. If they can be shown how to function more effectively, they will blame themselves much less. Second, by berating themselves and making themselves hostile to others and to the world, neurotic individuals sabotage their acquiring various social, recreational, and vocational skills; and they consequently can use some special teaching in these areas. Third, the acquisition of definite skills is usually linked with self-discipline and with the overcoming of low frustration tolerance. Consequently, when we give clients skill training, this kind of teaching often helps them become more disciplined and to change their self-pitying and low-frustration-tolerance philosophies.

You can use skill training by first noting major skills in which you think you are deficient. Then you can try to improve in these areas by reading, taking courses, getting personal instruction or simply practicing.

If you tend to cop out on learning any useful skill, watch your low frustration tolerance (LFT). Use rational-emotive Disputing to rip up your irrational Beliefs that acquiring this skill is *too* hard; that it *shouldn't* be that hard; that you *can't stand* the learning process; and that it's *awful* that it takes so much time, effort, or money to learn the skill.

Force yourself, along with your Disputing, to keep at the learning process until it becomes familiar and easier. Remind yourself that this skill will finally become easy and semiautomatic to use; that there's rarely any gain without pain; and that it's good to acquire skills that will benefit you later. Take it as an active, enjoyable *challenge* to get some useful skill training; and as you get it, keep looking at the doughnut instead of the hole!

Stimulus control. When you try to give up a pernicious habit or to acquire a good one, it is better to change your Belief System (at point B) rather than merely to change what is happening to you at the Activating Events (A's). But at times, especially when you are trying to overcome addictive behavior, it is also beneficial to exert some stimulus control and change some of the conditions at point A.

Suppose, for example, you are trying to lose weight. RET shows you how to look at your interfering irrational Beliefs, such as: "I *must* have the tasty foods that I normally enjoy! It's *horrible* to be deprived of food I like! It's unfair that I have to diet when other people can eat everything they want and the world is *a rotten place* when it is this unfair!" If you persistently and vigorously keep challenging these irrational Beliefs, you will surrender them and stop interfering with your dieting.

In addition, however, there are good reasons why you had better change some of the Activating Events, at point A, which encourage you to overeat and had better learn some methods of stimulus control. Thus, as shown in Ellis and Abrahms, *Brief Psychotherapy in Medical and Health Practice,* you can try some of these techniques to control your food intake:

1. Restructure your environment to reduce your temptations to eat. If,

for example, pastry is served during your office coffee breaks, you can take *only* the coffee and carry it to your desk to drink.

2. Avoid the purchase of problematic foods. Take a list of suitable foods to the grocery or supermarket and bring only enough money to cover their cost.

3. Do not serve desserts or other fattening foods to your family members, but train them to take their own.

4. Clear all plates directly and swiftly into the garbage pail and refuse to leave any tempting food to eat later.

5. Leave the table soon after you finish each meal.

6. Eat slowly and do not gulp down your food. The faster you eat the more you will tend to consume.

7. Eat at least three and preferably four or more meals a day so that your calories are divided and you do not feel tempted to eat too much at any one time.

8. Only eat at mealtimes and do not watch TV while eating or use other distractions that keep you from eating only the right amount of food.

9. Use relaxation exercises or other distractions that will keep you from feeling anxious and from eating to overcome your anxiety.

10. Use a small plate rather than a large dinner plate. This will help give the illusion of your eating more.

11. Do not use condiments at meals that have a high caloric content, such as chutney or other sauces.

12. Engage in regular exercise, such as moderate walking, that helps burn calories.

13. Eliminate from your diet various high-calorie foods such as alcohol, cake, bread and butter.

14. Encourage your family members to be supportive of your dieting efforts, and reward them when they are supportive.

CHAPTER 7

Ten Rules for Achieving Personal Happiness

You have the power to achieve personal happiness—if you decide to use it. You also have the ability to make yourself miserable—if you decide to do so. What is your choice?

You already know ours. We, in our own personal and professional lives, normally (not always!) choose happiness and we strongly advise that you do the same. Not that you have to. Not that you *must.* But we hope that you prefer to and that you will carry out that preference.

Here are ten rules that summarize the basics of achieving personal happiness. We hope you will take them quite seriously.

1. *Decide to strive primarily for your own happiness.* This is your right as a human; and, as we have noted throughout this book, there are many advantages to doing so. Consider the virtues of giving primary value to your own existence and your own enjoyment. And if you think that these virtues are worth it, decide—yes, *decide*—to strive for them.

2. *Decide to put ôther people's happiness a close second to your own.* Since you will probably choose to live among other people and to try to get along with them, and since your own happiness will, therefore, be tied up with that of these others, you had better decide to consider seriously the rights and privileges of all other humans and, in particular, to put some of them a close second to yourself. Enlightened self-interest includes the interest of others.

3. *Decide that you largely control your own emotional destiny.* As a human living in a social group, you are never completely autonomous but

give away some control to others. But you can still decide to think your own thoughts and feel your own emotions. Decide, therefore, which reactions and feelings you want to experience.

4. *When you feel disturbed or act self-defeatingly, look for your disturbance-creating Beliefs.* Find the absolutistics *shoulds, musts,* and *commands* with which you needlessly upset yourself. Assume that you implicitly or explicitly hold and strongly believe in these *musts* and look into your head and heart to find them.

5. *Actively dispute and surrender your self-sabotaging musts.* Don't merely parrot their irrationality, but use the scientific method to prove their falseness.

6. *Figure out a set of rational Beliefs that will help you live happily and keep reviewing them.* Teach yourself to understand and believe that "Nothing is *awful,*" "I *can* stand what I don't like!" "I am never a rotten, worthless individual, no matter how badly I behave!" and similar self-helping rational beliefs.

7. *Use several other cognitive methods of surrendering your irrational Beliefs*—such as, thinking homework, problem solving, semantic precision, referenting, imaging, bibliotherapy, and the use of humor.

8. *Work directly on your emotions to change them from inappropriate to appropriate feelings.* Use several or all of the methods outlined in Chapter 5, such as rational-emotive imagery, unconditional self-acceptance, shame-attacking exercises, self-disclosure exercises, role-playing, and the use of forceful and dramatic self-statements to feel more appropriately.

9. *Forcefully act against your irrational Beliefs and inappropriate feelings.* Use several or all of the behavioral methods outlined in Chapter 6 to change your feelings, beliefs, and actions. For example, give yourself homework assignments that make you face the things you needlessly fear and perform useful tasks that you foolishly avoid. Use self-management procedures to reward yourself for effective behavior and to penalize yourself for self-defeating performances. At times, consider using relaxation and other methods of physical distraction, skill training, and the use of stimulus-control methods to help yourself lead a less disturbed, happier life.

10. *Resolve to change, acknowledge that change means hard work, and keep working to implement your resolutions.* The ability to choose your own emotional destiny or to use will power consists of (1) a strong resolution to change; (2) determination to work at the process of change; and (3) actual work to implement that process. Only *practice* makes

perfect; and, as we say in RET, there's rarely any gain without pain! Careful thought plus work and practice are the essence of achieving personal happiness.

In the previous chapters, we have outlined some of the main techniques of rational-emotive therapy (RET) and have shown you how you can use them in your own life. To illustrate their actual usage, and how they were helpfully applied to the cases of a good many psychotherapy clients, the following chapters of this book will mainly consist of transcripts of verbatim dialogue from actual RET sessions. These transcripts will be interspersed with comments, so that the points made during these actual therapy sessions will be clearer, and so that you can see how these points can be applied to *your* own life. Each chapter will deal with a particular type of common emotional problem, and how the client was helped to use RET principles and techniques with this problem in order to achieve personal happiness.

CHAPTER 8

Overcoming Shyness and Feelings of Inadequacy

This area could be called the common cold of psychology because so many of us are affected by it. The emotional problem is shyness, which goes under many other names, including lack of confidence, fear of asserting oneself, insecurity, and feelings of inadequacy. In looking at the case excerpts that follow, you will see how certain core beliefs create the feelings and actions that we label as shyness. You will also see how overcoming shyness relates to personal happiness and what you can do to become less shy and more assertive.

The client in the first case is a 22-year-old female secretary. Since this is the initial session, the therapist knows little about the client aside from what the client writes on a biographical information form. What follows is the transcript of most of the session, along with comments pointing out how the principles taught to the client can help you with similar problems in your own life. Let us join as the session is beginning.

T = Therapist   C = Client

T. Okay, this [client's form] says "lack of self-confidence, feelings of inadequacy and shyness in certain social situations, need for perfectionism in myself and others." The perfectionism, you see, is probably the main issue. Because as long as you're a perfectionist, how could you not be shy?

C. I don't see how that follows.

T. Well, shyness is a high-class name for feeling scared. That's mainly what it means. It's too bad we use the word *shy* because it covers up the real feeling. The only things a person can legitimately be afraid of are some kinds of real harm or damage, such as physical injury. But that is hardly the issue here. You're not afraid that a person whom you just met is going to punch you, are you?

C. No. Hardly that!

T. So you're afraid of doing something imperfectly.

C. Right! Exactly!

T. You're probably afraid that you're going to act stupidly, say the wrong thing, or something like that, and afraid I'm going to think "What a nut she is for acting that way!" And you're going to believe you're no good—because you're a perfectionist.

C. Exactly.

T. Now if you weren't a perfectionist, if you really said to yourself, "Oh, yes, I see that my act is stupid but that doesn't mean *I* am." Let's just suppose you believed that and suppose you also told yourself, "He's wrongly downing me as a person for my stupid behavior." Would you be shy?

C. I guess not. I do feel shy when I wear glasses, so I wear contacts.

T. But let's suppose you forgot your contacts, and you therefore felt shy. It's not just because you wear the glasses. It's because, one, you view that as an imperfection, which it might *not* be. I might like you better with the glasses. Some people do, some don't. And, two, you're saying, "It's horrible to have that imperfection. I *should* be perfect." Aren't you?

C. Yes, I am.

T. Well, why *should* you be perfect?

C. It's really terrible. It relates to everything I do. It's probably because I expect too much of others. They don't live up to my image of them and I guess I don't live up to my image of me.

T. Let's take your own image of yourself, which is the issue. Why must you have an image?

C. I don't know.

T. Well, the answer is because you're human and humans foolishly make up images of themselves. They don't have to, but they almost invariably do. Let's get back to the issue of glasses. You could say, "Since I look worse to most people with·glasses, it is, therefore, a handicap to wear glasses." Right?

C. Yeah.

T. And if possible you could add, "So I'll get contacts, or not wear my glasses at times, or find a few people who like glasses." You see, that would be the way to overcome your handicap. But instead you jump from "I don't like *it*" to "I don't like *me*" for that dislikable behavior, wearing glasses. You start rating yourself as a human. Now that's nutty. And that's what we call an image. "Because my glasses don't make me look good, my image is no good." Or, "*I* am no good. My being, my essence, is worthless." Now, is your essence *really* no good because you have this bad defect—because you don't look well in glasses?

C. No.

T. But that's what you believe.

C. Yeah, I do believe it, but I don't know how to overcome it.

Shyness, and all the other names it goes under, really means being overly fearful of doing or saying the "wrong" thing and/or not looking as you "should." What is meant by "wrong" or "should" depends on your own definition. The most important thing to understand here is why you are overly fearful or anxious. The answer is that *others may criticize or not like you, and then you foolishly rate yourself as a rotten person.* You think that others *must* accept you and view you in a favorable light. This *irrational demand for perfection lies behind extreme shyness.* It is your *demanding* perfect behavior, looks, or some other trait that leads to self-*downing.* You have the idea, "If I have a lousy *trait,*" (which just about all of us do) "I am, therefore, a lousy *person.*" This is a false idea, as you will see as we return to the session.

T. Ask yourself a simple question: "How does my defect, whatever it is, make me less of a person?" "How does a defect of any kind make *me* a rotten *person*?"

C. Because it's a weakness.

T. Well, how does a weakness make *you* weak? You, for example, might have a blackness on your skin, perhaps a mole or something like that. Does that make you black?

C. Of course not.

T. Well, then how does a weakness make *you* completely weak for all time? Because when you have a weakness you say, "I *am* a weakling," which is an *over*generalization. "I have a weakness right now and that means I'll *always* be a weakling." Well, how is it possible for you to predict that?

C. I'm always condemning myself for doing certain things.

T. But condemning yourself is what we're talking about, because it's another way of saying, "*I* am rotten if my *act* is rotten." Now give me a rotten act that you do, for example.

C. I guess I'm passive at times.

T. All right. "I would like to ask *X* for something but I'm afraid."

C. Yeah, I'd like to be more aggressive but sometimes I don't know how to go about it.

T. Well, aggressive might mean hostile, so I don't like the word. You mean, you'd like to be more assertive—"I'd like to express myself, to ask for what I want, tell people what I don't want to do." A guy asks you to go to bed with him, and you would like to say "No" or something like that. And "If I meet a guy and I want to go with him, I'd like to ask him for his number, be assertive. And right now I'm less assertive than I'd like." Right?

C. Yeah, right.

T. So that's a handicap, that's a deficiency. Now how does that make *you* a deficient person?

The key lesson here is: *You do not equal your trait.* This is a simple yet profound key to reducing shyness. Most of us tend to overgeneralize and jump over the bounds of logic by believing that "If something about my *appearance* or my *performance* is defective, then *I* am defective." This implies that "I should (must) act or look perfectly, or else I can't accept myself."

C. I *should* be stronger.

T. Oh, wait a minute, wait a minute! Where'd you get the *should*?

C. I should accept myself as being the way that I am?

T. I'd *better,* not I *should.* Do you realize that *should* is almost always wrong? Because *should* means "I've *got* to, and if I don't do what I've got to, I'm no good!" Let me give you a simple illustration. It shows what human disturbance is, and it's a very good model. You go out of here in a half-hour and you say to yourself, "I'd like ten dollars in my purse, because I might want to take a cab, go to the movies, or eat something. I really *wish,* I *want* it, I *prefer* to have ten dollars." You then look in your purse and you have only nine. Now how do you feel? You'd prefer ten but you have nine. How would you feel?

C. That I'd like to have another dollar. Uh—disappointed.

T. Only disappointed?

C. Yeah, disappointed.

T. You wouldn't be happy?

C. No.

T. And you wouldn't be indifferent?

C. No, not at all.

T. You wouldn't be depressed or suicidal?

C. No, definitely not.

T. So you'd be *disappointed* and that's appropriate. "I'd like *X,* I have *X* minus 1, and I'm disappointed." Okay, suppose you are going out a second time and this time you devoutly believe, "I *must,* I *should,* I've *got* to have at least ten dollars. Not one hundred, not two hundred, but at least ten. I *must* have a guarantee of always having a minimum of ten." Again, you look in your purse and again you find nine. How would you then feel?

C. Terrible. Destroyed.

T. Yes, destroyed. "I don't have what I *must,* I don't have what I *should!*" You'd be anxious, destroyed, and maybe hostile. "The world's not giving me what I *must* have!" But mind you, it's the same nine dollars. It isn't the missing dollar that's upsetting you. One time you have nine and you're *disappointed.* The other time you have nine dollars and you're *destroyed* and *hostile.* Because of the *must.* As soon as you escalate a *preference* into a *must,* you make yourself anxious or depressed.

C. Yes, I can see that.

T. Now let's go one step further. You're still saying, "I *must,* I absolutely *must,* at all times have at least ten dollars"—the same hypothesis. And then you look in your pocket and you have eleven. Now how would you feel?

C. Great.

T. For how long? That's the right answer, but for how long?

C. Until I need the ten dollars again or until I use the eleven up.

T. No, even before that you would feel anxious. You still have the eleven dollars. You *have* to have at least ten and you have one more; but you're still anxious. Why?

C. After you spend it?

T. No, let's suppose you don't spend it. You're still anxious.

C. Why are you still anxious?

T. Because you're going to say to yourself, "Suppose I *spend* two, suppose I *lose* two, suppose I get *robbed*?" You see?

C. Yeah.

T. Because you know the world is such that you might *not* have ten dollars a minute from now. Right now you have eleven. That's great and you're happy. But how do you know you're going to keep it?

C. Yeah, I don't.

T. Whenever you set up a *must,* a *should,* an *ought,* or a *got to,* you're miserable when you *don't* have what you think you must and you will probably be miserable even when you *do.* Do you see that?

C. Yes.

T. A *should* equals a *must,* you see. "I should" means two things: One, "It would be better," and two, "Therefore, I *must!*" That's what the word means. Now that's what you're also saying about yourself. One, "It would be nice if I didn't have flaws, if I were perfect." And that's okay because that's not going to get you into trouble. But then you're saying, two, "And I *must* be perfect." Now how would you feel if you were not perfect?

C. Terrible.

T. Unless you arrange to be perfect. But is that likely?

C. No.

T. Suppose I wave a wand, a magic wand, and I wave it and you become perfect. You look gorgeous. Your body is exactly the way you want it. Your mind is brilliant. You're charming. Just like that, you're perfect! Now, for a while, you'll be happy. But what will you say to yourself after an hour or two? If you're perfect at this moment, what are you going to think a little later?

C. That I really couldn't be perfect.

T. No, let's suppose you know you're perfect.

C. How long will it last?

T. That's right. At this moment the therapist made me perfect with his magic wand. My breasts are the right size, my hips are marvelous, my height is great. But what is going to happen to me tomorrow? Do you know?

C. No.

T. Of course not. You're asking for two impossible things. First, "That I be perfect *right now,*" which is not going to happen because you're fallible, you're human. And, second, "That I *always* remain perfect."

As the ten-dollar example illustrates, *when you demand perfection, you will down yourself and feel miserable when you spot an imperfection.* Even if you now feel you are perfect, which is unlikely, you will become anxious over the possibility that tomorrow you may not be. Your demanding, which RET calls *shoulditis* or *musturbation,* leads to a no-win situation. As an antidote, you can vigorously challenge your ideas that (1) "I *must* appear perfect to myself and others;" (2) "It is *awful* if I don't;" and (3) "I am a *rotten person* if I have flaws." *Question these beliefs* by asking for evidence to support them, and you will see how irrational and self-defeating they are. *Act against these beliefs* by pushing yourself to do whatever it is you are insecure about doing—such as meeting new people, asserting yourself, or going for an interview. You will then begin to accept yourself with your imperfections. Enormously fearing other peoples' opinions and thereby making yourself anxious and unassertive is quite the opposite of striving for personal happiness. Often people will not approve of your looks or behavior, but you don't *have to* take them too seriously. *You* decide if there is some merit to their criticism, and act accordingly. *Negatively rating yourself, your totality, is why you fear criticism and demand perfection.*

C. I try to accept myself for being the way that I am.

T. All right. But what's the hassle?

C. I'm not happy with myself the way I am.

T. Well, we don't want you to be happy with your negative traits. We want you to be dissatisfied with *them,* but not with *yourself.* Name one of your traits you really don't like.

C. How about lack of assertiveness. I mentioned it earlier.

T. All right, let's take lack of assertiveness. Unassertiveness means, "I'd like to ask people for things I want but if I do, they may disapprove of me and I *can't stand* that." Now why can't you stand disapproval? Suppose you asked a man you really liked for something. You said, "Will you go to the museum with me?" And he said, "No, I won't go! People who go to museums are stupid!" Now why must you take that seriously!

C. Because I feel that he wouldn't want to be with me.

T. Well, suppose he said, "No, let's not go to the museum, let's go home and screw." Then how would you feel? He refused to go to the museum with you but he would gladly screw you. How would you take that?

C. That he just wanted my body. I would feel *awful.*

T. You see, you're putting yourself down. Let's suppose that he really liked your body and he didn't even know you. All he wanted to do was screw you. He's a male, and males frequently will go for your body. They hardly know you at all, and they might not even like your traits, but they want to screw you. Now how does that make *you* a worm if they only want your body?

C. Because they should want more than that.

T. Notice the *should.* They *should* want you for your personality, your mind, but they don't. Maybe they're sexually indiscriminate. Maybe you have a marvelous personality and mind, but they're only interested in your genitals. So you conclude, "If they don't like my mind, I'm a rotten person," instead of, "That's their taste. They're obsessed with sex."

C. I'd think that there must be something wrong with me.

T. But why must there be? Why can't it be *their* taste that they only go for women's bodies and not give much of a damn for their minds or personality? Some men only want to screw; that's all they enjoy. As soon as they see a woman, they don't care how stupid or bright she is. They only want to screw her. Now why does that mean there's something wrong with you?

C. It doesn't, I guess.

T. But you're saying, "If I were really noble, and great, and charming, they would want me for my mind."

C. Right.

T. But you're forgetting *them.* It's *their* taste. They may only pay attention to your mind *after* they screw you—which is true of many men. They're very excited. They look at your breasts and your ass, and right away they get an erection. And they say, "Oh boy, what a great piece she is!" And if you went to bed with them, some of them will really enjoy your mind and like you for it. But some won't. Now how does that prove *you're* no good?

C. It's their problem, I guess.

T. That's the point! You're not really facing that; that *they* have certain tastes. Suppose I meet you socially and I say to myself right away, "Oh damn, dark eyes. I really like blue!" and I completely reject you. Let's say I even say to you, "Oh, you have dark eyes. I only go for blue-eyed women." You're going to feel rejected, assuming that you like me. Right?

C. Yeah.

T. But does it really mean anything about *you?*

C. No, I don't think so.

T. Is it a flaw to have dark eyes? The next man you meet might mainly like you *because* you have dark eyes. He thrills to dark eyes, but I happen to like blue. Now how does my preference for blue eyes make you into a nothing?

C. No reason.

Some people, of either sex, might be interested in you only because of your body, eye color, or type of car. If so, don't jump to the false conclusion, "Something is wrong with *me.*" Instead, recognize that people have individual tastes and may like you or not like you for a great variety of reasons. If you believe "People *must* like me as a 'person,' before being interested in me sexually," and then down yourself when they don't follow your rule, you ignore human nature and demand that people act differently from the way they often do. Holding on to your rule will only lead to self-downing and anger at others. Surely a miserable state of affairs!

T. Suppose you're going to a party with your male friend.

C. If I don't know anyone there, I get very nervous and I clam up.

T. Because, "If I say the wrong thing—"

C. They'll think I'm stupid.

T. Well, suppose they do.

C. Well, I don't want them to think that way.

T. Well, that's undesirable, but will it really *destroy* you?

C. Maybe.

T. How will it? Let's suppose you go to this party and you say exactly the wrong thing, and everybody there thinks, "What an idiot she is!" Now how will that *destroy* you?

C. Because I want to make a good impression.

T. Fine. But you're believing, "I've *got* to make a good impression."

C. Because I want people to think highly of me.

T. You mean, "I *need* it!" You see, you're not being honest with yourself. You're not admitting that you don't have *wants* about approval. If you want an ice cream cone, that's a want; and if you don't get it you say,

"Tough! So I'm not getting it." But your search for approval is a dire *need*. You're falsely saying "I *want*" when you really mean "I *need*." Now unless you see that you have made this into a dire need and change it back to only a desire, you will continue to be anxious.

C. I see what you mean.

T. Most of the people you'll meet at the party are strangers whom you'll never see again. Right?

C. Yeah.

T. And the irony is as long as you have your *need* for approval, you're probably going to appear anxious; and they might say to themselves, "She's a weak, anxious person. How inadequate!" Some of them will. A lot of them will just say, "She doesn't talk well." But some of them will say, "She's a total slob because she doesn't talk well!"

C. I don't talk. I keep still.

T. Then some will believe, "She's dull, she's stupid, she can't talk." Which is not true, because you're talking very well to me. You're quite articulate right now because you're talking about your problem and you're not *focusing* on whether I like you. Isn't that true?

C. Yes. I want help from you but really don't care if you like me.

T. You obviously can do it. But as soon as you say to yourself, "The therapist *must* like me!" rather than "I *want* him to but he doesn't *have* to," you're going to go dumb even with me. So try to acknowledge your *need* rather than wrongly calling it a *desire*.

C. But why do I so easily escalate my desire for approval into a dire need or necessity?

T. Most people are born and reared with a strong tendency to create a dire need for approval. This is a natural, nutty, human condition. It has relatively little to do with upbringing, but upbringing makes it worse. This is the way you *easily* think and feel. Why do most people over 40 get fat? Because that's their biological tendency. Now they don't *have* to gain too much weight. Nobody *has* to overeat. But they *easily* do it. You are probably a natural perfectionist who normally *escalates your wants into needs*. And you'd better fight this tendency and keep fighting it because you're quite able to do so and to become a person who ultimately wants *without* needing.

C. Well, how do you go about doing that?

T. By first acknowledging your necessitizing. Don't say to yourself, "I'm not talking up at parties because I *want* people's approval." That's a lie. Admit the truth—"I *need*, or *think* I need, their approval." That's step number one. Look at your *got tos,* your *have tos,* your *musts,* your *shoulds,* your *oughts,* your *needs*. Then, as soon as you observe one, immediately ask yourself, "Why the hell do I *have* to win their approval?" Now what's the answer.

C. Well, in certain situations when I want something, I honestly feel that I do have to.

T. But you see! You just gave the *wrong* answer. "When I really *want* something, I *have* to have it." You're like a two-year-old. The two-year-old thinks she has to have a red lollipop and stubbornly rebels against accepting an orange one even if that's the only one available. Now does she really *have* to have the red lollipop?

C. No.

T. She *thinks* she does. Now aren't you in the same position?

C. I guess so.

T. And, incidentally, if she doesn't have the red lollipop and she thinks she *has* to have it, what happens?

C. She'll start crying.

T. She'll make herself terribly upset. But is it the lollipop; is it her desire for the lollipop which is upsetting her?

C. No.

T. It's her *dire need.* And you're not facing your needs, nor trying to give them up. Even when I was questioning you, do you see how you were hanging on to them?

The demand, the need for approval, is the core-problem in shyness. Desiring approval is fine and will only lead to disappointment if approval is not attained. But when you escalate a desire or a wish into a *demand* or *need,* you will be anxious about doing something and depressed or angry when you haven't met your goal for approval. When you tell yourself you *must* be liked at a party, you ironically make yourself anxious and are thus *less* likely to succeed.

You often refrain from going after what you want for fear others will not think well of you. And you then take others' neglect as "proof" of your worthlessness. A key thing to remember is: *Be yourself, don't try to prove yourself.*

The client in the following case is a 31-year-old male teacher. He fears being dominated by those close to him, which is directly related (as you will see) to insecurity, lack of assertiveness, and feelings of inadequacy. This case shows how such negative feelings can affect one's social and family relationships, and what one can do to become less susceptible to being, or feeling, dominated.

T. (Reading from client's form) "Difficulty in dealing with my brother and mother, run from relationships." All right, which one do you want to start with?

C. Run from relationships.

T. All right, you've never been involved, or you have been involved?

C. I have not been involved.

T. What's the pattern of your dating normally?

C. I date a girl who is safe for me. One that is not very attractive, one that I can screw easily, so that it's almost a nonrelatable type of girl. Because I say, "Well, she's not for me, and I don't like her that much because of her looks, but she'll screw, and that's as far as I want to go." That's one type of relationship, sexual. The other type is with someone whom I just won't touch. It's a nonsexual involvement. In other words, I categorize my women into sexual and nonsexual.

T. Why won't you touch these others? What's stopping you from touching them?

C. I believe that they'll get to like me more, and I'll get into a relationship. This scares me.

T. What are you afraid will happen?

C. That my mother won't be happy. This happened when I almost got involved with a certain girl, which is the problem. I enter into an area that gets scary.

T. But we're trying to find out *why* it is scary. Is it mainly your mother, that your mother is going to object to practically every woman that you get involved with? Is that what you're saying? And, therefore, you don't want to see her upset and you withdraw? Is that the reason, or is it something else? Suppose this woman had been acceptable to your mother. Would you then have withdrawn from her?

C. Yeah.

T. Because? What would *then* have been dangerous? You're *inventing* some danger. What would it be?

C. The real thing is that I'm scared they'll like me.

T. And if they do?

C. If they do, that means I may get married.

T. So, "If I get married—" Let's just assume that you do.

C. Okay, if I get married I will lose my identity.

T. How will you lose your identity if you get married?

C. I will not have any say.

T. Why is that so? You'll hurt her by refusing what she wants? She'll dominate you? Is that it?

C. Well, the domination point is part of it. I feel kind of weak in my own opinions. Thus, if I get into a relationship, I feel that I will be just knocked right out. I just will be taken over. I will be dominated, and my feelings will just not be considered.

T. As you are by your mother, for example? Are you dominated by your mother?

C. Yeah, I am.

T. And by your brother?

C. Yeah.

T. Well, let's suppose they thought poorly of you. They disapprove of what you do. Why do you have to take their views so seriously?

C. Because it's a habit.

T. Because you don't *stop* this habit and say, "Screw it! I am going to accept myself no matter who thinks what of me." And you have the belief, "Other people are correct if they think I am a worm, and it's awful if they think I am!"—It's that *belief* that leads to your weakness, your willingness to let women dominate you. You see that?

C. I'm not sure.

T. It's really your belief, "I need people's approval," that makes you so dominatable and as long as you have that belief, you will be afraid that women whom you care for will subject you and not consider your feelings.

C. And I'd better not marry any woman except a weakling who won't dominate me. But then I'll get bored with her, so that won't work out.

T. Yes. Your problem is to become firm. And the main way you're going to become stronger is by not giving *that much* of a damn what people, including women, think of you.

As the client has shown, when one has the problem of feeling weak and in danger of being dominated by others, this negatively affects many types of relationships. The core problem here, as in the previous case of shyness, is a *demand for approval.* The client is afraid that significant others will disapprove of his choices and will think badly of him; and that he, in turn, will then think badly of himself. He, therefore, will tend to do what *others* want him to and to please them rather than himself. This is what we generally mean by being "dominated" by others, and it is often opposed to choosing your personal happiness. The *thinking* part of challenging your fear of involvement includes *forcefully disputing* your irrational Beliefs (iBs) by asking for objective evidence to support them: These Beliefs usually are: 1) "I *must* have my partner's approval of what I do or say!" 2) "It is *awful* when, and *I can't stand* it if, I don't get that approval!" 3) "If my partner thinks badly of me, that proves that I am *a rotten person who does not really deserve to be happy.*"

Ask yourself the following questions: 1) "Although it is *nice* to have others' approval, where is the evidence that I *must* have what would be nice? After all, it would be nice to have a million dollars also but I hardly *need* it!" 2) "Although there are *disadvantages* to being disapproved of, why would it be *awful* or *horrible,* and where is the evidence that I *can't stand* it? Would I shrivel up and die?" 3) "How can someone's thinking badly of me ever prove that I am a *rotten person?*" Questions such as these, if asked with vigor, will help you see how irrational your beliefs are. The *behaving or acting part of disputing* your fear of involvement consists of practicing speaking your own mind and doing what you want to do even when your chosen partner may disapprove of you and reject you.

T. Apparently all the therapy you had still hasn't helped you to look at your demand for approval, because I doubt whether it's been philosophic.

C. What do you mean?

T. It showed you all kinds of things about yourself, right?

C. Yeah.

T. But those things aren't why you're disturbed. They had practically nothing to do with your rating yourself as a person. Do you know why?

C. No.

T. Let's suppose you know all those things about yourself—your child-hood, your past, and all the things you probably went through in life. Why would this knowledge do you little good? Suppose you now have insight and realize that when you were three, your mother looked at you cross-eyed and said, "You're terrible," and you hated her and loathed yourself. Why would that knowledge not change you?

C. Because I still have the habit of looking for approval.

T. Because you *still* have a three-year-old philosophy: "I *need* my mother's and other people's approval!" Until you give that up a thou-sand times—not merely understand that you have it but *attack* it and *give it up*—it'll always be around. You see, it's your *belief* that upsets you, not your experiences with your mother. And your strong tendency is to say, "I *need* people's approval, and if I stand firm, they won't approve of me" which is partially true. Some of them won't. But you go beyond that observation to the irrational Belief, "Wouldn't it be *horrible* if they didn't?" And you're not questioning that belief, are you?

C. No.

T. Well, you'd better! And the way to work against it is to get involved, especially with a "dominating" woman, and then to hold firm. How can she dominate you? How can she really rule you?

C. Yeah. It's amazing how I've stayed clear of those women.

T. Because you're convinced that they would *have to* dominate you. But let's suppose that a woman really was very dominating—most really aren't, but let's suppose she was. And suppose that if you got close to her, she would try to run you by the nose. You wouldn't have to *let* her, would you?

C. No, I wouldn't.

T. But how are you going to know that, unless you risk it?

C. Yeah. I see that.

T. And if you told me right now that you know a very dominating woman, that she's quite attractive to you, and that you're afraid she will make you do everything she wants, I'd say, "Try to get involved with her. Get some *practice* in relating to her and standing firm. For if you run away from a thing all your life, you're never going to get practice in coping."

Insight into your past, although it can be interesting, will do little to help you recognize and work against self-defeating beliefs. *These beliefs are behind your disturbed feelings and actions and lead to increased emotional pain* and decreased happiness. Doing what you fear, such as dating "dominating" partners, is a key way to work against irrational beliefs, because you begin to see that you don't *have* to be dominated, and that you *can* risk disapproval.

C. Regarding clothes—I want to buy my own and pick them out myself. I don't like my brother giving me a suit and won't wear it if he does. He's my same size and thinks I should love to wear his cast-offs.

T. That's okay to refuse, as long as you don't *overly* rebel and say to yourself "I'm not going to wear the suit *because* he gave it to me." "I'm not going to wear it because it's not my style," is very different. You see the difference? Suppose your brother just happened to buy a suit you like? Does he wear the same size as you?

C. Yeah.

T. Let's suppose, for some reason or another, his woman friend hates this fine suit so he won't wear it. It's just your size and you like it. Why would you refuse it, if that's so?

C. Well, he did give me one suit I really liked. But I had it in the closet for months and I fought him about it. "I don't want it, I don't want it!" Finally, one day I put it on and I wore it. At that time I think my head was in good shape.

T. Right. Because you were saying, "Do I *like* this suit?" And not, "Who gave it to me?" If he gives you a suit, there's no magic about his giving it that makes him run you by the nose.

C. He had a sexual problem once where he couldn't get a hard on. Okay, so he used to tell me this. So all of a sudden I couldn't get a hard on either.

T. Well, that's self-suggestion, probably. "If my brother can't get it up, maybe I won't be able to either." And then you don't because you're worried about it.

C. So that has set a rebellion in motion in my head, by my saying, "I don't want to know anything about you or do anything you want."

T. But that's *over*rebellion. You think—wrongly—that just by hearing about his doings, you will automatically become overinfluenced. So you make yourself afraid to hear anything about him.

As is the case with this client, when you feel that you are weak and that, therefore, others dominate you, you may compensate by swinging all the way over in the other direction. This leads to overrebellion (frequently seen in adolescents), which means you're trying to do the *opposite* of what others want, even when what they ask you to do would be beneficial. This behavior is based upon the irrational idea, "If I do *any-thing* they want me to do, I will surely become hopelessly dominated by them."

C. With women, I feel the need for support before I can stand up to them.

T. But again you're saying, "I can't do it myself." But you *can* run your own life. You're quite able to take chances and risks, stand up to people, and go with so-called dominating females. And if things get rough, you can just calmly hold your ground. You don't have to rebel, but just hold your ground and do what you want to do. And if they don't like it, that's tough! So they don't like it! The point is not to do things because others do them, and not to *not* do them because others do them. Just find out "What do *I* want," and take a chance on that. And if it works out, great, and if it doesn't, too bad! "I'll do something else." You'd better take risks, and you're avoiding them—especially emotional risks.

C. But the big risk is that I came in here to see you, and I'm happy that I did.

T. Right! What's the worst thing that could have happened to you, seeing me?

C. You could have been a screamer who yelled at me.

T. But let's suppose I did yell at you. "You're a ninny! You've had all this therapy, and you're still kissing people's asses!" Suppose I yelled at you like that? Then what would have happened? Let's suppose that I was even right, that you were acting inadequately, and I said, "You're a dumb cluck! You *shouldn't* behave like that!" How could my yelling affect you?

C. Well, by my inside feeling that I'm a dumb cluck.

T. By your *agreeing* with me that you were. There's no other way I can affect you.

C. Yeah, by my agreeing.

T. That's right. Your *agreement,* which *you* control. You don't control me. I can call you every name under the sun, and you can't stop me. But you do control your agreeing with me. When a child, a two-year-old child, listens to his mother, the problem is not so much what she tells him: "You're no good! You're a louse! You *shouldn't* do this!" It's his nutty *agreeing* with her. And then he *continues* agreeing with her for the next 20 years. That's what's affecting him, *not* what she did or said.

C. His agreeing.

T. That's right. The same thing goes with your brother, your mother, and with other females. If you feel awful because they say you're no good, you're *agreeing* with them. They can say exactly the same thing, and you can tell yourself, "Well, maybe they're right about my behavior, but I'm not a worm for doing it. So I *acted* crummily. Now how am I going to *change* these acts?" You never have to put *yourself* down, no matter who says what. Suppose the whole world says you're a dummy. They'd all be wrong. Now do you know why they'd be wrong?

C. Because I don't have to agree with them.

T. And because there are no dummies. They may be right about your poor behavior, but to call *you* worthless labels you as a person who can *only* and *always* engage in dumb behavior. It also means that your *totality,* your *essence,* is damnable, contemptible. And that's a nutty idea. No human, including you, is contemptible. Your *behavior* may stink, but *you're* no *stinker.* Do you see the difference between those two views?

C. Yeah. I *am* not what I *do.*

T. Right! And some people will damn you, there's no doubt about that. They'll put *you* down when a few of your *acts* are incompetent. That's *their* craziness.

C. This is the basic meat of my problem. If a person says something bad about me, I agree.

T. Right. Instead of saying, "Well, he might be right about my deed or trait. I did that job foolishly, but I am never a rotten person. I'm *a person who did a rotten job.* What the hell am I going to do next time to do a better job? You can't rate *me,* I'm too complex, I'm an ongoing process." You can't rate a *process,* you can't rate a *human.* You can only rate his or her deeds, acts, performances. And you're spending your whole life rating *yourself* instead of rating your *behavior.*

C. Yeah, I'm my own worst enemy.

T. Right. You rate your traits, and you say, "That was good or that was bad," which is correct. Because you want to do better in life, do things more efficiently. But then you foolishly tell yourself, "If my traits stink then *I'm* no good. If my traits are good, *I* am a great person." They're both incorrect. You cannot really rate humans; you can only rate their acts. People are processes, like the process of evolution. *You can't rate a process.* Another way of saying this is: You can rate your acts, but you can't rate *that which acts*—you. Humans are born and reared with this nutty tendency to give themselves a report card; and you've indulged in this tendency all your life. It's hard not to do it because it is a strong tendency. When you meet a woman, you're not merely saying, "Would it be enjoyable for me to be with her?" You're saying, "Can I *succeed?* Suppose she dominates me! Suppose I fall on my face! That would be horrible! I'd be a slob!" So you make your relationship with her too "dangerous."

The previous dialogue represents a most important lesson in overcoming your shyness, insecurity, and fear of domination. Your *acts* can be legitimately rated but your *person,* your *self,* cannot be. Fear of disapproval stems from *agreeing* with the idea that you, the total person, can be rated on the basis of one or several of your many deeds and traits. We wish to make it clear that we are not advocating a policy of not caring at all about people's opinions, since there are real advantages to having certain people like us. What we are advocating is a philosophy that leads to that golden mean between the extremes; namely that you *desire* rather than *demand* approval and that you attempt to please significant others *only at certain times* (such as when you love them or want to get something from them). We question your *compulsively* and *invariantly* striving to please them.

C. Sometimes I feel it's dangerous to see a "strong" woman.

T. The "danger" is that she might try to dominate you; and you'd better either hold your ground and refuse to be her slave—or else get away. That's all that would happen, if you weren't telling yourself, "Yes, she's right! I am a worm who should be dominated, and she's got my number! So I'll let her put a ring through my nose for the rest of my life." If we can get you to see your *agreement* with people who put you down, to listen to their name-calling but refuse to *agree* with it, you would then be undominatable. Your *agreement,* and not their putting you down, enslaves you.

C. Only now am I beginning to realize that I am allowed to have my own opinions.

T. Right. *You* allow yourself to. The universe doesn't care one way or the other whether you have your own opinions or kiss others' asses. But *you choose* to either kiss their asses and adopt their views or to stand on your own feet and hold your own opinions. If others don't like your views, tough! You can always find some people who do.

C. And there are a lot of people out there.

T. Right! And there are lots of women, some of whom won't see you for dust, especially if you're firm and strong. But others will think you're great that way. Why not go through enough of them until you find those who don't need to be dominating?

C. Yeah, it's my choice.

T. Right, your choice. That's what you'd better tell yourself a thousand times. *Your* decision, *your* choice. It's their choice to try to dominate you and your choice, which you can always take, to stand firm.

C. I guess I've chosen so far to stay and be dominated—and then make myself angry. Or to cravenly run away.

T. Yes, and even when you do run, you don't have to put yourself down. Instead of, "Suppose I let them dominate me. What a weakling I'd be!" you could tell yourself, "Suppose I let them dominate me, I'll then stand firm and go back to my own views." You always have a choice. Also: "If they won't stop being so dominating, I'll leave the relationship."

C. I see. But I had to flee from this last girl before I really gave the relationship a chance. The pain of being dominated was too much. The pressure started to build up.

T. But it was *your* pressure. You *let her* dominate you, which you didn't have to do. And then you told yourself, "I'm a weakling!" which you weren't. You were a human being who acted weakly some of the time. And you probably said to yourself, "If I let this relationship continue, I won't be able to escape!" Nonsense! Of course, you're able to escape. You can always escape, even if you are legally married to a would-be dominating woman!

The key point here is that you can choose to become assertive and to achieve personal freedom and happiness rather than to make yourself insecure, self-downing, and "dominatable." Ironically, most people will tend to have more respect for you when you stand firm; and *you have the right to seek out this type of person.* Assertiveness is a sort of middle ground between (1) always doing what others want to gain their "needed" approval, and (2) aggression, in which you believe that others have no rights and must behave as you wish. Assertiveness simply means seeking what you want and avoiding what you don't want, without downing yourself or others.

These two cases have demonstrated some of the problems associated with having a belief system based on the *need* for approval and the demand for perfection. This type of belief system, and the self-downing that goes with it, leads to the feelings and behaviors we call shyness, insecurity, fear of asserting oneself. If you suffer from those problems, your solution lies in (1) *forcefully attacking* the irrational beliefs we have mentioned and (2) *acting against* these Beliefs by practicing contradictory behaviors. This will help you to a more secure (no self-rating) existence, and to achieving considerably more personal happiness.

CHAPTER 9

Overcoming Feelings of Guilt

We shall now leave the problem area dealing with insecurity and turn to an area that represents great difficulty for many people. This is the problem of overcoming guilt about leaving a marriage or close relationship. Once the guilt is greatly diminished, the client can *logically* discuss the pros and cons of the relationship, and have a much greater chance at making the best decision. As you will see in the following case, the therapist does not begin by discussing the details of the relationship, but starts with a direct attack upon the guilt.

The client in this case is a 37-year-old accountant whose problem involves his fear of terminating his marriage.

T. The paper here says, "Can't terminate marriage." Why can't you terminate the marriage? Does anything special stop you?

C. I don't know. I'm anxious. Maybe it's guilt. I've been trying to get out of the marriage, feeling I should, for maybe six or seven years.

T. All right. Now why would you be guilty if you left?

C. I guess because it's something I never thought I should do.

T. But why *shouldn't* you leave a marriage if you don't want to stay in it?

C. Well, it's hard for me to come to grips with that, although I know other people do it, and one out of every three people gets divorced.

T. Right. So if everybody—.

C. But I can't identify with that. It goes back. My father died when I was six months old. I had a stepfather who was very weak. I grew up with my grandparents in their home; it was a mess and I always promised myself that if I had a wife and family and all that, I would keep them together.

T. But that was a foolish promise, since many people are worse rather than better off in a bad but undissolved marriage. Now why don't you give up on it?

C. I can't give it up. I can't.

T. Then suffer the consequences of keeping this promise. But you obviously *can* give it up if you really want to do so and try.

C. How can I? I feel it in here (pointing to his heart) that I *have* to keep my marital promise. How can I change that deep inner feeling?

T. By changing your crazy philosophy of life and accepting the fact that you have one damned life to live, approximately 75 years of it. That's all. And if you devote it largely to promises to others rather than to enjoying yourself, is that what you really call *living?*

Here the therapist quickly picks up on one of the client's major irrational beliefs: that he *shouldn't* leave a marriage even though he is very unhappy in it. The idea that you *should* (meaning *must*) do or not do anything, such as staying married against your will, is really absurd. There is no law in the universe which states that you *can't* leave an unhappy situation that you no longer want. And because this client has learned, in the past, that he *must* keep marital promises is no reason why he cannot change that belief today. RET shows him that he *can* examine any of his irrational Beliefs and *can* change them.

C. I know that it's crazy to feel I *must* stay married.

T. Not exactly! You don't *know* it's crazy. You mean that once in a while you know it's crazy. But most of the time, *strongly,* you believe it's sane.

C. Yeah, right. But I'm very uncomfortable.

T. You're uncomfortable with the marriage, but you're convincing yourself that you *have* to stay married. Now, unless you give up that stubbornly ingrained belief, you're going to suffer. Anybody who has nutty beliefs pays the consequences; and you want to get rid of the consequences while keeping the beliefs, so you're really not trying very hard to give up the belief. You will keep subscribing to it—and therefore either stay miserably married or feel exceptionally guilty if you leave your wife. The important point here is to see that your beliefs create self-damning emotions (such as guilt), which block effective action. Giving up such beliefs begins with seeing why they are irrational and replacing them with beliefs that are rational—and that, therefore, enhance your personal happiness.

C. What about my relationship with my children? I feel close to them. I feel like I want to be there with them. I live on my own, and have for three years, but I visit on the weekends. So I'm still half in and half out of the marriage. Also, my wife's in the hospital now, and I have to go home every night. She has back problems. I have no social life of my own. I'm in independent practice as an accountant and I haven't had any income in five months. I'm $18,000 in debt. Wherever I turn—business or social life—nothing seems to work. I have a sense of obligation to my kids, but I can't talk to my wife about anything except who's going to go for the groceries. I do take the kids to visit her in the hospital, and this compounds my sense of guilt. How can you leave a woman that's in the hospital?

T. The answer is that you can. There's little question about it. How long will she be in the hospital?

C. She may come out in two or three weeks.

T. All right, so let's talk about that. Let's suppose she's out of the hospital, and she is somewhat better. Why can't you leave then?

C. Why can't I leave the marriage?

T. Yeah, why don't you have the right to be happier at the expense of your wife?

C. Okay, let's say I'm not sure that—somehow it must be a lack of confidence in myself.

T. Or, "If I got a divorce, I wouldn't be a happy, happy human being?"

C. I've had glimmers of happiness. When I am alone and can meet people or pick up women I'm pretty happy. You know, for the evening or a couple of days. But that quickly goes down the drain because I go to visit my kids and so on and I'm right back into the same pattern.

T. But you're ignoring the basic philosophic issue: that as a human being, you have a right to put yourself first, even if your wife wants you to put her and your family first and feels deprived if you don't.

C. That I can't come to grips with.

T. Well, then suffer. Put yourself second. You see you have two choices—put yourself first or second. If you put yourself second, your wife will want you to stay, so you'll stay. Put yourself first, and you'll say, "Too bad!" and leave.

You have the right to put yourself first just as others have the right to put themselves before you. This does not mean to deliberately seek to hurt another. You can *choose* to be happy by primarily thinking of your interests and secondarily considering those of others. You thereby can decide whether you stay in a poor marriage, poor job, or poor anything. In essence, choosing the belief, "I cannot leave something because someone else will feel hurt or deprived," guarantees your staying in an unpleasant situation. The key is to challenge the beliefs which lead to unhappiness and replace them with more appropriate ones.

Your irrational beliefs ("I *must* not leave a marriage"), which you are often unaware of, create self-defeating emotions such as guilt and anxiety. *Guilt keeps you from doing what you enjoy, and can make you a slave to others.* Downing yourself, which is a major part of guilt, is never necessary. Weigh the real consequences of an act, and if they are poor, seek to do better next time. You can seldom make logical decisions or correct past errors until you accept yourself fully.

C. What's going to happen if I put myself second?

T. Well, the heavens will open and you'll rule the universe. Is that what's going to happen?

C. Something like that.

T. On the form you filled out, you say you're an atheist; but actually you're not.

C. How is that?

T. Well, you are not devoutly religious in the conventional sense, but you are still a devout believer in hogwash. That is religiosity.

C. Religiosity?

T. Yes, your religiosity is that you believe that other humans *must* come before you. That's a devoutly held belief with no empirical evidence to support it.

C. Yeah, but you see this was the way my mother controlled me. Because she constantly said, "Be a good boy and go to school and make your grades, and set yourself up in business; go to graduate school; serve others; become proficient at your work. The world and the universe— God—will reward you." She didn't even think about money. It's only in the last two years that I even thought about having to earn money to survive.

T. That's what I call hogwash. The world and the universe hardly give a damn about you. They are impartial and *won't* necessarily reward you for being "a good boy." You can distinguish, as we try to help people do in RET, between being religious (or philosophic) and being devoutly religious (or dogmatic and absolutistic). Devout religion, or religiosity, is irrational and tends to interfere with your life goals and values while less rigid religious views may not.

C. I know. Well, that's my programming.

T. That's your *acceptance* of your programming. We are all programmed.

C. Okay, but from the day you're born—a long period of time, 12, 16, 18, 20 years—you get programmed with this garbage. You marry a wife because you see others conforming to that custom. She likes to tread upon you, so you go through eight or 10 years allowing her to do that.

T. No, that's not true. You can *choose* to go through it—or not!

C. Okay, but I accepted this programming.

T. Suppose you were programmed to only vote for Republicans. Would you keep doing it?

C. It took me a long time to stop voting Republican.

T. Right. But you changed.

C. I did change. The point is how to overcome this very heavy trip I've laid on me, not only around me but inside of me? Just to suddenly say I can be myself won't do it.

T. No, I am afraid that only very hard work will do it.

How you are "programmed" (conditioned by your upbringing) over the years often does influence you. But change is very possible if you are willing to work at changing false or irrational Beliefs. This is basically done by asking for the evidence for a Belief such as, "I can't put myself first and leave a marriage without feeling guilty." You will see that there is really no supporting evidence for that Belief. After going over this numerous times, you then will begin to recondition yourself and develop a saner Belief System.

C. I will not change quickly.

T. No.

C. But how can I take positive steps so that I can reprogram myself without going through 10 years of psychoanalysis or something like that?

T. The answer is to stop and vigorously challenge your irrational ideas many times. If you do, there's little doubt that you can give up your hogwash because it's now *yours,* not your mother's, not society's. You *accept* it. In the past, you have agreed with this nonsense and you're still actively agreeing.

C. I am, but now you have helped me see that it *is* nonsense. I've identified it. I've been to three different therapists in the last two years, but the effect of their advice lasted only a few months. We finally got to the same point that you got me to in 10 minutes, which I appreciate.

T. So either you're going to work diligently to give up the nonsense or—.

C. There must be some way, some other insight, something you can tell me to help me. You just can't sit in that chair.

T. There's no insight that works by itself. *You* either reiterate a belief or *you* vigorously combat it, and now you'd better work at this combating! You're a bright guy, and if you vigorously combat your belief that you must put others first, you will give it up. If you don't combat it, you will continue to have it for years.

As the client has just been shown, there is no magical way to change a Belief. Only hard work will lead you to see that you can accept yourself and refuse to down yourself. Since your subscribing to false beliefs is often reinforced during your upbringing, you had better vigorously challenge them in order to make any basic personality change.

C. I have to get out of this environment that I'm in, picking a woman up on Monday or Tuesday night, sleeping with her, going to visit my kids, not getting any new business this week, going deeper into debt. Now what can I do to change this deadly routine?

T. The RET model of change is very simple. Let's suppose that you believe that black cats are unlucky and you live in a neighborhood of black cats. Let's suppose that. Now that's a nutty idea. Right?

C. Yeah.

T. Now you can do two things to get rid of that idea. What do you think they are?

C. To get rid of the idea?

T. That black cats are unlucky.

C. Well, you would move away from the neighborhood; that might be effective action.

T. No, that's the opposite of effective action. That's usually the wrong action.

C. Yes, I see. To get rid of the idea, you would have to change your idea that the black cats were unlucky.

T. Yes. You would first counterattack it vigorously many times, asking yourself "How the hell could a black cat actually hurt or harm me?" Second, your action would not be moving out of the neighborhood. It would be the opposite.

C. Moving out would be running away.

T. That's right. So you already see what the right action would be. It would be patting innumerable black cats on the head; or perhaps getting a black cat as a pet. You could thus show yourself over and over, empirically, that black cats won't harm you.

C. Well, that's an action, getting closer to a black cat and patting it on the head. And I thought that I was beginning to take that kind of action by taking the step of moving out.

T. Right, that is the first step.

Once you recognize an irrational Belief (one that helps create self-defeating emotions and behaviors), such as that black cats are harmful, you had better work against it in two major ways. The first is through thinking, and the second is through behaving differently. In regard to the Belief, "I must not put myself first and leave a bad marriage," the thinking part would consist of vigorously questioning it by asking what evidence supports it. The behavioral part would involve taking specific actions, such as dating, consulting a lawyer, and so on. This may require much effort, but unfortunately there is no magical or easy way to change your philosophy.

C. When I moved here alone for a year, I should have separated from my wife at that point.

T. It would have been wise to do so, but watch your *shoulds* and *musts!* It would have been wise, but there's no reason why you *must* act wisely! Right now there are two obvious steps you can take which are somewhat similar to your overcoming a superstition about black cats. One is, as I've said, vigorously contradicting your nutty philosophy, over and over, every time it comes into your head—that is, the philosophy that others come first and that, compared to them, you don't count.

C. In my situation, what would be analogous to my starting to pet the black cat?

T. Oh, that's simple. Doing the opposite thing to what you're now doing. You could gradually start staying away from your wife and family.

C. I've had six years of gradualness!

T. Yes, but that's been *too* gradual. A better but still gradual plan might be that during the next few months you could see them fewer weekends, make less frequent telephone calls. Thus, you could call your children on the phone and speak to them for only five or ten minutes a day. And you could firmly let your wife know, "Look dear, this is it. You'd better go out and find somebody else." Try to convince her by action, because actions speak louder than words.

C. So I'd better do two things: *one,* think against my put-yourself-last philosophy; and *two,* act against it, which I have done only slightly.

T. Yes. And to help yourself act, you could employ operant conditioning or reinforcement. Do you know what that is?

C. No, not by that term.

T. Operant conditioning is a body of self-management principles created by the famous psychologist, B. F. Skinner. Using it, you reward yourself when you take a self-promised action, such as breaking away from your wife. You can also penalize yourself if you don't take it. Suppose you make an agreement with yourself, for example, to only spend one day a week with your wife and family. Then if you spend two days or more, you immediately—and I mean *immediately*—refrain from some rewarding activity (such as reading), and you immediately—and not 10 weeks from now—do something obnoxious (like sending $100 to a cause you hate). This technique is called reinforcement or aversive conditioning, and many people use it to good advantage. Thus, you could bargain yourself, "*After* I stay away from my wife for six days, I will allow myself to date another woman whom I would really like to see."

C. Yeah, I understand. It's interesting.

T. But you're not doing it, you see. You're allowing yourself the good things you want while *still* weakly doing your wife's bidding. If you made some of your enjoyments contingent upon your being firm with her, you'd be surprised how firm you might soon become!

In order to help yourself meet your goals (such as the goal of challenging irrational Beliefs every day), you can use rewards and penalties. Only *you* can really decide what would be a potent reward or penalty for yourself. After deciding that, you try immediately rewarding yourself upon meeting your daily goal. If rewards work, then fine. But if they don't, you can use a potent, immediate penalty when you fail to meet your goal. But remember—reward or penalize yourself in order to diminish self-defeating thinking and acting, *not* because you are a "good" or "bad" person.

C. I'm in a pattern, and I'm sure it must have something to do with what screwed up the whole business.

T. Yes, your pattern is that you have hope, faith, and charity that something will happen to change you. But you're in the saddle seat; *you* control your own destiny. And only *you* can really change yourself.

C. Yes, but to have faith in any given action, to see whether it's working or not, I have to experience achievement.

T. Yes, you're largely right. But you often have to *force yourself,* quite uncomfortably, to *get* learning experiences. And only when you force yourself will you *see* that you can change.

C. I believe it. This idea of taking control of my life and being the captain of the ship and taking the consequences. I'll try it, but I have not had the experience yet that works.

T. Because you haven't tried. If you try it, you'll get the experience.

C. What are the guarantees that it'll work?

T. There are *no* guarantees in the universe. Zero. No guarantees. That's what sanity means: accepting that reality. There's only probability and chance in the universe, as far as we can tell. No certainties, no musts, no absolutes.

C. Well, I just don't have that experience—of taking the responsibilities or the consequences.

T. I know that.

C. I guess I'm saying that if I take the consequences, if I act, if I jump ahead, if I hit some problem out there and get knocked down a couple of times, I want somebody to help me.

T. But the only one who can truly help you is you. It's the same thing with the black cat. You can say, "But I've never gone toward a black cat, therefore I can't." You never approached a black cat, therefore you have no experience but that doesn't mean you can't *get* it.

C. But in my life I have done something like approaching black cats. I have been trying to force myself away from my wife and kids.

T. You've been doing it, but much too gradually. It'll take 20 more years at the rate you're going.

C. Yeah, I won't last that long!

T. Well, you might, but you'll probably have a miserable existence.

Two important points are brought out here. One is that there are no guarantees about *anything;* and the other is that only by *your* hard work can you begin to make desired changes in your thoughts, feelings, and actions. Therapy sessions can show you how to make changes, but no one can make them for you.

The client in the next case is a 35-year-old editor who feels guilty about leaving her alcoholic husband. Although the theme here is similar to that of the previous case, some important and different points are brought out.

T. [Reading the form the client filled out] "I love my husband, but he is dependent on alcohol, and I resent our lack of sex and togetherness resulting from this condition; I seem unable to leave him or help him to free himself and, therefore, us from alcohol." Now let's just suppose he stayed alcoholic, which is certainly possible, why couldn't you leave him? Why are you dependent on him?

C. Well, I think there are two reasons. One is because I feel that if I leave him, I worry about what's going to happen to him: you know, smoking in bed and his health, sleepwalking, and that sort of thing, and I just worry about him and his safety from that point of view.

T. Yeah, but why don't you worry about *you* more? Now let's assume he may harm himself or may get into trouble. Why aren't you more concerned about *you?*

C. Because ultimately I don't want to live with guilt if something should happen to him. I feel like I'll be guilty for the rest of my life if something bad should happen.

T. Let's suppose you left him for your benefit, because you saw he's not going to get over the alcoholism, and then he harmed himself. Why would you be guilty? Because you picked you over him? Why should you pick him over you?

C. I don't know.

T. Well, that seems to be your nutty standard. "Another human being is more important than I am." That's what you're saying, aren't you?

C. Yes.

T. Well, what makes another human being more important than you?

C. I guess it's just a philosophy of life that I have, that ultimately I feel as though we are responsible as human beings for each other, and that if we always choose ourselves then that's a very isolated way to go through life.

T. But if you *never* choose yourself, what kind of way is that to go through life?

C. I guess I want the best of both worlds, to have my cake and eat it too. I want to be well, I want to be happy. I want to be able to fulfill myself and see his potential fulfilled as well.

T. But the obvious best answer would be for him to stop his drinking and other self-defeating acts. But you'd better face the fact that he may never do that. How has he been for the last year?

C Just exactly the same. Our relationship has improved slightly because I had been seeing other men outside. We had separated for a year, and after we got back together I continued to see one other man for a while. But I haven't for about the last month and a-half or two months. Ever since I stopped seeing the other man, our relationship has gotten better in terms of no heated arguments or tremendous anxiety and all that on his part. But, on the other hand, that deep feeling of unhappiness is stronger in me. Because I don't feel fulfilled. And I can't when he falls asleep drunk almost every night.

The client quickly admits that guilt prevents her from leaving her husband, even though his alcoholism has shown no improvement. In order to make an important decision such as this, you had better use a "hedonic calculus." This means you carefully weigh the pros and cons involved and thus make an enlightened choice. Self-defeating emotions (such as guilt, anxiety, depression, and hostility) *interfere* with a sensible decision-making process. When you feel guilty, you do two different things. First, you decide if you really did something wrong or irresponsible. Assuming that you did, then, second, you down yourself for it. This second part is not rational, because you can really only rate each *act* you do as good or bad, not rate *yourself* globally. "You" really are a highly complex and changing process composed of many positive and negative traits and acts. Downing *yourself,* moreover, actually prevents you from dealing with correcting your mistakes and making fewer of them in the future.

T. You're an attractive woman. Why don't you get another man if the one that you were with didn't work out?

C. Well, it's not that it didn't work out. He wants to see me and I still want to see him, but it's too painful.

T. What is painful?

C. Well, he's married and I'm married. I don't seem capable of leaving my husband, and it's so difficult for us to see each other.

T. Because your husband would find out? Is that why it's difficult?

C. No, he knew that I was seeing this other man. I couldn't lie about it.

T. And what was his attitude while you were seeing the other man? Your husband's attitude?

C. Terrible.

T. So that seeing this man would lead to marital disruption?

C. Right.

T. But why, if you wanted to work it out with your husband, didn't you secretly see another man and not tell your husband, so that he wouldn't upset himself?

C. Because he keeps such close tabs on me.

T. Oh, so it would be impractical?

C. Yes.

T. What sort of work do you do?

C. Well, right now I edit children's literature.

T. Is it regular hours?

C. Yes, regular hours.

T. So he would find out if you weren't home. And you couldn't find any excuse, like being in the library or something like that?

C. Well, I'll tell you very frankly, I've lived through that sort of a life for so long that I'm really exhausted about it. I just can't stand it anymore, this lying and having to make up stories. I'm just exhausted with it, and it really takes too much away from my profession. I want to take this energy that I needed for hiding my relationships outside of my marriage and put it into my work.

T. All right; but there's another thing you could do, if you wanted. You could say to your husband, "Look, dear, I'm going to have outside affairs until you stop the drinking."

C. Yes, I've done that. That's what I did this last time when I came back to him and I said, "All right, this is it, you know." And he said it was unfair trying to compare drinking to my having an affair and he couldn't accept it. He just won't accept it. In other words, he wants me on *his* terms.

T. Yes, but on his terms he's going to keep drinking and he's going to keep not having sex with you. Isn't that what his terms really are?

C. Yes, that's what they've always been.

T. And that's not going to work out, is it?

C. No, and that's my problem. I really don't know what to do anymore. I felt almost silly this morning coming in to see you, because I really feel like I understand this whole thing clearly, and I realize that I either have to commit myself to living with him according to his standards, be very unhappy living with him, or separate from him. And yet I don't seem to be able to make a move.

T. Well, let's just talk about separation. Why couldn't you separate and once again give him the option that just as soon as he stops the drinking, you would then go back? Now what would stop you from doing that?

If a serious and long-standing problem (such as alcoholism with lack of sex) exists in a marriage, and especially if previous efforts at reducing the problem have failed, then it is reasonable to examine other alternatives that may lead to a happier existence. These may include seeing other partners, either secretly or as part of an ultimatum, or possibly leaving the marriage on a trial basis. Decisions such as these can best be made when you do not feel guilty, depressed, or hostile. In essence this means without downing yourself or your partner. If you feel guilty, your feeling stems from the belief, "*I* must not behave in a certain manner, and *I* rate as a rotten person if I do." If you feel angry, your feeling comes from the belief "*You* must not behave badly to me, and you are a rotten person, deserving of punishment, if you do." Once you are aware of having these beliefs, you can forcefully challenge them by asking yourself, "Why *must* I or anyone else behave as I demand?" You will then conclude that there are reasons why it would be better if you and your partner behaved well but there is no support for your *must.* You also can ask yourself, "How does anyone rate as a *rotten person,* even if he or she does rotten things?" Answer, "No one really does, since it is next to impossible to rate complex humans in a global way. A person is an organism who performs many acts, good and bad, an organism that is an everchanging *process.*"

C. I spent one year away from him. We've now been back together in our marriage for six months, and I feel as though I've done everything that I could to try to help him get out of this need for alcohol. But I haven't done everything to free myself from my guilt and anxiety about leaving him.

T. Right. But what have you done then?

C. Well, I had seen other men on the side, and I was getting my own needs gratified and therefore not forcing the issue with him, you see. I was able to live a double life. But I'm getting too old for this kind of thing, I guess.

T. But right now for the last month or so, have you been doing everything you could to help him? In the last month? Let's talk about that.

C. Yes, I've tried to help him.

T. And he's not changing.

C. No, though actually he's a much happier human being.

T. But he's still drinking and he's still not having sex with you. Right?

C. Right.

T. Then why can't you leave him? Couldn't you tell yourself, "I'm trying to do everything and it still doesn't work." Why couldn't you convince yourself it's okay to leave him?

C. I think perhaps I could.

T. It seems to me you could do something like that. Spend a few months refraining from having affairs; devote your time to him; be as good as you can, giving him a chance to stop drinking. Then, if he doesn't, leave him. In that way, you give him the option, even after you've left him, of getting off the alcohol, having sex with you regularly, and working his way back to a relationship with you. You can still give him that option.

C. You see, the thing is this tremendous need that I have. We met when we were at college, when we were in our teens, and we've been together ever since, even though we haven't been married all that time. It's just that he's been so much a part of my life and I a part of his, and we've been so dependent on each other for so many years, that this move to give up on him—that's really what it is, you know—is what I can't face. I don't think I am able to do it. I feel like it's a great defeat of my life, not to have been able to pull him out of it.

T. That's nonsense, utter nonsense! It's not a defeat on your part, it's really a defeat on *his* part. He refuses—in order to retain the marriage with you that he wants—he refuses to stay off alcohol. Which is the only way your marriage is going to work. So why do you see it as *your* defeat?

C. That's what I thought. But he keeps on believing and he keeps on trying to convince me that it can work with him on the alcohol.

T. Well, he'd better get rid of that idea! Either he stops drinking or else. It's not going to work while he's drinking. You've had years knowing him with the drinking. Has it ever worked?

C. Of course not.

T. Will it?

C. Never.

T. All right. If he wants to unrealistically think, which almost every alcoholic or pill-taker does, "I can remain on the pills and get along with my wife," or "I can drink and get along with her," if he wants to believe that, then let him believe that; but it's utter nonsense!

Even after the therapist suggests the option of the client devoting herself to her husband for the next few months and thus giving him another chance at drinking less, she feels it would still be *her* defeat if she left. Her conclusion follows from a philosophy that places one consistently second to others. In your own case, this would be okay if you really want to spend your life making others happy at your expense. If not, then you had better work to acquire a belief system that places a few significant people in your life as *close seconds* but not necessarily *before* you. Achieving personal happiness stems from mainly doing what is best for you without needlessly and deliberately hurting others. Another way of saying this: Be self-interested (primarily devoted to your own health and happiness) but not selfish (working against the interests of others).

C. Right. I've come to this point of forcing the issue now. I stopped the escapism of living the double life and getting my surface needs fulfilled while living with him. But I need to get over this hump of coming right to the point and facing the issues now. And I'm saying that something has got to be done, and I see everything for what it is, which I never wanted to do before. But now to make the move, to just make the move! I hoped that I would be able to convince him that it was absolutely essential for him to stop drinking for us to be able to have a good life. Then, once he would stop doing that, I could start living my life.

T. Let's suppose he's not convinced, which obviously he still isn't. You haven't convinced him, I haven't convinced him, nobody has convinced him to stop drinking. We don't know whether he'll ever quit. But don't you think he has a better chance of stopping if you stop your vacillation? If you're really out for *you,* and no nonsense, don't you think you might help him stop drinking?

C. Yeah, I thought of that. I realized that I've often been a deterrent to his stopping.

T. Yes. He may use you, possibly as a cop-out. And if you stop being a cop-out and he knows that you are determined to put yourself first and him at best second, then maybe that will help him stop. We don't know if it actually will. But this way, being weak yourself, you haven't helped him stop drinking.

C. No, of course not. But the issue here is finding myself, now that I'm 35, and going out on my own. I've never had trouble finding male partners and that sort of thing. I really think in terms of myself as a female, as a quality person. On the other hand, there is the problem of my having children at the age of 35. What if I don't find a man that I want to live with for another six years, and it's going to be too late to have children? I really do want to have children.

T. And that would be unfortunate, if you never had any. But again, that's all the more reason why maybe you'd better get going and not be dependent upon him; because as long as you're dependent on him, the years will go by and you still won't have any children.

C. I know. I haven't had children all this time because of the problem. Both his brother and sister are alcoholics, and so is his father.

T. Right. So it wouldn't be the wisest thing in the world to have children with somebody who, even if he got over the alcoholism, still has the tendency to be that nutty. Consequently, considering the strong tendency of his family members to be severely disturbed, any children you have by him might possibly inherit this tendency.

The therapist points out that if the client lets her husband know, in no uncertain terms, that she will leave if he does not improve in several months, she can actually help motivate him to change. If your alcoholic mate feels that you will consistently put yourself second, you may actually contribute to a lack of improvement. Regarding the issue of children, there is evidence of their being born with a predisposition (ease) of becoming disturbed when one or both parents are seriously disturbed. So if having children is one of your goals, you had better weigh this factor carefully.

C. What about him?

T. What about him? What do you mean, "What about him?"

C. That he's an important human being. He's extremely important to me.

T. He's important, but is he more important than *you?*

C. But is that the only issue in life?

T. No, but it's one main issue. We'd better usually put ourselves first and others second. And second doesn't mean last; it means second.

C. Yeah, I know. You're right.

T. But?

C. But if I leave him, then I'm abandoning him.

T. But if you stay with him, don't you abandon *you* if he's not going to change? Not if you stay with him and he changes. But if you stay with him and he remains an alcoholic, isn't that your abandonment of you?

C. Yes it is. But what I'm saying is this: Let's say that I make the choice for me, which of course will be the rational one to make. Still, if your mother were dying of a disease and what was right for you at that moment was to go to another city and accept a good job, you might well not do it. You are involved with her, too—and what happens to her if you leave?

T. Yes. But don't forget that your mother would not be voluntarily choosing to die of cancer—while your husband *is* choosing to remain alcoholic.

C. Well, I understand that. But what I wanted to ask you is how do I deal with the feelings that I have about abandoning him because he has no friends?

T. *Your feelings come from your ideas.* You'd better say, "How do I deal with my philosophy, my ideas," because you don't have feelings without ideas. You can deal with your feelings by dealing with your ideas which create the feelings. You see?

C. There seems something inhuman about that.

T. No, on the contrary. Let's just suppose, for example, that you didn't have a husband but that you were guilty about sex, because you were raised to be guilty about sex. Let's suppose that. So here you are guilty about sex and not doing anything about your sexual desires because of your guilt. Your guilt comes from *beliefs;* feelings just about always come from beliefs. Now how would you handle your beliefs which lead to the guilt? Because really that's what you have: guilt about abandoning your husband.

C. Yes, I do. But I have other feelings that maybe don't stem from guilt, but just may be pure concern for him as a human being.

T. Fine, but which concern comes first? Your concern for him or your concern for yourself? There are two concerns.

C. But if I choose the concern that's best for me, it doesn't mean that I have no ideas or feelings of concern for him.

T. No, you do have some; but which had you better put first? There are two concerns: concern for him and concern for you. We know what concern for him has done for your concern for yourself so far. Now which is *more* important, not which has importance? Of course you have concern for him because he's a human being and you care for him. That has some importance, but how much? And how much concern do you have for you? That's the issue.

C. Yes, I see the difference.

T. Especially since he is probably going to continue to destroy himself, and your concern for him isn't going to stop that.

C. I know you're right, but it's hard to think that way.

T. Yes, it's *very* hard. But if you don't, you are not facing what had better be one of your paramount goals—concern for you. That had better be first; not exclusive, but first. *To thine own self be true* had better be one of your slogans. And you are not facing *that* concern, as far as I can see.

C. Let's say that I dissolve the problem with my husband and I take up life on my own. I have a job and I can support myself. And at this point in my life I am able to handle everything. My question is—

T. What's the question?

C. The question is that he's going to be sitting up in that apartment by himself, with no outlet to life.

T. Because he *chooses* that. You're not *forcing* him to do that. That's *his* choice.

Trying to achieve personal happiness sometimes *includes* making sacrifices for significant people in your life. This may benefit both parties, since these people will often tend to make sacrifices for you. This is largely what close, caring relationships are about. The key question is: What *degree* of sacrifice to make? If you find that certain feelings (such as guilt) block you from doing what you really want to do, the most important thing you can do is recognize that your beliefs create those feelings. By changing these beliefs, you can change the feelings and the actions that impede your achieving your goals. We will elaborate upon these beliefs and ways of changing them as we look at other problem areas in which a happiness-creating philosophy can be most helpful.

CHAPTER 10

Coping with Depression and Low Frustration Tolerance

We shall deal in this chapter with the common problems of depression and low frustration tolerance, particularly when they occur in connection with the break-up of a relationship or with a divorce. Feeling very much alone and depressed after a relationship (marriage, living together, dating) ends is a frequent occurrence, and we will examine the basic causes of such feelings and ways of ameliorating them.

The client in the next case is a 43-year-old unemployed real estate agent who is separated from her husband. She is depressed and has even tried suicide.

T. [Reading from the form that the client filled out] You say, "I am separated from my husband and cannot cope with it. I took an overdose of sleeping pills." Now why can't you accept the fact that you're separated from your husband?

C. Because it just seems to be very difficult for me to do it.

T. Well, it *is* difficult. But why shouldn't there be difficulties in the universe?

C. I do think there should be.

T. That's right; and if you really *accept* the fact that there should be, you'll say to yourself, "It's too damned bad I'm separated from my husband, but I am." Why did you separate?

C. Because he began to go out with other women.

T. So you don't want to be with a man who's going out with other women. Right?

C. Yes. And then I told him that he really shouldn't be married, so he left.

T. But why do you bother yourself so much, if you married an unmarriage-able man, and then you separated from him?

C. I don't know.

T. Well, because you're probably telling yourself, "I *need* him, even though he's no good to me. I *must not* lose him."

C. Yes. I guess I am.

T. Well, why do you *need* him?

C. Because I feel like half a person without him.

T. But obviously you look like you have two parts. You have not been sawed in half! Now why do you convince yourself that you're half a *person,* instead of a person with half a *marriage*?

C. I'm not sure.

In stating that she feels like half a person, the client is expressing a common idea: "When I separate from somebody I care for, I really lose part of *me*." Although this idea may sound romantic, it is not true and contributes to feelings of self-pity and depression. You can be *frustrated* when a relationship ends, but you don't lose *you*.

T. You're saying, "I'm nothing without my husband." Well, prove it. How does it make you a zero to be without him?

C. Because I don't go out; I stay home.

T. No, that's *because* you think you're a rotten person, a worm. If you think you're a worm, you'll say, "How can a worm like me go out in public?" But why *are* you a worm? You think you're one, but how does that *make* you one—just because you're not with him?

C. I am not sure.

T. This is important. Why should you think it makes you a rotten person just because you're not with him?

C. I don't know.

T. Well, because you're rating yourself as a person, and you're saying, "I'm only a good person when he, or other people whom I choose, care for me." And that's going to get you into trouble. You're going to be reliant on him, or somebody else, caring for you. Now it has disadvan-tages, being away from your husband, I'm sure. But why are those disadvantages so *terrible, awful*?

C. Because I'm lonely.

T. Well, you're alone. But *loneliness* means aloneness. *Are* you less of a person for being alone?

C. No. I guess I'm not.

T. You'd better believe that. It's *unfortunate* to be alone, but it hardly makes you unworthy! And if you don't like being alone, why aren't you out looking for more companions?

C. Because I can't do it.

T. Why *can't* you?

C. I don't know.

T. Because you're defining yourself as a zero. We're back to that again. Suppose you did go out to look for other companions. Now what would you predict?

C. That I probably wouldn't be accepted.

We begin to see the basic cause of the client's depression—her *self-downing*. She is defining herself as being rotten because she is without her mate. She sees being alone as proof of her worthlessness and feels helpless and hopeless about changing the situation. When you begin to feel depressed, it is most important to realize that it is your *Beliefs* (ideas) and not the events of your life that create your depression.

If a hundred people got separated, would they all feel depressed? No! Some would be happy, others would feel sad, and some would be depressed. Their ideas *about* separation, and not the event of separation, determine how they feel and behave. The person feeling *sad* would have beliefs such as: "It is frustrating to be separated. I am deprived of certain benefits. It won't be easy to start with other potential partners. Life is tough." Beliefs such as these lead to the appropriate feeling of sadness—appropriate in that it leads to trying to change the annoying situation or to gracefully lumping a situation that can't be changed.

Depression, on the other hand, is created by such Beliefs as: "It is awful and horrible that I am now alone; I can't stand it!" "Things *shouldn't* and *must not* be this way; the world is *too* hard for me." "Because the relationship failed, I am a rotten person." These irrational Beliefs (not based on logic or evidence) lead to a state of despair and inaction and thus are inappropriate to the goal of achieving personal happiness. These beliefs lead to *not* accepting yourself and to *not* seeking minimal pain and increased pleasure. In short, they lead to *self-defeating* emotions and behavior.

We will now return to the case and look at how to work against such Beliefs.

T. Why wouldn't you be accepted by people? What is unacceptable about you?

C. My looks.

T. Well, what about your looks? You look attractive enough to me. What do you find wrong with them?

C. I'm heavy.

T. Yes, but some men like heavy women. You'd do better, probably, if you were thinner; but why should *no* people like you just because you're heavy?

C. Because I don't talk to people.

T. But why don't you talk to them?

C. Because I have nothing to say.

T. Well, you obviously have *something* to say. You mean that what you say wouldn't be good enough?

C. I find it very difficult to talk.

T. Because you're probably watching yourself talk and you're saying, "I should be a marvelous talker, and isn't it awful that I'm not what I should be?"

C. But I was a much better talker before.

T. Because you're probably telling yourself, "What a no-goodnik I am. Nobody will like me if my own husband left me. Now I won't be able to talk well to anybody." Are you saying things like that to yourself?

C. Yes, especially since my separation. Also, I'm putting myself down because my friends don't call me.

T. And you're saying, "Isn't that *awful* that they don't call me?" Aren't you?

C. Yes.

T. Well, why is it *awful* if your friends don't call you?

C. Because I'm so alone.

T. That's why it's *uncomfortable,* but why is being uncomfortable *awful?*

C. Because I'm unworthy, I guess.

T. Because you're *defining* yourself as unworthy. You're saying, "If I'm alone, it's because they think I'm unworthy. And they're right!" You see, you're agreeing with them and thinking that if people aren't calling you, it's because they think you're worthless. It's possible that that's the reason. But why would you *agree* with them if they thought that you were no good?

C. I'm not sure.

T. Probably because you're demanding that you gain worth through acceptance. And, by definition, you're saying, "I'm only worthwhile when people like me and accept me, and if they don't, *I'm* a no good slob." That's your definition of yourself, and that's not going to get you anywhere, is it?

C. No. I see that it won't.

T. In fact, it'll make you anxious all the time. Because even if people accept you, really accept you, what are you likely to worry about then?

C. Oh, I'll find something.

T. Yes. I think you'll find the same thing: "How do I know they'll accept me *tomorrow?*" The only thing that would satisfy you, with your philosophy, would be a *guarantee* of acceptability. But how are you going to get that? How are you going to get a *guarantee* of acceptability?

C. I can't.

T. That's right, you can't. Guarantees don't exist. Therefore, you're going to be miserable all your life, even when you're accepted. You're going to be even more miserable when you're not accepted, because that "proves" to you, "I'm no good." But even when you are accepted today, you're going to worry about being accepted tomorrow!

When people find themselves alone, they often conclude, "How *horrible* it is to be rejected! I must really be a rotten person to be alone!" Both these ideas are self-defeating, for although it is annoying to be alone, it is hardly *horrible.* And being alone can't possibly prove anything about your self-worth. Even if it is your fault that you are alone, you can logically conclude that, being a *fallible human,* you will make countless errors and, therefore, often get rejected. But instead of downing yourself, the best course is to accept yourself in spite of others' disapproval and to see how you can improve your current situation and make fewer errors in the future.

T. Your philosophy isn't going to work. Now why retain it if it isn't going to work?

C. Because I just can't seem to get rid of it.

T. Well, how are you trying to look at it and get rid of it?

C. I'm not really.

T. That's right. If you say, "I can't play tennis," and I ask, "Why can't you?" and you say, "Well, I'm not trying," that never proves you can't. It just proves you're not yet playing. Now you're not looking at your philosophy of unworthiness and disputing it, contradicting it, as far as I can see. Therefore, it will remain. If you ask yourself 20 times a day, not "Why am I doing poorly?" but "Why am I a worm when I do poorly and people don't like me?" what would the answer be?

C. That it's because I'm unworthy.

T. No, the answer is: "Because I *define* myself as such." There are no shits. You and Lee Harvey Oswald are not shits. Why was Oswald *not* a shit?

C. Well, I thought he was.

T. No, that's a mistake. He wasn't. He acted shittily, but how did that make *him* a shit?

C. I guess it didn't.

T. All right, why didn't it? That's the correct answer: "It didn't." But why didn't it? A lot of people foolishly think that it did. Now why are they wrong?

C. Because he was entitled to do what he wanted to do.

T. *Because human beings do wrong things, that's their nature.* And he didn't do *all* wrong things. A shit would have an *essence* of manure and would *only* and *always* do wrong things. Did Oswald only and always do wrong things?

C. No, I guess not.

T. And, also, by doing those wrong things a shit is *damnable*. That's what the term really means. Now why should we damn *him,* Oswald, for his wrong deeds?

C. We shouldn't.

T. We'd better not, because if we damn him, we'll damn ourselves when we behave badly, and that's what you're doing. You're damning yourself, instead of telling yourself, "My *deeds* stink, but not my total *person.* What, therefore, am I going to do to change those deeds?" Assuming that you really did perform rotten deeds, and that your husband consequently left you, you're sitting at home and bemoaning your fate. That's foolish behavior, because it's not going to make you happy, nor help you change your poor performances.

This is a tough concept, but a very important one: *We can rate one's deeds, but we really cannot rate the person who performs those deeds.* This means that we can penalize someone for serious violations, but once we rate that *person* as being rotten, we risk rating ourselves when we make mistakes. This rating leads to anger or depression and is counterproductive and hardly helps us to make positive changes. When you depress yourself over an event, you tend to do nothing to make things better. It is, therefore, important to *look for your depression-creating Beliefs* (the ones we mentioned a little earlier) and to *forcefully challenge* them each day. You can do this by writing out your Beliefs and asking for evidence to support each. Also, *act* against your Beliefs, especially against the idea that you are helpless to change things. Pick up the phone and call friends, join a class, meet new dating partners, do some things alone and see that you can still accept yourself.

C. I should get out and get a job.

T. "I'd better." You'd better watch the "should," because if you say, "I *should* do it, and I don't do what I should," that's how you damn yourself. "If I *should* do something, and I don't, *I'm* no good." "If I *had better* do it, and I don't, *it* is not good." You see the difference?

C. Yeah. I am not my acts; I am more than that.

T. Right. Now if we could only get you to think that way consistently! "My behavior, staying in and remaining alone, stinks because it's not enjoyable, because it would be better if I were active. Therefore, *it* is bad, but *I* am never bad. Nor am *I* ever good. I'm too complex to be globally rated." Also, you're a process. And you can't rate or evaluate an ongoing, ever-changing process. But that's what you're doing. You're not only evaluating your acts, you're evaluating your ongoing *youness.*

C.   It sounds so easy when you say it.

T.   It's simple. But simple doesn't mean easy. People confuse the two. It's very simple, and you obviously understand it, which shows that you're bright and that you could change. The simplest thing in the world that almost anybody ever invented is dieting. Now, is it easy?

C.   No.

T.   But you know how to diet. You just consistently reduce your calories. That's quite simple—but hard! And you're not doing another hard but simple thing—*not* rating yourself.

C.   It seems very easy for me to say, "I am no good because I act poorly."

T.   Right! But it seems much harder for you to say, "Prove it. Where is the evidence?" You could, however, do this hard thing. Every time you feel depressed, anxious, lonely, or self-downing, you could say, "I'm demanding that I should do better. Why should I? How does it make me a worm if I do act poorly?" You're not asking that simple question. But you could, even though it's hard to ask it, because you're perfectly able to. Are you blaming yourself for taking the pills?

C.   Well, I guess so.

T.   All right, let's take that as A, the Activating Experience, that you took the pills. The emotional Consequence is your feeling guilty, ashamed, and depressed. Right?

C.   Yes.

T.   Now, what do you think B is?

The therapist is showing the client how to look for her irrational Beliefs. You start with the Activating Event (A), such as a suicide attempt, and your emotional Consequence (C), such as guilt about this attempt. You then ask what you are telling yourself about A that creates your depression. This would consist of your Beliefs (B) about the event. Usually you will have both rational Beliefs (rBs) and irrational Beliefs (iBs). Take the irrational Beliefs and prove again and again that they are false, and gradually the rational Beliefs will dominate.

T.   What are you telling yourself *about* taking those pills?

C.   It was wrong for me to take them.

T.   Yes, but that's a rational Belief that would make you feel sorry or regretful but not guilty. What else are you saying? You're saying, "It was wrong to take the pills." But then what are you *additionally* saying about yourself for taking them?

C.   That I'm unworthy.

T.   That's right. You see, "I'm unworthy" follows from "I *shouldn't* have taken them" instead of *"It would be better* had I not tried to commit suicide." The latter idea would only make you feel *sorry* about taking the pills.

C. Actually I'm only sorry that I survived.

T. That's because you're predicting that you'll always feel like a nothing and have no happiness in life. Aren't you?

C. Yes, I really feel that way. I've done *many* bad things. And I am afraid I'll have to continue that way.

T. But is that a true prediction?

C. As far as I can see, it is.

T. Well, if you insist on *making* it so . . . You see, suppose you predicted that you'd stop walking and instead always hop. Well, you could follow up that prediction and insist on hopping. But the prediction itself isn't going to make you hop, is it?

C. No.

T. You see, *you decide* whether to follow it up. So you're saying, "So far I have demanded that I do well, and when I don't, I call myself a worm instead of calling myself a human being who acted poorly." You're also saying, "Because I've done that, then I have to keep doing it." Now why do you have to *keep* doing it?

C. I'm beginning to see that I don't.

T. That's right! It's your choice. And do you see that once you make that choice—to put yourself down for acting badly—you will feel depressed and suicidal? Do you see that part?

C. Yes.

T. Then why do it? Because you can act just as badly and *not* put yourself down. Right?

C. I suppose I can.

T. Now how would you do that? Let's suppose you act badly. You certainly did try to commit suicide; and you probably did all kinds of foolish things with your husband. You made lots of errors. Now how could you *not* put yourself down for those errors and still acknowledge that they were errors? What could you say to yourself?

C. "I took the pills, that I did bad things, but I'm not unworthy. My *acts* were bad, but I'm not a bad *person!"*

T. That's right! "I did those bad acts, whatever they were, and it's unfortunate that I did. *It's* bad, but *I'm* neither good nor bad." Right?

C. Yes. I never saw that before. But I'm beginning to see it now.

T. Great! Do you believe that you could really fully believe that?

C. No, not yet.

T. Now why couldn't you? You do believe the opposite—that you are no good. But suppose you continue to do bad acts. Let's suppose that you mainly continue to do bad acts: act stupidly, be lonely, be overweight, and so on. Why must you maintain the proposition, "I'm a worm for doing those acts?"

C. I don't have to.
T. But then why do you keep insisting on downing yourself?
C. Because it's easier, I guess.
T. Correct! It *is* easier—meaning that you know how to do it, and you're well practiced in doing it. But what about the *results?*
C. The results are terrible.
T. Then why do it?
C. I guess because stopping is easier said than done.

Several interesting and important points have been brought out here. The first is that a person who really feels depressed (as opposed to sad) *often* believes that he or she will always feel that way and can do little to change things. This irrational idea had better be challenged by logical thinking and by appropriate actions. A second point is that it is easier to believe old ideas, even if those ideas create negative emotions and actions. This is true, but it only indicates that *hard work* is required to replace irrational, dysfunctional Beliefs with more rational ones.

If serious depression is a problem for you or someone you know, professional help had better be considered. When you believe that there is no hope, a professional can help you work against that idea, via both thinking and action. Downing *yourself* over anything is foolish, but to down yourself for seeking help is especially so.

T. I would like you to say to yourself: "Well, I see that I have choices. I don't have much choice about making mistakes, because I'm quite fallible, and will continue to make them. I could make fewer, but I'll always make some. Once I make a serious error—like dealing badly with my husband or trying to kill myself—I have a *choice* of telling myself 'I'm a rotten person' *or* 'I'm a person who did a rotten deed.'"
C. Yes, I see that I have this choice.
T. You're saying that right now, but do you really *believe* it? I'm not sure that you do. But you *do* have that choice, and saying "I'm a rotten person" will make you depressed while saying "I did a rotten deed" will help you. Because then you can look at your deeds and try to change your behavior in the future. Why do you think you couldn't learn to say, "I did a rotten deed" instead of "I am a rotten person"?
C. I guess I could. It would be better if I did.
T. Are you *determined?* You just said it would be better to do that. Are you *determined* to do what would be better—meaning more enjoyable, more happy—for you?
C. No, not really.
T. Because you want to be unhappy?
C. No.

T. Why aren't you determined to think the way that will make you happy?

C. Because I can't.

T. Rot! You obviously *could.* You mean it's *difficult?*

C. Yes.

T. But why *couldn't* you do that difficult thing?

C. Well, for instance, I have a fear of going by myself to social groups. And I can't find anyone to go with me, so I don't go.

T. But you're saying again, "I can't go," instead of, "I find it difficult." Now why couldn't you *force* yourself to go by yourself, no matter *how* difficult? It's therapeutic; and will help you get over your idea, "Isn't it awful that I might go and be alone!" Why couldn't you force yourself?

C. It's just because I find it easier to stay home.

T. Well, that's not quite true; it's only partly true. *At the moment* you find it easier to stay home, but then you'll be bored at home and you'll probably start downing yourself: "Oh, hell. I goofed! I didn't do it, I'll never get anywhere!" Then you'll remain depressed at home. Right?

C. Yes. That's exactly what happens time and again.

T. Now which is *really* easier? Forcing yourself out and being *temporarily* uncomfortable? Or remaining home and feeling uncomfortable *for the rest of your life?*

C. I guess going out.

T. Is really easier in the long run?

C. Yes. I have to admit it, though I often see the opposite.

T. That's right! What you're saying (and that's largely the human condition) is that you usually pick what's *immediately* more comfortable, at the expense of what is later more comfortable. Now if you refuse to do that and force yourself to do what's immediately *un*comfortable, you would solve the problem.

The major point here is that *there is no gain without pain.* The client begins to see that *short-range hedonism* (seeking immediate pleasure) will bring comfort now but results in great discomfort later. The solution is *long-range hedonism,* and this involves suffering some discomfort now so that things will be better in the future. Although it would be quite hard for her to go out to meet people, it would be harder, in the long run, for her not to. Let us now see how this concept applies to the client's overeating.

T. The same thing is probably happening with food. When you are about to put food in your mouth, and you know you've had enough and that you're going to get fatter and not lose weight—what do you tell yourself about eating?

C. That a little more won't hurt.

T. But that's a lie!

C. Yes, I guess it is. I realize it's a rationalization.

T. But what's your real belief under "a little more won't hurt"? Because a little more will hurt—it will make you fatter—and you don't want to be fatter, do you?

C. No, not at all. I hate being fat!

T. So a little more *will* hurt. But what do you think your real belief is? "If I push away this food"—what?

C. I'll be unhappy. And I can't stand being deprived and unhappy!

T. Another way of putting it: "I can't stand being unhappy *right now,* so I'll risk being unhappy *forever."* Do you *have* to be a short-range hedonist?

C. No, I suppose not.

T. Let's suppose that you're back to eating extra food, you're about to put it in your mouth, and it tastes good. Now what could you say as you think of putting it in your mouth? What could you tell yourself?

C. This will make me fat.

T. "This will make me *fatter,* which I don't want to become!" And—?

C. "And in the long run, I'll be better off if I don't eat it. Therefore, I don't need it!"

T. Right! "It'll make me fatter and happier right now, but more unhappy in the future." Now you probably do sometimes convince yourself of that, don't you? But how often?

C. Not often enough.

T. Right. Isn't that the story of your life?

C. Yes.

T. It's the same when you think of going out to a social group. And when you think of dealing better with your husband but don't take the trouble to do so. And you probably do the same thing in other areas of your life. You do take the easy way out, don't you?

C. Generally. Not always, but quite often.

T. And then you beat yourself for the poor results. You see, that's the second thing you're doing. You're doing two self-defeating things. Let's just take the food again; it's a good example. One: you're saying, "At the moment it's hard to push away this food," which is correct. Then you say, "It's *too* hard, I *shouldn't* have to do such hard things!"—which is irrational. Then you rationalize and say, "Well, it really doesn't matter. A little bit more won't hurt"—which is sheer nonsense. But the real irrational Belief is that "It's *too* hard to push away this good-tasting food! I must have it right now!" So then you eat it.

C. Then I severely blame myself.

T. Yes, once you eat the food, you take your symptom, overeating (which we call C, a dysfunctional Consequence in RET), and you make it into a new A (or Activating Experience). And then you make yourself feel guilty, at a second C (Consequence)—because you're telling yourself what, at B, your Belief System—what do you believe about your over-eating? What irrational B is causing your secondary feeling of guilt, at C?

C. That I'm going to get fat.

T. No, that wouldn't cause you to feel guilty. The fact that you're going to get fat would tend to be seen as unfortunate and would only make you feel sad: "Well, I ate that food and it was wrong, and I'm going to get fat. Isn't that too bad?" So you'd feel sad, sorry. But you're actually feeling guilty. Why?

C. Because I ate that food which I *shouldn't* have done. So I'm a *rotten person!*

T. Exactly! That's your nutty, irrational belief that leads to your self-damn-ing and guilt. Ironically, blaming yourself right after you've eaten the extra food isn't going to help you diet. Because then you're going to feel anxious and want *more* food to distract you from your anxiety. And you're going to feel hopeless, unable to diet. For a rotten person presumably *can't* behave unrottenly. Isn't that what the term means? You're *always* a crumb, and cannot possibly do good things, like dieting.

C. Yeah.

T. So then you eat still more, and probably blame yourself more. Now if we can get you to start there, with your guilt feeling, and say, "Yes, that was a rotten *act,* but I'm not a *rotten person.* Now what the hell am I going to to about that *act?*", you start to solve your problem. You finally get back to acquiring a higher frustration tolerance. You refuse to de-fine dieting as *too* hard, but only accurately define it as hard. Because it *is* hard. You're saying, with your low frustration tolerance, "When I'm hungry I *must* eat" instead of "I'd like to, but I'd better not! It's hard to diet but, in the long run, it's harder to overeat!"

Although eating too much is the example in this case, the lesson about low frustration tolerance can be applied to many behaviors that require giving up some short-range pleasure in order to achieve long-term plea-sure or comfort. Some of these behaviors include going out to meet people despite the discomfort of shyness, studying in order to enter a worthwhile profession, and exercising to promote health. When you feel depressed, it is hard to take effective action—but important to do so. Since low frustration tolerance (LFT) blocks your road to long-range pleasure and to truly achieving personal happiness, it is important that you be very familiar with the basic irrational Beliefs creating it. These Beliefs basically include: "It is *horrible* to suffer discomfort now! It is *too hard* for poor me. I *can't stand* such discomfort! It *should* be easy to achieve worthwhile goals. I *must not* be frustrated! People who make me do difficult things are *rotten people.*" These ideas do not match reality, and it is important (especially if you are depressed) to challenge them again and again so that you can cope with short-range discomfort. Use self-imposed rewards and penalties to help you take effective action, but be careful to see that you don't down yourself as a person when you fail to do something constructive. This will only make you more depressed and less likely to try again. We again emphasize how important it is to *forcefully challenge your irrational Beliefs on a daily basis, in both thought and action.*

C. I haven't gone out, I stay home and watch TV, and I haven't done any exercises, so I put on a lot of weight.

T. Now why haven't you exercised? What stops you? Isn't it the same thing?

C. Yes, I see it as being too hard.

T. Is it really *too* hard? It's just hard. So you start with low frustration tolerance—"It's too hard to do the exercise that I don't want, in order to get the weight reduction I do want"—and then you damn yourself for having that low tolerance, and that makes it worse. If you'd accept yourself *with* your low frustration tolerance and work against it, then you'd lose weight, you wouldn't be alone because you'd be going out to social functions, and you'd start getting better results. Not immediately or in a second, but you soon would. But even right now, when you're doing all the wrong things—overeating, staying at home, looking at television—you're just a human being who's *acting badly;* you're not a *bad person.* You now are shaking your head affirmatively, but do you really believe that?

C. No.

T. Why do you insist on believing in *bad people,* which is almost equivalent to believing in devils?

C. I don't know, but I guess I do believe that.

T. The answer is: that's the way you normally think. That's the way almost all humans tend to think.

C. Uh-huh.

T. Again you're saying uh-huh because you see it *right now.* Now your problem is to get to see it *regularly.* And you could do this if you questioned yourself the way I'm now questioning you. Suppose at A you make a mistake, and at C, a Consequence, you have a horrible feeling, which we'll call worthlessness or inadequacy. Look for B, your beliefs about A. First, look at your rational beliefs: "It was wrong to screw up. I made an error, and that's too bad." Second, look at your irrational beliefs: "What an awful person I am! I *shouldn't* make those errors!" Then you go to D, Disputing, and ask, "Why *shouldn't* I make errors?" And what's the answer?

C. There's no reason I shouldn't.

T. That's right! Don't say, "It's good to err." Say, instead, "It would be better if I didn't. But I should do what I do, even when I'm wrong in doing it. I'm a fallible human, and humans make errors!" Now if we can get you to do that consistently, that kind of disputing, you'll give up your feeling of slobhood. But the question is: Will you do it?

C. Well, I can try.

T. That's right. It's the one thing any human can do—try!

After a love relationship (marriage or otherwise) ends, you would expect to feel sad for a while. If, instead, you find yourself faced with prolonged depression, look for the *irrational Beliefs* creating the feelings of worthlessness and hopelessness, look for the escalation of a *desire* into a *must* and a *bad* into an *awful*. *Attack these ideas* without mercy, and act against your low frustration tolerance. Once you start taking effective action, possibly with the help of a professional, your depression will begin to become less intense and the fight against it easier. Also remember that *prevention* of depression is possible by changing your Belief System to a more rational one *before* an unpleasant event takes place. This requires hard work, but you can do it!

CHAPTER 11

Coping with Anger and With Mating Problems

By looking at the current divorce rate, it is easy to see that people are having serious problems getting along with each other. This leads us to the next area, which is how to get along better with your mate. Although we are dealing in this RET dialogue with a married couple, almost everything being said here can also be applied to the couple living together or seriously dating on a regular basis. Although sex is often mentioned as an area of conflict within a relationship, we will not look at that now, since we have reserved a separate chapter for that topic alone.

Couples argue, and at times physically fight, about a great variety of issues. These may include money, in-laws, sex, household chores, criticism, and the amount of attention received from partner and friends. As we shall see in the following two cases, the *real* problem in the relationship is the *anger* and *self-downing* which prevents people from finding intelligent solutions for the inevitable disagreements couples have. Therefore, it is most important to first deal with the emotional problems (mainly anger and self-downing), and then to seek practical solutions. Achieving your personal happiness really means getting rid of a self-defeating philosophy, which stands in the way of your getting maximum pleasure and minimum pain from your relationships.

The client in the first case is a 38-year-old female who is angry at her husband. Let us join as the session begins.

T. Do you frequently get angry?
C. Yes. I often get angry at my husband.
T. Yes?

C. I spent the entire last weekend with him and that made me feel lousy.

T. Okay, now, what did he do at A (Activating Event)? What did he do *before* you felt angry?

C. Not very darned much; nothing. I mean, he doesn't do *anything*.

T. Yes, but is that what you're angry about?

C. That's why I'm angry—I'm angry because I'm spending my whole life watching this man sleep in an armchair, and it's making me mad.

T. All right, so he did something at what we call point A in RET. He slept in an armchair.

C. Right.

T. At your home?

C. Yeah.

T. So you were at home, and he doesn't work on weekends, and he slept in an armchair.

C. Mmm-hmm.

T. So we know A (the Activating Event)—his sleeping. And we know C (the emotional Consequence)—you felt angry all weekend. Now how did you behave?

C. Oh, I made a perfect ass of myself. I carried on and screamed and yelled and told him I hated him, and just . . . just really put on an act, realizing that I was putting on an act, and I felt that it was a pretty lousy weekend. I only have every other weekend off, and I felt like I kind of blew it for myself, you know.

T. All right. Now, what do you think you were telling yourself at B (your Belief System) to make yourself angry? And let's assume he really did sleep around the clock, did lie in the hammock all weekend, and acted exactly the way you said he did. He might give us a different version, if we asked him. But let's accept yours. Now, what did you say to yourself about his sleeping to make yourself feel angry?

C. I said to myself, "I'm putting more into this marriage than he is. I'm not getting anything out of it. I deserve more than I'm getting." I guess that was it.

T. All right. The first part of your self-statement wouldn't make you angry—"I'm putting more into it and I'm not getting anything out of it." That would just be an observation, which you could or could not choose to anger yourself about. You might just think, "Well, isn't that too bad. I think I'll look for another man if this one won't change," or something like that, and thereby choose to feel sorry but not angry. See?

C. Yes. I have a choice about what I tell myself and feel.

T. Exactly. Of course, that may not be the right thing to do. I'm just showing you that the first part of what you told yourself wouldn't make you angry. Do you see that? "I'm not getting much out of this" wouldn't make you angry. Do you see that that is so?

C. No, it made me hurt. It made me . . . it made me nurse a grudge. It justified the fact that I was acting badly toward him.

T. Right. It "justified" the fact, but it really didn't *make* you have a grudge, feel hurt, or feel anything. It just was a *description* of what was happening. But then you probably added to it the rational *evaluation,* "I don't like the way that he's behaving." Right?

C. Yes. I assigned badness—uh, rottenness—to his sleeping.

T. Yes, you *assigned* it. And how would you feel if you *only* stuck with "I don't like his sleeping?" If you only said, "I don't like his acting that way and wasting our time on weekends." How would you feel if you only said *that* to yourself? "I wish he wouldn't nap like that. I don't like it. I prefer him to act differently."

C. I'd probably just get on with . . . with my life, and not . . . not spend so much time yelling and screaming.

T. Right. And you'd probably only feel sorry and annoyed at his behavior. Wouldn't you?

C. Yes, sad but not terribly upset.

Keep in mind that although the client is angry at her husband for "doing nothing," her anger could apply to any type of marital or relationship disagreement. The rational-emotive therapist starts by helping her see that in between what her husband does (or doesn't do) and how she feels lies a set of *Beliefs.* Some of these are *rational,* in the sense that they are supported by evidence and lead to appropriate (self-helping) emotions, such as disappointment and regret. This is demonstrated by the client's reaction when she was asked how she would feel if she stuck with Beliefs such as "I don't like his sleeping. I wish he wouldn't nap that way." But, alas, most of us then add some *irrational,* anger-producing Beliefs.

T. You wouldn't feel angry if you only told yourself rational Beliefs. So, to make yourself feel angry, you proceed to another—and highly irrational—evaluation or set of evaluations of his sleeping: namely, "I don't *deserve* this kind of behavior!" Why is this idea irrational?

C. Because I mean, "He and the world *shouldn't* give me this kind of unlikeable behavior." I'm demanding that he do what I like.

T. You certainly are! So, if you want to eliminate your anger at *him* and go back to feeling only sorry and annoyed at his *behavior,* you can go on to D (Disputing) and ask yourself, "Why *shouldn't* he act that crummy way?"

C. Why *shouldn't* he?

T. Yes, why *shouldn't* he?

C. Because I have it set up in my mind that I give a certain amount, and he gives a certain amount, and he's not.

T. Not what?

C. And he's not fulfilling it.

T. He's being unfair?

C. He's being—yeah, very unfair!

T. Why *should* he not be unfair? Let's suppose he is. Why *must* he not be?

C. There's no reason. There's no logical reason he shouldn't be unfair, except that I have set up these expectations.

T. "There's no logical reason that he shouldn't be unfair. But the bastard still *shouldn't* be!" Right?

C. Yes, because I'm a good wife. I really am.

T. Oh, and that's . . .

C. More than he deserves.

T. Do you see how you just dragged a non sequitur—a thought that doesn't follow a prior thought—into your thinking? "*Because* I'm a good wife, he *shouldn't* act badly and go to sleep on me!" Does that follow?

C. No, it doesn't always follow.

T. It *never* follows! The second thought really has nothing to do with the first one. If you were a bad wife, it still might be unfair of him to go to sleep so much on weekends. And even if you are the greatest wife in the world, he doesn't *have to* stay awake and treat you fairly. Do you see that?

C. Mmm-hmm.

T. Can you give me *any* reason that he *shouldn't* act the way he does? Can you really think of any reason he *must* not, *should* not, act the way you find undesirable? Can you think of any reason that he *shouldn't*?

C. I see it as . . . ah . . . it comes between our relationship.

T. Yeah.

C. A marriage is something that we're both carrying—a load, a board. We're both carrying an end of it, and he's let his down.

T. Right.

C. I'm carrying the whole thing, and it just . . . it just kind of ruins the relationship.

T. But now you're giving me reasons why his behavior is abominable. I'm sure you can give me five or ten reasons why you find it stupid, abominable, and unfair. But why *must* he not act unfairly? You see, it's that *second* statement that you use to make yourself angry.

C. Yes. There's no reason why he *must* act fairly.

T. Right. But you'd better say that *more convincingly,* you see? There's no reason why he *must*. As a matter of fact, he *should* act unfairly. Do you know why he should?

C. No, why?

T. Because he *does.* That's the way he behaves. It *should* be raining if it *is* raining.

C. Well . . .

T. Shouldn't it?

C. Yeah, I guess so. Well, I'll go along with the rain.

T. Yeah, the rain doesn't give us a choice. But you could say, "Yes, but *he* has a choice. He could *decide* not to sleep all day—therefore, he *shouldn't!*" But if he's deciding to lie in the hammock, then he *should* lie in the hammock. Right?

C. I wouldn't go so far as to say *should.* But I'd say it's his decision. It's his life.

T. It's his decision and *should* means that. He's done it. He decided to lie in the hammock. It doesn't mean it's *good* that he makes this decision. But he *should* lead a crummy life *if* he picks a crummy life.

C. It's his thing.

T. Because he does it. It's his thing. That's his nature, and those are the conditions under which he chooses to live. And you're saying, "He *shouldn't* pick those conditions!" But as long as he picks them, he picks them; and as long as he is that way, or chooses that way, then those conditions will exist. And demanding or commanding that they *must* not exist and that he *has* to please you, is real grandiosity or gall on your part!

We now come to the major anger-producing irrational Belief; *"My mate should not, must not, act the way s/he is acting."* Whenever you are really angry, this Belief is present. It represents an irrational demand upon the other person and is contrary to reality. We therefore call it the *nobility* or *chutzpah factor*—your *insisting* that what would be better *must* exist. If you were God, it probably would be rational to hold this belief. Since most of us (who are sane) admit that we don't have God's power, it is safe to say that the Belief is irrational. Although we often find it hard to accept, it is true that, by definition, whatever exists *should* exist.

This does not mean that we can't try to change bad situations, but that we won't usually achieve workable solutions if we anger ourselves about those situations. You may have good, logical reasons why your partner's behavior is annoying or frustrating, but there is no law of the universe stating that annoying behavior *must* not exist. If you find yourself angry, rather than irritated or annoyed, look for your *shoulds, musts,* and *oughts* and begin asking yourself why your partner *must* act as you would like. This unrealistic *demand,* as opposed to a *desire,* is the root cause of anger. A little later we will look at other Beliefs involved in creating anger.

C. His behavior makes me mad, and in getting mad I act like an ass, and then I feel bad because I acted that way.

T. We will get to your "assininity" in a short while. But *it* doesn't make you mad. Do you know why *it* doesn't make you mad?

C. No.

T. Do you have any idea?

C. It doesn't make me mad because it's his life?

T. Well, yes. But, more importantly, if he lived with a hundred other women, and acted the same way with them, would they all feel mad?

C. Probably not.

T. It's unlikely. Most of them would feel sorry and displeased. But that isn't madness, anger.

C. Mmm-hmm.

T. You see, you're *making yourself* mad when he acts displeasingly. I take it that you've told him that you don't like his lying in the hammock, and he continues to do it. So he chooses to do what you don't like, and therefore he's frustrating you, depriving you. But you're pigheadedly *making yourself* mad about that frustration.

C. And realizing it, and then I feel so guilty.

T. That's right, you see. You have the primary symptom of anger and the secondary symptom—which, again, *you* bring on—of making yourself guilty about your anger.

C. So I do myself in *twice!*

T. Yes. But first, do you see what you could do to not feel mad? We'll look at your guilt or your shame about your anger in a few minutes. But do you see what you could do to *not* feel mad about your husband's crummy behavior, his goofing? Do you know what you could do?

C. I could realize it doesn't have anything to do with me. It's *his* behavior.

T. Right! It's *his* behavior; it's what he chooses to do; and he's not doing it *against* you.

C. And I'm only responsible for my own behavior.

T. That's right. He's responsible for his, and he is acting irresponsibly in the marriage. How long have you been married?

C. Fifteen years.

T. And for 15 years he's been lying in a chair or on the bed, to your displeasure?

C. It's getting worse. I've become his mother, you know, instead of his wife.

T. All right. But certainly for the last few years he's not been acting as a responsible husband. So we're not exonerating him at all, we're not saying that he's acting well.

C. No. He certainly isn't! And never has!

T. But that doesn't make you mad. And we don't know that he's doing it against you. Even if he were deliberately doing it to goad you, he still has the right, the privilege, to act that way. And whenever you're angry, you're saying, "He *must not* be doing what he is undubitably doing. He has no *right* to do wrong." Well, doesn't he have a right to do wrong?

C. Yes, I guess so.

T. You'd better say that *stronger.* He damned well does!

C. Okay, he has a right. Yes, he definitely has a right to do his own thing.

T. Correct! *All* humans have a right to act wrongly, and they frequently exert that right. Let's face it. So if you kept telling yourself many times, very vigorously, "He *has* a right to sleep away his life. I wish to hell he *wouldn't,* but he *does!*" you'd feel displeased, or annoyed at his behavior. But you wouldn't be downing *him* nor screaming and yelling that *he's* no good. Then you would decide whether you'd better calmly leave him or do something else. But not with anger, just with displeasure. Do you see?

C. Mmm-hmm. Quite a different view than what I usually take.

T. Yes, quite different.

Once you begin to see how you create your own anger by maintaining certain Beliefs, you begin the job of proving to yourself that these Beliefs are indeed irrational. Along with the major anger-creating Belief, "My mate *must* not behave the way he or she is behaving" are usually a few more false ideas. These include: "The way my mate acts is *awful* and *horrible!* I *can't stand* that way! My mate is a *total louse* for acting in that fashion!"

When you really feel angry or in a rage, you can be almost sure that you are telling yourself some or all of these statements. If you spend a little time each day *challenging* these beliefs by *vigorously questioning* their validity, you will make yourself feel disappointed and annoyed instead of angry. Irrational beliefs will be replaced by rational ones, so that you will see that although it is *frustrating* to have your mate behave in a manner you don't like, it is not *awful.* You always can *stand* what you don't like. There is no reason anyone *must* behave as you see fit (since all humans are fallible). And your mate does not magically rate as a rotten *person* even when he or she commits rotten *acts.* Also, when you don't allow another person the right to behave wrongly, you run the risk of downing *yourself* when *you* act wrongly, as we shall now see.

T. After making yourself feel needlessly angry, you've taken your anger and made it into an A (Activating Event). You're noting at A, "I am stupidly acting angrily, yelling and screaming," and then at C (Consequence) you're feeling guilty and ashamed. Now, what are you saying at B *about* your anger to produce your guilt at C? Let's assume that you are foolishly making yourself angry. What are you telling yourself at B, to make yourself feel this guilt?

C. What am I doing to make myself—? Well, I'm feeling that my husband's behavior is really not directed against me, and I know this. So therefore I have no right to carry on so angrily, the way I do. I have gone through this act, the same enraged song and dance, time and time again, and I know it. I can almost tape-record it. And it's, it's just fruitless. It gets me nowhere. There's no point to it.

T. That's right. So?

C. And I feel—.

T. Yes, go ahead.

C. I feel that it's pointless.

T. Right. It's pointless. But I also hear you telling yourself, "I *shouldn't* act that stupid, pointless way!" Is that right? "I have *no right* to, I *shouldn't.*"

C. Yes, I know better.

T. "And because I know better, I *shouldn't* do what I know is worse!"

C. Right. That's what I believe—and feel.

T. Why *shouldn't* you act stupidly, pointlessly?

C. Because it doesn't gain me anything. I've been through this whole thing before and it always makes me feel bad, and I know it makes me feel bad. There's no sense in getting so angry and upset.

T. That's why your anger is foolish.

C. It's pointless.

T. That's the reason for *its* stupidity. Some people would say that it's good for you to be angry, but you're saying, "Oh, no, it doesn't get me anywhere, and it's pointless." But why *shouldn't* you—a bright woman like you—act stupidly and pointlessly at times?

C. Well, there's no reason I shouldn't.

T. "But I *shouldn't!*"

C. The anger is a mistake.

T. "And I *shouldn't* make mistakes!"

C. But I shouldn't make the same mistake over and over again.

T. Oh? Why *shouldn't* you?

C. Because there's no sense in making a mistake if you don't learn from it.

T. That's true, but why *should* a fallible human like you be infallible?

C. Well, because I like myself when I don't do things like that—when I don't make myself angry.

The client sees that her anger does not help solve the problem of her husband doing nothing. (We assume the worst—namely that he really does nothing—so that the client can be shown that even *that* doesn't have to result in anger.) And then she slips into using the same anger-producing idea against herself by insisting that she *should (must) not* act the way she acts. Although there are good reasons why her anger is foolish behavior, this never proves that one *must* not be angry. The semantic difference here is crucial, because "it would be better" leads to trying to improve behavior, whereas the "must" just leads to self-downing and blocks improvement. Self-anger leads to shame and guilt.

T.   But you see, you're damning yourself. Instead of damning your *behavior* and saying, "*That's* sinful, *that's* bad," you're saying, "*I* am an errant sinner, *I* am a no-good person for doing that stupid act." Now, will that self-flagellation help you act less stupidly?

C.   It helps me for a while, but then I go back and repeat the same thing again.

T.   That's right.

C.   And I'm in the middle of feeling anger and I think, "Oh, my God, I've been here before! I've said this before, and done this before."

T.   Right. And by making yourself guilty about your anger, that will distract you rather than help you. Do you know why the guilt will distract you from changing your anger? Do you know why it will also hinder you?

C.   No.

T.   Because when you down yourself and feel guilty, you believe that a louse like you can't change, and you don't try.

C.   I see. I also realize that anger has a payoff.

T.   That's right. There is a payoff, and what is the payoff of anger?

C.   Depression?

T.   No, no, I don't think that is a very good payoff. The one I'm thinking of is *nobility.* See what I mean?

C.   That I feel that I'm right and he's wrong, you mean? Therefore, I feel noble.

T.   That's right. You're ascending to heaven, and we know where he is!

C.   But it doesn't work out that way, because I feel guilty.

T.   Because you *make* yourself guilty and thus put yourself in hell along with him!

C.   After I feel guilty about my anger, I apologize profusely to him. And he is noble and says, "I forgive you." You know?

T.   So he's gotten one up! You wind up as the villainess. But the reason your guilt isn't going to do you any good is that it encourages you to spend considerable time and energy damning yourself. And how is that going to help you recognize your anger and say, "Oh, hell, he does have the right to act stupidly or lazily! That's the way he behaves. Too damned bad"? How is that going to help you do that, when you're obsessed with, "I'm no good, I *shouldn't* be angry at him! There I go, screaming and yelling again. Oh, my God, what a fool I am!" Is that going to help you change your behavior?

C.   No. It only makes me worse.

T.   And isn't your guilt a vote of nonconfidence in you? "I am unable to conquer this anger! What a worm I am! I'll always be this way!"

C.   Mmm-hmm.

T. How can the worm turn? If you would give up your guilt and say, "Yes, I'm still a fallible human; isn't that fascinating? Still as fallible as I was before. That's the way I often behave, but I'll work on it and try to act somewhat less fallibly," then you could give up the guilt, first, and work on the anger, second. But your guilt is stopping you from really working that hard on your anger.

The therapist indicates the payoff for anger. What this means is that for the moment angry people feel superior to those at whom they are angry. Let us not also forget that when enraged, we also experience a "pain in the gut," and our obsession with this feeling distracts from finding solutions to problems. As the client correctly points out, *anger does not change the other person's behavior.* In fact, your rage can foster hostility in your mate and thereby create an escalating conflict. Your guilt about your anger (which is a common reaction) helps create *a problem about your problem.* Having the problem of anger, you may believe that because anger is self-defeating, you *must* not be angry and are a *rotten person* for feeling that way. Your secondary problem (self-blame and guilt) actually blocks your working on your original problem of anger. Therefore, if you are downing yourself over your anger, look for your guilt-creating beliefs and forcefully work against them. You will then be able to work on reducing your anger and to seek practical solutions to your relationship problems—which we investigate later. Now back to the case.

T. Let me show you how to use rational-emotive imagery on your anger. Close your eyes and vividly imagine your husband next weekend, lolling around as usual and wasting away the entire weekend. Can you vividly imagine that?

C. Oh, God, yes!

T. And how do you honestly feel, in your gut, as you imagine that?

C. Angry. Quite enraged!

T. All right. Keep the same image, and really get in touch with your anger. Feel it strongly! Okay? Now change it *only* to a feeling of disappointment, only disappointment. Let yourself *merely* feel disappointed, but *not* angry. Now, let's see you do that. You're able to do that.

C. Okay.

T. Did you do it?

C. Yes, I only feel disappointed as I imagine him lolling around.

T. All right. Now, you can open your eyes. *How* did you change your feeling?

C. I thought about him as if I were his mother.

T. Yes?

C. As long as I'm his wife, I'm angry at him. As long as I'm his mother, I feel sorry for him, and that's what he wants anyway.

T. But what's the end of your sentence? "I feel sorry for him because—?"

C. Because he is a loused-up human being. I mean, he's just got problems, you know?

T. And isn't that—?

C. Disappointing. Quite disappointing, but he's got good points, too; and I can still love him.

T. And his napping is not awful?

C. No. That's his way.

T. Yes. That *is* his way. Right. Now, you can for the next 20 or 30 days, if you want to help yourself, repeat this rational-emotive imagery exercise every day. Imagine your husband sleeping away the weekend. Make yourself as angry as you can be. Then change your feeling to only disappointment. In this way you'll keep practicing feeling *disappointment* rather than, as you now do, *anger.* And you don't even have to do it by seeing yourself as his mother. If you want to do that, you can. But you could be disappointed if you were his sister, or a friend, or even a wife. You could be disappointed at his *behavior* rather than angry at *him.*

C. Mmm-hmm.

Rational-emotive imagery is a technique invented by Dr. Maxie Maultsby, Jr. and adapted by Albert Ellis. It is designed to help break the habit of irrational thinking. What you do is close your eyes (this aids imagery) and vividly imagine a disturbing event—one about which you often feel anger, anxiety, guilt, or depression. For example, you can imagine your mate doing or saying exactly what you don't like. By imagining this "terrible" event, you get yourself to feel quite disturbed. Then keep the same image but *change your emotion* to just annoyance, disappointment, or frustration. You will find that the emotion changes when you tell yourself different things (Beliefs) about the event. For example, anger is mainly created by the demand that your mate *must* behave in a certain way. The anger can be changed to annoyance by convincing yourself that although such behavior by your mate would be nice, there is no reason he or she *must* behave that way. Once you see how to change your emotions, even if it's only for a minute, you can practice this each day until the Beliefs about a particular event begin to change. This is another tool to use in changing irrational, self-defeating beliefs to more rational ones. Try it!

T. Now, once you get to the point of being just disappointed, you might then decide to look for practical solutions. You might decide not to be with him on weekends or something like that, you know. You don't have to stay with him all weekend, do you?

C. No. No, I guess I don't.

T. Why do you? If he's going to sleep away the weekend, why do you sit around and watch him do it?

C. Well, there are certain things that have to be done. See, I work full-time and he works full-time. And on the weekends, there are certain things like, oh, laundry and ironing, and housecleaning, and refrigerator defrosting, and things like that, that have to be done. So I do them.

T. But if he were doing other things, you still would do your things, wouldn't you? What does his sleeping have to do with your doing those things? How does it deprive you if he's asleep?

C. It deprives me of companionship. I've got nobody to talk to.

T. Yes, I see. Well, invite some other people in to talk to. There are various things that you could do *if you weren't angry.*

C. Yes, I could.

T. You see? And you're whining and telling yourself, "But it's his *obligation* to talk to me while I'm doing the housework or whatever I'm doing. And that bastard *should* be companionable!" You certainly don't have great companionship while you're telling yourself that, do you?

C. No.

T. So if you got rid of your guilt first (which stems from, "I am a louse for feeling angry") and your anger second (which stems from, "He's a louse for neglecting me!") you could do something about *changing* the situation. You see?

C. Mmm-hmm.

The key point here is that the best time to work out practical solutions to your relationship problems is *after* you have greatly reduced, first, your guilt over being angry and, second, the anger itself. We are *not* advocating that you just accept a frustrating situation but rather that you remove the emotional blocks (anger and self-downing) so that you can be more effective in your attempts to change the situation.

Practical solutions can be very simple (such as inviting friends when your mate is uncompanionable) or complex (such as ending a relationship). The type of solution depends greatly on the specific nature of the problem, as well as on the personalities of the couple.

Professional help may be useful when problems are serious and/or numerous. For example, couples can learn the fine art of compromise, which can include making *contracts.* A contract involves one partner making some change, contingent upon the other partner making a change: "I will agree to help you with the dishes, if you agree to visit my mother." Each partner gives something in order to get something. Many issues over which couples argue really involve *opinion* rather than fact. Neither partner is right or wrong, but is of a certain *opinion.* Realizing this makes compromise easier.

C. I do feel that he doesn't give a damn about me. I mean, I look at myself in the mirror and I think, "There you are, lady, nobody cares about you." You know? It gives you kind of an icky feeling.

T. Well, does his laziness prove he doesn't care about you? Is that true?

C. Yes.

T. Does it?

C. Yes, I think so.

T. "Because if he really cared he'd get off his ass?"

C. If he really cared he wouldn't sleep all the time. You know? I mean, he sleeps in a chair with his mouth open. You know how disgusting that looks? If he'd at least close his mouth! I mean, I've even said to him, if you'd just go upstairs and sleep, so I don't have to look at you with your mouth open. I mean, that's little enough to ask. He won't even do that.

T. Do you think he's deliberately doing that to bother you?

C. No, I don't think so.

T. You're giving evidence for his low frustration tolerance, his laziness. He won't bother to go upstairs to sleep. He won't bother to keep his mouth closed. But I don't believe it has anything to do with you.

C. That's it. It has *nothing* to do with me! I think that's the thing that really gets me. Nothing he does has anything to do with me.

T. He's indifferent?

C. Yes.

T. But he's not indifferent to his own laziness, you see? He's so intent on doing things the easy way that you get lost in the shuffle. If you wanted to make that observation, wouldn't it describe how and why he acts against your wishes?

C. Mmm-hmm.

T. But let's assume that you are correct: that he *doesn't* care about you. Why *must* he?

C. He—there's no reason. There's no reason that he *must* care for me.

T. You see, you give the right answers when I force you to think about things. But you'd better force yourself, whenever you feel hurt, which we're talking about now—.

C. Yes.

T. —to see that there's *no* reason that he has to care for you. And if you stopped accusing him of mayhem and arson, and of being a louse for not loving you, maybe he would care a little more.

C. Maybe. But the reason that I'm angry, the reason that I put on this act and dance around and carry on like a banshee, is because I get a rise out of him. It's the *only* way that I get his attention!

T. Yes, but is that rise *love?* Is that the *kind* of attention you really want?

C. No, that's just like hitting somebody over the head with a board, you know? It's just getting his attention, not his love.

T. Yes; right. But you use this method because your anger distracts you momentarily from your feeling hurt. You rush from experiencing disappointment to making yourself feel hurt. Disappointment would be the Beliefs, "It's very frustrating that I'm not getting what I want, not getting more of his attention. But it's not the end of the world." Hurt follows from the Beliefs: "I *should* get what I want, and it means I'm a rotten person if he doesn't love me and give me more attention!" Now, isn't that in there when you feel hurt?

C. Yes. I feel put down.

T. You're putting *yourself* down. *Disappointment* is not *hurt,* because it doesn't include self-blame.

C. I guess I feel both—but especially hurt.

T. When you're just disappointed with his behavior, you're not magically rating yourself, your you-ness. Even if he were deliberately inattentive to you, because he dislikes you, you would only feel very sorry and frustrated and probably tell yourself, "Who needs a husband who's deliberately doing me in?" But you wouldn't down yourself because he was treating you badly. You see?

C. Yes. I see the difference.

T. And your guilt, again, is self-blaming—both your hurt and guilt are self-downing.

The client feels that if her husband really cared for her, he would act differently. This brings up the issue of *attribution,* which means the reasons you think lie behind your partner's behavior. If you believe that your mate is *deliberately* trying to hurt you, which is often *not* the case, it will be easier to anger yourself. If, on the other hand, you recognize that his or her low frustration tolerance ("It's too hard to change, you and the world *should* make things easy for me") is often at the core of his or her reluctance to change, you may conclude that being accepting of your mate (not of the poor behavior) is the best approach. Even assuming the worst—that your partner doesn't care about you—you could adopt the philosophy of accepting that lack of love as *unfortunate* rather than *terrible,* and then take appropriate action without downing yourself or making yourself really angry.

We shall now look at excerpts from another client's therapy session which also deals with the problems of getting along in a close relationship. The client in this case is angry at his wife for criticizing him for not doing housework.

C. My wife feels like I ought to do more around the house, housework and stuff like that.

T. So she says you're not doing enough?

C. Right.

T. What's your feeling when she gets after you? What's your honest feeling?

C. I really feel angry. I feel like she . . . she's just bitching at me, and the bitching drives me away from doing more.

T. And do you feel that she's unfairly after you, unfairly criticizing you for the lack of housework?

C. Yes.

T. Why is she unfair, then, if you don't do the housework?

C. She doesn't accept my being a slob.

T. Oh, I see. So she's after you too much about your sloppiness. She doesn't give you unconditional positive regard about it. Right?

C. Right.

T. Okay. So we have A (an Activating Event). Let's assume that you're describing A correctly—that she's after you too much and criticizing you severely, calling you a slob for not cleaning up enough. Right?

C. Right.

T. And at C, the Consequence, you're angry when she does this?

C. Right.

T. All right, now, what do you think you're telling yourself at B, your Belief System, *about* her doing this? What are you telling yourself to create your anger? You're doing something at B. Let's see if you can figure out your anger-creating Belief.

C. Well, I think it is: "I'm okay and she's giving me a message that I'm a slob. She doesn't accept what I am."

T. All right. So the first part is, "She doesn't accept what I am." But you're telling yourself something else about that. Because you could just say, "Well, screw it! So she doesn't accept what I am," and then you wouldn't be angry. So you're saying something in addition. What are you saying about *her* for not accepting you the way you are?

C. That she's a bitch.

T. "She's a bitch!" Right. And are you also saying, "She *should* accept me the way I am, and because she doesn't she's a bitch"?

C. Yes. Precisely!

T. Okay, now we come to D, Disputing: *Why* should she accept you the way you are? Why *must* she?

C. If she did, I'd probably do more.

T. All right. But you see, you answered the question the way most people do: "It would be *preferable* if she really accepted me, because she'd get better results. I'd probably do more." So you're giving a good reason why it should be preferable; but why *must* your wife act preferably?

C. I can't come up with anything except that when she doesn't, it just makes me mad, drives me away.

T. No, no! "*I* make myself mad." You see? *It* doesn't make me mad. And "*I* drive myself away. *She* acts annoyingly, and *I* make myself mad." Do you see the difference between those two statements?

C. Yes. *She* can't really make me feel anything. Only *I* can.

T. Now, ironically, you're doing to her what you accuse her of doing to you. Do you realize that, when you're angry?

C. I am?

T. Yes. You said before, if I heard you correctly, that "She's not accepting me the way I am—slobbish." Well, are you accepting *her* the way she is—critical?

C. Ah, no.

Once again we see that *anger* is the main problem. In the previous case a wife was angry at her husband for doing nothing. In this case, a husband is angry at his wife because she nags him (and is probably angry) about his not doing enough housework. The husband correctly points out that his wife's criticism (and probable anger) encourages him to do *less* work. The solution? First get rid of, or greatly reduce his own anger. This is done by *recognizing* and then *attacking* his anger-creating Beliefs. In this case, his Belief is: "My wife *must* accept me, and she's a bitch if she doesn't!" It would be great if she did accept him and not criticize, but it would also be great to have a million dollars, and he doesn't *need* either. Anger comes from not accepting reality, from *demanding* that people or things be different than they are.

If anger worked, then it would be beneficial. But usually it helps make the situation much worse and blocks practical solutions to the problem. In this case, and in most, each partner is angry at the other, *demanding* certain behavior, and *downing* the other for not meeting the demands. She demands that he not be a slob, and he demands that she not be critical of him. Then they both feel angrier. Here we have an almost perfect vicious circle.

T. Your anger comes from your refusal to accept your wife with her critical behavior. You see? Doesn't she have the right to be critical?

C. She's been critical. Very critical!

T. That's right. She's talented in that respect, isn't she? And she was probably this way for many years before you ever met her.

C. She's good at it!

T. And she practices every day, right?

C. You got it.

T. Now, if you'd give her the right to be critical, you still wouldn't like it, but you wouldn't feel angry.

C. I guess that's true. But it's not easy!

T. Also, you're saying, "She's a bitch!" Well, I want evidence that she's a bitch. Let's suppose she goes on criticizing you for the next 20 years— let's suppose that. How does that make her a bitch? I want evidence. I'm a scientist, and I want some hard data to support your hypothesis that she's a bitch.

C. It just doesn't go along with . . . what I think she *should* be like.

T. That's true, but all the evidence that you've given me—and I'm assuming you're describing her correctly now—is bitchy *behavior:* that she acts bitchily *at times,* when she's angry.

C. Right.

T. Now, how does that make *her* a bitch?

C. It doesn't.

T. You see, that's a label. Just like when she calls you a slob. Are you really a total slob when you *act* slobbily some of the time?

C. Well, no. I'm not a slob.

T. That's right! *Why* aren't you? She thinks you are, or she says you are. Now, why aren't you a slob?

C. I also have nonslobbish behavior?

T. That's right! You act in many ways, sometimes slobbily, and sometimes not. And she's saying, "*You're* a slob," implying that you practically always act slobbishly; and that's incorrect. And you're doing the same thing to her when you say *she's* a bitch. She's a human who unfortunately at times acts bitchily. You see?

C. Well, I just don't . . . Now I'm drawing a blank. What I hear you saying is that neither one of us has to change. She can be bitchy if I act slobbish.

T. No. Let's deliberately assume the worst—that she continues to act bitchily. If you give her the right to be bitchy, you will stop angering yourself at her. She's wrong if she keeps calling you a slob, so we're not saying she's right. If she were correct, she'd just say, "Look, dear, that was slobbish behavior; I wish you wouldn't continue it." Then, as you said before, you'd probably do less of it. You can try and talk with her, get her to change. But if she keeps on for the rest of your married life calling you a slob, castrating you, you can still accept that without liking it or putting yourself down. Are you sometimes putting yourself down when she calls you a slob?

C. Most generally, yes.

T. Now, how are *you* no good even if you steadily exhibit slobbish behavior for the rest of your life? How does that make *you* a no-goodnik?

C. Oh, it doesn't . . . But it really does.

T. "But it really does." You see! You'd better watch that! Your behavior doesn't make *you* a slob; but you slip into thinking it does at times. If she were here screaming, "You goddamned slob! You cleaned the house crummily for the eightieth time!" you probably would tell yourself, "Well, she's right. I *am* a slob!"

C.   I told myself that this morning.

T.   You see? And that was a mistake. Not "I acted slobbily" — you probably did. But *you* are not your *acts*. You *do* your acts, and we're not defending some of your acts. But you are *you,* and you have the right as a *fallible human* to do fallible acts.

C.   Good.

T.   Yes, but you'd better believe it! You'd better correctly rate your *acts* and stop incorrectly labeling *you* and *your wife,* until you habituate yourself to this new, constructive type of thinking and thereby minimize your anger and your self-hatred.

The key lesson here is that you can *accept,* not down or blame, yourself and your mate while not accepting certain *behavior.* A human is a complex process with many acts and traits, and, therefore, really can't be given a *global* "good" or "bad" rating. If you put down your partner for not living up to your expectations, anger results. When you put yourself down as a total person, guilt and/or depression result. It is most important to work at eliminating the idea that you or your partner is a rotten person for having certain traits. Once you make progress in this area, practical solutions can be tried. We mentioned contracts and the art of compromise earlier. If, after a *reasonable period of time and effort,* your mate will not change certain very annoying behaviors, and on balance you are getting *more pain than pleasure* out of the relationship, you might consider ending the relationship. It would be wise to seek *professional guidance* before taking this step.

Many disagreements relate to the issue of *power.* Both partners are fearful of "giving in," because that would mean they were "weak." Actually, the reverse is often true, because "giving in" on noncrucial issues can be a sign of strength. *Achieving personal happiness in a relationship does not mean needlessly and deliberately hurting your partner.* It does mean standing up for your rights, without hostility and blame and it means seeking maximum pleasure and minimum pain from the relationship. Part of this consists in treating your mate with kindness and consideration, while accepting some faults. This generally leads to similar behavior towards you, and a better relationship. The lessons taught in this chapter have helped many couples achieve a more beneficial relationship. The same can be true for you, if you *work* at it!

CHAPTER 12

Overcoming Sex Problems

Although one of the greatest pleasures in life, sex provides many people with significant problems. The "sexual revolution" has helped some achieve a happier sex life, but at the same time many complain of new pressures and anxieties. Sexual-performance problems are widespread, and numerous ideas about cause and treatment currently exist. Except for the small percentage of cases in which a true physiological problem exists, we have found that in most cases clients' irrational Beliefs create their main emotional and performance problems.

If you have a performance problem, such as lack of arousal and/or orgasm, you are usually *anxious* or *guilty* (sometimes angry) about sex. This results from placing *demands* upon yourself or others and then *downing* yourself or your partner when these demands (rather than preferences) are not met. Your anxiety and guilt are frequently part of a general lack of assertiveness in seeking pleasure.

The cases which follow will demonstrate how RET helps the client (and can help you) see and challenge the self-defeating Beliefs which are at the root of many sex problems. In RET, behavioral techniques are also presented, as well as basic sex information and advice.

The client in the first case is a 48-year-old engineer who complains of being impotent.

T. [Reading from client's form] "Sexual inadequacy, general feelings of failure and insecurity." What kind of sexual inadequacy?
C. Well, that's impotency. It's just that I can't remain stiff when I enter the vagina. I was successful with a couple of women in the past four years or so, but otherwise it's generally a problem.

T. First of all, do you get an erection?

C. Yes, I sometimes get an erection, but I don't maintain it.

T. But suppose you don't try to have intercourse, and you just pet, what happens then?

C. I can have an erection. I can have an ejaculation by just pressing against her, and so on.

T. Okay, so if she handles your penis, or you press against her, you will maintain an erection fairly well, and then you'll ejaculate? Is that so?

C. Right.

T. But if you try to enter her, then it often goes down. Before entry or after?

C. I'm not able to enter her, because it goes down before.

T. So what's happening is that you're anxious.

C. Yes.

T. And what happens in masturbation? Suppose you masturbate?

C. I can do that all right.

T. There's no trouble maintaining an erection?

C. In masturbating, no.

T. And coming to orgasm?

C. No.

T. And how many times, if you masturbate, could you have an erection and an orgasm a week? About how many times?

C. I haven't tried it lately, but I imagine if I wanted to, once a day.

T. So there's no problem there.

Although most cases of impotency in men (or "sexual inadequacy" in women) are caused by psychological problems, it is important to rule out physical causes. A checkup by a competent medical doctor is a good start, but you can also ask yourself certain questions. For example, if you can become aroused (erect for the male) when you are alone, this obviously proves that you are capable of arousal. Likewise, if you masturbate and achieve orgasm, this proves that you are physically capable of having orgasms. Most sex problems occur with a partner (or a certain type of partner), and this indicates either a psychological problem or poor sex techniques. As we will now see, this "psychological" problem mainly arises from a few irrational Beliefs (iBs).

T. What happened sexually with the women you were successful with?

C. You see, it was the very first night with them; and the difference, as I tried to analyze it, is that in my own mind, in some way they showed me that they wanted me. I was confident that they wanted me. I didn't have to be the aggressor.

T. They wanted you not just sexually but generally? Is that what you mean? I'm not quite sure.

C. They wanted me sexually.

T. They wanted you sexually; and because they wanted you, and didn't care that much whether you failed, you were able to make it?

C. That's true. There was no pressure; they were very uninhibited, and I may have been at times impotent with them. But I was able to satisfy them orally, so I didn't feel as though they wouldn't come back.

T. They let it be known that they didn't need intercourse. Is that right? So that you could satisfy them one way or another?

C. I would say yes.

T. And because they didn't need intercourse, you were actually able to get it up and screw them.

C. Right.

T. While you assume that some other women do want intercourse, or need it, and then you get anxious?

C. Yeah.

T. All right, why would it be awful if they did require satisfaction through intercourse? Suppose you go with a woman, and she definitely wants intercourse. She puts the pressure on you for intercourse.

C. This is what I had in my last relationship.

T. How long did you go with her?

C. Between two and three months.

T. So you go with this woman two or three months, and you're quite sure that she wants intercourse; and then suppose you start worrying, "Wouldn't it be *awful* if I failed." Well, why *would* it be? Suppose this woman wants intercourse but you aren't able to have it? You're only capable of satisfying her with your tongue, or your fingers, or something like that?

C. But unfortunately I wasn't able to satisfy her with my tongue or fingers; that was the difficulty.

T. Because she wouldn't allow it?

C. No, she regarded the tongue as a preliminary, but I couldn't bring her to orgasm with it.

T. The only way she comes to orgasm is in intercourse?

C. Right. And she ended up, after breaking the relationship, by telling me that as well as we got along in other areas, she had the feeling that there was some kind of, I can't remember the exact words, but it seemed to be like an antagonism on my part, that I was punishing her by denying her my penis.

T. But, she's merely *assuming* you were hostile and punishing. That's *her* problem, isn't it?

C. Yes, but I wonder if other women that I failed with, or that I lost, were just not quite that outspoken. I had another case where a woman said she enjoyed it orally, but that our sex life wasn't really that good. So she, too, ended our relationship.

The client, although physically capable of arousal and orgasm, is frequently impotent with a partner. The basic cause of this really is best understood in two parts: (1) the female's *demand,* rather than preference, for intercourse as the only way to achieve satisfaction; and (2) the client's *acceptance* of that condition, along with the ideas that "it would be *awful* not to be able to have intercourse. I *should* be able to have it and I rate as a *rotten person* if I can't." These self-defeating beliefs *create* anxiety and actually block sexual arousal. The ironic part is that the women who didn't *demand* penile-vaginal copulation from this client were actually the ones to get it. *When you accept another's definition of how sex must be, you are often setting yourself up for failure.*

T. The last woman you mentioned is really saying, "You can go down on me, and you can manipulate my clitoris, but I *have to* end up with intercourse to really enjoy it and come." Isn't that her hypothesis?

C. Yeah, right.

T. Now let's just suppose you really were impotent, that you couldn't ever get an erection. Why couldn't she be satisfied with your having your fingers in her vagina rather than your penis?

C. I don't know.

T. Well, did you ever try it that way?

C. Yes.

T. Did you ever try to convince her that that was okay, having fingers in her vagina?

C. Not convince her verbally, but I tried to prolong it until perhaps I could make her come. But she would say, "Well, I enjoy it more if you're just lying on top of me," and she knew that I couldn't put my penis in her. She seemed to enjoy my full body lying on top of her full body.

T. But why couldn't you put, in her case, your full body on top of her body, and put your fingers in her vagina, and get her to come that way if she wanted vaginal intromission? What would stop that, if she really wanted orgasm with something in her vagina?

C. I don't know.

T. Because obviously if she won't let that kind of intromission work, *she* has a problem. That's what I'm trying to show you: That she's arbitrarily telling herself that you *must* have your penis in her vagina, and it *must* be erect in order for her to come. That's her *demand.* And I'm trying to show you—though I don't know if you'll be able to convince her of this—that any woman who can come with a penis inside her can also come with fingers inside her. There isn't that much difference. And your fingers can remain perennially erect! Isn't that true?

C. Yeah.

T. So she is arbitrarily defining sex in a certain way. Because you could lie on top of her, put your fingers in her vagina if your penis went down, and presumably she would come that way. And she has a one-track view; that unless your penis remains erect, and you keep screwing her, she's not going to come. And that's her silly *idea;* but I don't think you realize that.

C. Well, I realize from what you say that that can be true. However, unfortunately, if it was just one woman, then I would not be that concerned. I would say, "Well, all right, there's something wrong with her." Right?

T. Right.

C. But it has happened with others.

T. But if it does happen with them, then they're defining sex in a certain fashion, and *that's* the pressure they're putting on you. Suppose, for example, a woman arbitrarily thought that the only way she could come was to have your penis in her anus. Let's just suppose that. Well, that's wrong. She's making that up, because if your penis can give her an orgasm that way, your fingers could also do so. In fact, you could probably do it better with your fingers! But if she views it in one limited way, and if you *accept* that "fact," then you're going to have a problem. And you're going to say, "Oh damn! I'll never be able to satisfy her in the way she wants; therefore, it's *awful!*" And then your penis will go down—if you accept this nonsense. Whatever a woman arbitrarily defines as absolutely *necessary,* if you accept that, you're going to get anxious about not providing. Isn't that right?

C. Yeah.

T. Suppose, for example, a woman believed, "You have to keep your tongue inside my mouth for a half-hour, then I'll come." Let's suppose she believed that, and you didn't like tonguing her mouth for such a long period. Then you're not going to make it with her. You could do what she wants—keep your tongue inside her mouth for a half-hour. But suppose you don't like it, you start gagging, or find it unpleasant. Well, obviously she's not for you. Because of her *demand.* But I don't think you see that. You say, "Oh, this woman who demands intercourse is right, because a lot of women are this way. They think my penis must be inside them." And you tell yourself, therefore, "If I don't maintain an erection there's something rotten about me!" and then you make yourself anxious. Instead, you could say, "Hell, that's *her* problem or taste, and she's not for me. But it has little to do with me. Because any woman who wants a penis inside her could also accept fingers inside her. But she's not allowing that. Therefore, that's her problem, and I'll try to help her get over the problem. But if I never succeed, I can seek other women. She's putting pressure on me, and I have the right to accept or reject her pressure." You're guilty, because you think she's right; that you're *supposed* to keep your penis in her vagina. You make yourself anxious, and that isn't going to work. You see what I mean?

C. Yeah, I put pressure on myself by agreeing with her pressure.

T. Right! There are many women who realize they don't *need* a penis inside them. They *like* it from time to time, but they don't *need* it. They can get an orgasm from clitoral manipulation; or from your fingers inside them, which would serve as a substitute for a penis. But if they don't allow that, then you'd better teach them to allow it—or go on to a woman who isn't that pressuring. If you took that attitude, then you would teach most of the women you were with that they don't *need* a penis all the time.

The point here is that although penile-vaginal intercourse is enjoyable, it is *not* the only way for the female to achieve pleasure and orgasm. This is true for the male also. When a female doesn't want intercourse, she can help him come to orgasm in other ways. If you convey to your partner that you enjoy a certain type of sex but can be happy without it, you actually help this partner have sex the way you want it. If your partner insists upon a narrow definition of sex, you can recognize that, realize that there is *no* reason why you must meet those demands, and that your self-worth certainly doesn't depend on it. Once you are less anxious, because you don't view "failure" as *awful,* you will often succeed. Achieving personal happiness also may mean leaving partners who keep *demanding* sex in a way that you don't prefer, and seeking more open-minded partners. If you like certain people, you can try to have them change their sexual ideas. But there is also no reason why you can't seek others if you are not successful. Your and your partner's basic goal is to enjoy sex, and certain partners will further that goal, and some will hinder it. Which will you choose?

T. There was a woman I had intercourse with years ago, and she was convinced that the only way she could come was with a penis inside her. That's what she was convinced. And we had intercourse once, and she came that way. But then to her surprise, I tried putting my fingers inside her vagina, because after intercourse I wasn't that capable of becoming erect again. So I put my fingers inside her, and started manipulating her vagina with my fingers, and she had one of the best orgasms in her life. This greatly surprised her, because she didn't realize that she could do that. She was prejudiced. And if people maintain any kind of sex prejudice, they're often going to create a self-fulfilling prophecy. They're only going to allow themselves to come in that one limited fashion. Some women are convinced that they can only come, they've told me, with a man sucking their clitoris. But if they give up that prejudice, they see after a while that there are other ways too, and they start enjoying these. If you let your sex partners sell you on some special way of coming, such as only during intercourse, you're both going to be stuck on that notion, and you're going to worry. And then *because of that pressure in your head,* you're not going to be able to keep your penis up. And if you realize that there are women like that, but it's *their* problem, *their* taste, and that's the way *they* are, you'll either try to teach them otherwise, or you won't make it with them. But you won't put yourself down, which you are now doing. When you meet such a woman, like this last one, who was convinced she could only come with a penis inside her, and you foolishly agree with her, you're going to think, "Oh, will I last, will I last?" And that's deadly, because then you're *not* going to last. But we know that with women who don't *require* intercourse, you're able to do it. That's the irony! Isn't that so?

C. Yes.

T. Because you are not putting pressure on yourself. But you *let* this last woman intimidate you. You probably thought she was right—that you had to screw her with your sacred penis up—and then you made it go down. Isn't that right?

C. Yeah, I now can see that I really pressured myself.

T. Intercourse is *one* way a woman can be satisfied; but she's bigotedly saying that it's the *only* way. And you're agreeing! If we could get you to see that that's her idea, and that practically any woman who can come with a penis inside her can also come with fingers, you would feel and act much differently, less anxiously. You see?

C. Well, I have the feeling that she would think, "Oh, well, if I can't have your penis, then what do I need you for?"

T. But that's her problem; and either you'd better talk her out of that belief, or you'd better get another woman.

C. It's generally accepted that vaginal intercourse is a normal thing.

T. It's generally accepted, but it's not the *only* way. In the old days, let's say fifty or a hundred years ago, it would generally be accepted that going down on a woman was wrong, and most women wouldn't allow it. They would say, "Oh, you're a pervert," and they would get little satis-faction from it. But that was the result of their ignorance. Today, women generally like intercourse, but many never have an orgasm that way, as Shere Hite shows in her book, *The Hite Report.*

C. I couldn't satisfy my wife. I mean at that time I wasn't impotent, and so I was able to get into her, but I came quicker than she could have an orgasm. I used to try to get her to come with my hand, and it was a long, tedious process. And finally one time she went to a doctor, and she came back to me with a story that the doctor asked her if she ever tried oral love. Now I had never tried it yet, and I felt that if the doctor suggested that, then maybe it's okay. And if she suggested it to me, maybe she wanted me to try it. So I tried it, and it was great. She had an orgasm the first time, and she was like out of her mind.

T. She had an orgasm from oral sex?

C. Yeah, right. And then the second and third times I did it with her, I had to more or less win her to this method. She resisted, and she said that it isn't right this way and all this sort of thing, and after about the third time I had the feeling that she thought that I had power over her, and she didn't want to get into this oral situation.

T. But the point is that was her problem. Did you finally see that it was her problem, or did you still think that it was yours?

C. No, I did realize that it was her problem.

The important lesson in this case is that there is no law of the universe stating that sexual satisfaction must result from only one prescribed type of sexual activity (such as intercourse). Some people will even wrongly insist that intercourse *must* be done in one particular position. This is utter nonsense! Individuals have different tastes, and *experimentation* with different positions, oral sex, and other methods, is the way to discover what you like best. Many women find that they have much better orgasms via direct clitoral stimulation, and therefore *prefer* their partner's tongue or hand, instead of regular intercourse. There are numerous ways to achieve satisfaction, and it is foolish to feel that you *must* perform in any one way.

In this case, the client's impotence is related to his partner and himself *demanding* potency. Many men are impotent even when there is no pressure from the woman. If no physical problem exists, the basic problem is then *self-imposed pressure.* This pressure consists of the following irrational ideas: "It would be *horrible* not to get an erection. I *must* get one, for if I don't, it proves I am not a real man, and no woman could be sexually satisfied by or care for me." These *anxiety-creating ideas* will actually prevent an erection.

On the other hand, thinking about your partner's body, fantasizing about exciting sexual situations, and concentrating on pleasurable sensations will help you become aroused. You are then an active participant without *demanding* erection or orgasm. When you demand, you become a spectator, since you *watch yourself* and worry whether or not you will function "properly." This is antisexual, and you had better work against this tendency by challenging your irrational Beliefs, and then practicing fantasizing and other methods of sexual arousal.

C. When I attract a new girlfriend and then I lose her, I wonder how far off the day will be when I cannot attract another.

T. You forget that you never can attract certain women, but there are always others that you can attract. Some women allow themselves to be attracted by a man your age. With such women, you will tend to do wonderfully. Isn't that true, that because they have that taste, you will tend to do well; while with those who only let themselves be attracted by a younger man, you won't do well?

C. Right. Well, usually when a young woman is attracted to an older man there has to be something material they're looking for. They want things.

T. Often, but women are different. They usually have prejudices, pro and con. Some will go absolutely batty about you, like these women you told me about before, because they like someone like you. And others, like this last woman, won't accept you. Now if you are going to get hung up because of different women's tastes and prejudices, you are going to knock yourself down when you meet women like the last one, and you're going to raise yourself up when you meet the ones who favor you. You'd better face it—it's *their* taste, and that's the way *they* feel and act.

C. I have feelings of insecurity. I've never been successful as far as money is concerned. I really struggle all the time. I've always struggled in anything that I did. In fact, I graduated from engineering school with honors, but I spent the day and night studying and just working and not getting in any kind of socializing. I mean, it was very one-sided, because I was determined to get through school.

T. Right. But can you see that your general feelings of insecurity come from your belief, "Unless I succeed, I'm a worm!" Isn't *that* your belief?

C. Well, I don't know if I exactly think of myself as a worm.

T. But don't you believe, "I'm not a good person; I'm not a great person"?

C. You see, the trouble is that I don't even know what a good person is.

T. It's what you believe it is.

C. It's easy enough to say that money is not important and so on, but in this society you really have to have it to get along.

T. You have to have it with *certain people*. With some women, if you don't have money and power, you can't get along. But then there are some who don't give a damn. In fact, there are some who are the opposite. If you had money and power, they would immediately feel inadequate, and you couldn't make it with them. I've seen lots of women like that. The only men they'll go for are those who *don't* have money and power.

C. So that they can dominate?

T. No, they think they're worms if a man does have money and power. So they only look for one "schnooky" man after another. And I'm not saying that's good. I'm just trying to show you that that's their taste. Others are like you're describing—they have to dominate. So if a guy has money and power, they run away. There are women like that. There's a wide range of women, and most of them think it's necessary to have a certain kind of man. And you're not going to satisfy all of them; no one is. Now if you meet such women, you'd better say to yourself, "I'm not their cup of tea." But that doesn't mean it's *awful,* or that there's anything *rotten* about you. But I think you do think you're no good, when you meet these women whom you will never satisfy. And, therefore, you end up with feelings of insecurity. Because you're not saying, "It's too bad I can't satisfy them." You're saying, "It's *awful; I must* satisfy them!"

C.   Yeah, I really do often say that.

T.   In my own case, I've failed with some women because they think I'm too short, too tall, too thin, too this, or too that. But I just say to myself, "Hell, that's the way *they* think and feel! They're not for me." I don't put myself down. I think you do. Isn't that true?

C.   Yes. I definitely do.

T.   Because of your beliefs. Instead of saying, "Too bad, I'm not for them," you say, "Maybe I'm not for *any* good woman! How terrible!" Then you put yourself down.

C.   You see, intellectually I understand all this, but how do I get myself to really believe it?

T.   "Intellectually" means *once in a while lightly.* "But most of the time, *very strongly,* I believe what I've always believed—that I've got to satisfy practically every woman I meet and if I don't for any reason *it's terrible!*" That's your *real* belief. But once in a while, lightly, you believe the opposite: "Okay, so I'm not satisfying this current woman. Tough! On to the next!" Once in a while you "intellectually" believe that, but *most* of the time you *powerfully* believe the opposite: "I *must* satisfy every new woman whatever the hell her thing is—*any* woman that I really like! And if I don't, it's *terrible!*" Now if we could get you to say, "*It would be nice* if I could satisfy every woman, but I can't—because there are too many of them, and they all have different tastes. That's the way it is!" If you would strongly think *that* way, you'd do much better, and would have full self-acceptance. And once you get that, I think your potency problems will go away. You will then accept *you,* even when some women don't. Because many women never will! So to really change your beliefs requires going over your false, or irrational, ones *vigorously,* each day, and substituting rational ones.

It is interesting to see how the client's self-defeating Beliefs about sex, namely, "I *must* perform well, or else I am a *rotten person,*" are applied to all desirable women he encounters. This relates to our discussion of insecurity (on pages 64-81) where it was shown how these types of Beliefs make you anxious. The people that you come in contact with will have a great variety of preferences. Therefore, it is important to realize that, in all probability, you will only please a small percentage of them. The example about money and power in this case illustrates this point. Some women actually would prefer a man without such characteristics, due to their own psychological makeup.

The client asks how to "really believe" more logical, rational ideas. We spoke about this in earlier chapters, but since it is so important, here is a brief review. When you have an emotional problem, such as anxiety with impotency, *look for your irrational Beliefs* (after finishing this book, you will be aware of them). *Write them out, and ask for logical evidence to support each one.* As you begin to see that there is no truth to an idea like "I am a *rotten person* if I don't get an erection tonight," *forcefully think about why it is false each day,* and substitute more logical Beliefs for it. Also, *act* against these ideas by meeting different partners and convincing yourself that you do not *have* to satisfy each one's individual preferences. All of this requires work, but there really is no shortcut to acquiring a philosophy that will not guarantee, but will notably increase your chances of achieving personal happiness.

In the next case, we have a single woman with a sex problem. She usually doesn't achieve orgasm with intercourse, but does via other means. The real problem is her guilt and anxiety about this and about her fantasies. It is interesting to note that the previous client had trouble with women who *demanded* intercourse as the only way to have sex, and here we have a woman who finds, as is not unusual, that intercourse is not necessarily the best way. Whenever one feels that sex *should* or *must* be a certain way, emotional and performance problems follow.

Let us join as the session gets under way.

C. I have orgasms with masturbation, but seldom with a partner, and with a partner it's mainly with oral sex.

T. And while you're getting aroused with a partner, and occasionally coming to orgasm, but usually not, are you thinking anything as the sex is going on?

C. Well, I'm nervous that I can't have an orgasm. When I masturbate alone, I'm thinking I'm going to have an orgasm, and when I'm with a partner, I think, "I'm not going to be able to have an orgasm."

T. And when you do it alone, about how long does it take to do it, to come to orgasm.

C. Maybe ten minutes, maybe less.

As was true of the last client, a few questions usually indicate whether a physical problem exists. Since this client has an orgasm when she masturbates, it is clear that she is capable of arousal and orgasm, but something is blocking her when she is with a partner. Could it be what she thinks about during sex?

T. There's not that much difficulty in having an orgasm with masturbation—What are you thinking about then?

C. Well, I used to have erotic fantasies that had to do with very impersonal sex, that had to do with being forced, or . . . being kind of an object that was being raped.

T. And now?

C. And now I . . . I just concentrate on the feeling, and on the sensation of coming.

T. And that works?

C. Yes.

T. So you see, you have at least two techniques—similar to the ones that most people have. They either have fantasies such as the one you had; and/or they focus on their sensations. But, naturally, when you're focusing on "I don't think I'll come!" or "Wouldn't it be *awful* if I didn't come?" what is going to happen?

C. I block myself from coming. I've tried to avoid having these fantasies, of being forced or . . . being raped.

T. Well, what would be bad about having them, if you had them while a man was trying to give you an orgasm? Why would that be bad to have those rape fantasies or any kind of fantasy?

C. I feel . . . that it's bad.

T. Yes, but why?

C. Because it's impersonal and it's . . . I should be able to have an orgasm without thinking about—uh—.

T. Impersonal things?

C. Yes.

T. Why *should* you? Who said so?

C. It's more social. It's more socially oriented.

T. But you notice that you think of your sensations when you masturbate, and is *that* socially oriented?

C. No; I see what you mean. I guess it's my belief that it's better to have fantasies about either another person, or about myself.

T. But aren't you arbitrarily dividing your fantasies into "good" and "bad" ones and saying, "If I get an impersonal one that works, that's not cricket?"

C. Right.

T. But is there any real evidence for that belief?

C. Well, it feels more socially acceptable.

T. Do you think your partner cares what you're thinking about?

C. No.

T. See? So, after all, it doesn't involve him. Dr. Lonny Myers, a female physician and sex therapist in Chicago, pointed out at one of our sex therapy practicums at the Institute for Rational-Emotive Therapy that, as both men and women get closer to orgasm, they become less intimate and get more and more into themselves, into their own sensations and physiological reactions. Do you see that that's probably true?

C. Yes. Yes, I can see that in myself.

T. Then why are you worrying about being less personal or less intimate in your fantasies if your body requires that you get into *you* and *your* sensations?

C. I feel . . . Well, I don't know.

T. As we said, your partner doesn't know or doesn't really care what you're thinking about. But you keep telling yourself, "My fantasies, my thoughts *have* to be intimate, *have* to be personal." Well, why *must* they? Aren't you putting an extra pressure on yourself?

C. Yes, I guess I am.

T. And we already know in your case that the *un*intimate fantasy works pretty well.

C. Yes, it definitely does.

T. So I would say, why don't you let yourself have *any* kind of fantasy that you want, as long as the fantasy doesn't include a self-downing philosophy, such as: "I *must* be beaten, or I *must* be raped because I don't deserve sex otherwise." You see? That kind of fantasy would be destructive because it would tend to lap over into the rest of your life and make you feel worthless. But as long as a fantasy works for sex satisfaction, really works, what difference does it make what kind of fantasy it is?

C. It doesn't really make any difference.

The client finds that fantasies involving "impersonal sex" work well, but she feels they're wrong. This idea, although false, is common to many women. It is arbitrary, and there is no evidence to support the idea that one type of fantasy is okay while another is not. The basic guideline we would recommend is, *if the fantasy helps arouse and satisfy you, use it.*

The only caution here, and it doesn't apply to most people, is to see if masochistic fantasies are part of a *general self-downing philosophy.* This would include the idea, "I must be beaten or hurt because I am a rotten person." If this is the case, work on challenging that idea by asking for evidence to support it. Achieving personal happiness involves doing what is best for you, without needlessly and deliberately hurting another. Surely your fantasies hurt no one.

The client has trouble having orgasms with a partner. Aside from the problem of not using fantasies that work, she creates anxiety by believing, "It would be awful not to come, and therefore I must." If you have irrational Beliefs (iBs) like these, you can forcefully challenge them, since there is no reason you *must* achieve orgasm (although it would be preferable to). And although it is inconvenient and frustrating not to climax, it is not *awful.* To help work against these ideas while having sex, utilize exciting fantasies and concentrate on your pleasant sensations. This will distract you from observing yourself and will interrupt your telling yourself, "I *must* become excited! It would be horrible if I don't!" This self-observing, or being a spectator rather than a participant, is deadly. Sex can be great fun, but not if you set up arbitrary rules and performance standards.

C. As a child I was taught that sex is bad and that men only wanted sex from me.

T. But is that true? Is that verifiable? Is sex *all* they want from you?

C. No.

T. And even if it were true, you could still enjoy yourself by having orgasms for *yourself,* for your *own* pleasure. Couldn't you?

C. Yes, but I reject that. I feel like I resist that. If that's *all* they want from me, I'm not going to give it to them.

T. "And I'm going to cut off my nose to spite my face!"

C. Yes.

T. But is that smart?

C. No.

T. Let's suppose men only wanted sex from you, but you were having good sex, too. Why not have the good sex and let them keep whatever nonsense they have in their little heads, such as the nonsense that you are *only* good for sex. You see? I don't see that you're much interested in sex for *you,* because you have these arbitrary notions of what you *should* do and how men *should* be. If you gave up those notions, you'd be more focused on *you.* And what is right for you is whatever works, so why not use it? Wouldn't that be a broader and more self-helping outlook?

C. Yes. Sometimes I'm afraid that I'll lose control when reaching orgasm.

T. And now let's suppose that you *do* lose control. You think of great fantasies, such as the ones you used to use, and you really let yourself go. What do you assume that the men are going to think as you let yourself go and "lose control"?

C. That I'm ugly and loose and . . . unattractive.

T. And have you checked that out with any male partners?

C. No. But I . . . When I've had orgasms, the man has been pleased.

T. See? So it's unlikely that he'll focus on your unattractiveness! Or on how awful it is for you to lose control!

Again, we can see how powerful ideas can be in determining feelings and behavior. The client in this case has anxiety about "loss of control" if she were to have an orgasm with a partner. This idea could certainly block an orgasm, so it is important to examine it.

The first part of her Belief is that men will see her as "loose or unattractive." Where is the evidence for this? The vast majority of men seem to love it when a woman has a great orgasm.

The second, and unstated, part of her irrational Belief (iB) is that if her partner were critical, she would *accept* his criticism and down herself. There are two things wrong with this. The first is that she doesn't have to agree with anyone's idea of what her sexual response *should* or *shouldn't* be; and the second is that she is incorrectly rating *herself* as bad when she rates her total self on the basis of a few sex *acts*.

The client indicates that she would also put herself down if she had sex with a man who only interested in her body. She can of course avoid such men and choose to seek partners who are interested in other aspects of herself, too. But if she discovers that a partner is only interested in sex, her rational attitude can be, "That's too bad. Look what he's losing in not appreciating more of me. I guess I went to bed with the wrong partner, and had better seek a new one. I certainly don't rate as a *rotten person* for doing this. It only proves once again that I am a *fallible human being.*" This attitude would lead to correcting the situation, instead of creating guilt (not to mention hostility and anxiety) which blocks effective action to help her achieve orgasm and a good human relationship.

C. I've had the experience of asking for oral sex and being refused.
T. And the reason was? Why the refusal? Do you know?
C. That . . . well, for one person . . . he was outraged. And . . . I don't know why.
T. All right, that can happen.
C. He didn't want to be asked. He only wanted to start things himself.
T. You don't need any partner like that.
C. No.
T. He sounds like something of a male chauvinist. Let him be outraged! But with most of the men, you've asked for oral sex? They went along with it?
C. Well, I seldom ask for it. I . . . I feel like I'm . . . I'm in a difficult position if I ask.

T. Because they might refuse?

C. Right. They might refuse.

T. And if they do?

C. They might not like to do it. If they wanted to, they would do it.

T. Well, but isn't that quite an assumption—that if they wanted to, they would? They might want it second or third, and want something else first. But left to their own devices, they might only go for what *they* most want and not what *you* prefer. Or they might think that *you* think that it's wrong. You see, there are many possibilities. Now, why not ask and risk refusal? What could you tell yourself if you asked and got refused? What could you say to yourself?

C. Well, I'd say I shouldn't have asked . . . I shouldn't need oral sex.

T. Why is that *wrong*? That's the wrong thing to say. That will get you in trouble with yourself. Now, why is that wrong?

C. Well, because it . . . I won't get satisfied.

T. Yes; and you'll also feel ashamed if you're refused.

C. Yes, I always feel very ashamed if they refuse me.

T. You see? Now, what *could* you say? What would be a better thing to say to yourself if you asked and got refused?

C. Well, he didn't want to.

T. He didn't want to, and that's—?

C. I'm disappointed, but it's okay.

T. Right. "It's not really okay. But he's not a louse. And it's too bad; and I'd better look elsewhere for somebody who will do what I want." Wouldn't that be a better thing for you to tell yourself?

C. Yes. It really would!

T. And: "He's entitled to his preference. He's entitled to that. But that's he, and he is not that good for me. Therefore, I'll look for somebody else who likes to do what I like to do." And there certainly are men who are in that category. See? So you can find and stick to them. But the main thing is to accept the notion that whatever you do that is satisfying to you is a good thing. I mean, you have every right to use any fantasy, or seek any kind of sex, like oral relations. Anything that really works to satisfy you! But you seem to say, "Oh, no. Either sex is bad, or it's okay, but I don't deserve this good thing!" Which do you think is the more powerful thought: "Sex is bad," or, "It's okay, but I don't really deserve to go after what I want?"

C. I don't deserve to go after what I want.

T. All right. Prove that statement, that you don't deserve it.

C. Well, I can't prove it. I feel it and . . .

T. You feel it, but where will it get you?

C. It won't get me anywhere.

T. That's right. "I feel it," usually means, "I deeply believe this." Now, if you deeply believe this, and follow that view, as you have just said, it won't get you anywhere.

C. Right.
T. Now, why not take a different view: "I deserve all the pleasure I can get, and if it is short-range pleasure which does me in later, I might not try for it. But as long as it's pleasure that's good now, and not bad later, why should I not get it? And as far as the partners are concerned, as long as I can get those who perform the sex acts I want, why should I waste my time with those who don't?" See? You do have choices, alternatives. And it doesn't sound to me like you're exercising as many options as you could.
C. Right. I see that I could do better.

In your efforts to achieve personal happiness, we advocate going after what *you* want, without needlessly and deliberately hurting another. In the area of sex, this means asking for what you want as well as being willing to try reasonable things your partner suggests. If oral sex is your cup of tea—as it is for many people—try to persuade your partner to oblige. He or she can't read your mind, and, therefore, it is important to let your desires be known.

If you are angry at your partner for not wanting oral sex or some other sex act, you are foolishly *demanding* that he or she do what you want and then *downing* him or her for frustrating you. Your partner has the right to refuse you, but you have the right to try and persuade him or her to be more openminded, or the right to seek others.

Many people are afraid to let their desires be known for fear that their partner may say something like, "I would never engage in oral sex, and you must really be perverted to even suggest such a thing!" If you fear such rejection, you have two irrational ideas. One is that it really is "wrong" to desire some form of oral sex, and the other is, "I really am a *rotten person* for having such a desire."

To take an extreme example, if you desired sex while sitting on a tenth-story window ledge, this obviously would be dangerous and therefore self-defeating. But this does not mean it is "wrong" in any moral sense of the word, and it certainly doesn't prove that you are a rotten person for having this silly idea. You have the choice, and the right, to adopt the view, "I deserve, just because I am alive, to seek maximum pleasure and minimum pain. If at times my behavior is foolish, I can still accept myself, and seek to improve my behavior in the future."

T. Now, if you were to summarize what I have said to you that's helpful, what would it be?
C. To widen my fantasies to include everything that gives me pleasure . . .
T. Yes, right.

C. And to . . . to work on feeling that I deserve pleasure, and to look for a partner who can give me pleasure . . . with whom I can feel pleasure.

T. Right! And we could add: even if you sometimes do the wrong thing— you pick the wrong partners and you stay with them too long, or you refuse to ask for what you want—you don't ever have to put yourself down. You can just say, "*That* was wrong—the *act*. But I am a human who did a wrong thing; let's see if I can do it better next time." See?

C. Could you explain what you mean by saying that having a philosophy that I must be raped or beaten, is bad.

T. Yes. The trouble with masochistic thoughts or images—and you sometimes use masochistic fantasies of being raped or beaten—is not the sex part, because such thoughts and fantasies are sexually exciting partly because they're different. The reason why we resort to masochistic and sadistic thoughts, probably, is that they're unusual. They're more dramatic than everyday sexual thoughts, which may get boring after a while. So we dream up unusual fantasies; and it's hard, really, to think of very many fantasies which are unusual other than sadism, masochism, transvestism, or something like that. They're rather dramatic.

Now, in themselves, they usually work. They're exciting and therefore useful. But *if* they mean—*if* you really mean by this masochistic thought, "I'm really a rotten person, and the only way I deserve sex is if he rapes me and he puts me down as a human"—then that would be a part of your general philosophy of life, and that would be disturbed self-downing. It would work sexually sometimes, but the gain wouldn't be worth the loss. You see? Just as if you had a class in school and you told yourself, "I'm no good. The professor is a good person, and shouldn't be plagued by a louse like me. So I'll break some of the rules and let her scream at me, put me down, because I deserve this. And then, after getting this punishment, I can allow myself to get a decent mark." Now, that wouldn't be a very good philosophy, would it?

C. No. I see what you mean.

T. So any kind of self-downing, or what is called philosophic masochism, is not good. But some sex masochism or sadism really *doesn't* carry that connotation. It just takes the form of an unusual fantasy, which people often use. I frequently ask women and men, "Do you have sadistic or masochistic fantasies?" and they reply, "Yes, I do." Then I ask, "Now, have you ever tried them in practice—let yourself actually be beaten, for example? Or have you really beaten somebody?" And they usually say, "Yes, once in a while." And I say, "What happened?" And they reply, "It turned me off." You see, they don't really enjoy the sado-masochistic act, but the *idea* of having it is exciting. It's different. It's novel. And you may use that idea sexually and not put yourself down. Or you may use it to put yourself down. Now, don't use it if you really believe that you are no good, that you don't deserve enjoyable sex. If that's the reason for the fantasy, change the fantasy. Or get rid of that self-downing idea, and then you can keep the fantasy just because it arouses you sexually.

The client begins to see that she has the right to seek pleasure, to look for partners who will help give her satisfaction, and to utilize a variety of exciting fantasies. She can do these things without putting herself or anyone else down. Seeing these things during therapy is one thing, but to really incorporate them as *Beliefs* requires going over them each day while *challenging* and *acting* against the irrational ideas.

Masochistic or sadistic fantasies are quite common. If your attitude toward sex includes the idea that you deserve pleasure, and you don't down yourself, these types of fantasies can be helpful to you in achieving sexual satisfaction. A problem arises for the few people who see themselves as worthless and only deserving of pleasure if they are punished in some way. This means that their masochistic fantasies are part of a philosophy which is in direct opposition to achieving personal happiness.

If that is your case, work on changing your philosophy (in the various ways we have shown you) so that you can use sexual fantasies in a more rational way. Meanwhile, use other types of fantasies while you are working to change your masochistic philosophy.

You *do* deserve the great pleasure which sex has to offer. If you are not getting it, examine your *demands* upon yourself and others and replace them with *preferences.* Learn to accept yourself with your inevitable errors, and begin to free yourself of arbitrary or irrational ideas. A tall order? Yes, but well worth it!

CHAPTER 13

Coping With Work Problems

Most of us are, or will be, involved in the world of work. Achieving personal happiness includes preparing for and actively seeking the type of work that you feel will be most rewarding. It also includes minimizing the emotional problems commonly associated with the job itself and with the people you work for and with. The two most common problems are *anxiety* about your job performance (along with a fear of losing your job) and *anger* toward your boss, supervisor, employees, or other coworkers. These emotional problems minimize pleasure and can also cause practical difficulties for you, such as the loss of a job or a business. They therefore are *self-defeating* emotions, and you would be best served by replacing them with more appropriate ones. This means looking for the irrational Beliefs (iBs) which create self-defeating emotions and working to eradicate them. The following two cases will help demonstrate which Beliefs are involved and what you can do about them.

The client in the first case is a young woman who is anxious about her job performance and blames her boss for this.

C. I have a problem with my boss.
T. Yes, what is it?
C. He makes me very nervous.
T. You mean you make yourself very nervous about him. Now, what does he do?
C. He's also nervous.
T. Yes.
C. I make him nervous; we make each other nervous.
T. Well, let's suppose that he starts by making himself nervous, and that

you're then telling yourself something about him being nervous. Now, what do you think you're telling yourself in order to upset yourself?

C. Emotions are contagious. Therefore, I am catching his nervousness.

T. Wow! That's a great thing to tell yourself! So, "If he jumps off the bridge, I have to jump off the bridge!" Is that what you mean?

C. But I don't know how to change myself.

T. Well, first let's find out exactly what you're telling yourself. One thing seems to be, "If he is nervous and upset, I have no other alternatives than to imitate him. I must feel nervous and upset." Now don't you think there is some other possibility? What else could you think and do? Let's suppose tomorrow you go in—.

C. I could ignore him.

T. Yes. By saying *what* to yourself? It's Monday morning and you're there—.

C. "Who cares about him anyhow?"

T. And about his nervousness?

C. Yeah.

T. All right. That's one thing you can say to yourself.

C. "He can be as nervous as he wants to be. I don't *have* to be."

T. Now, what stops you from doing exactly that? It's Monday morning, and for an hour he's been very fidgety and nervous.

C. He . . . he sits behind me.

T. Yes.

C. If he would stay in his office, it wouldn't bother me.

T. But he's sitting behind you, being nervous. Is he spying on you?

C. No.

T. But—?

C. I'm not doing as much as he would like me to do.

T. That's right. "And isn't that horrible if I'm not?"

C. Yes.

The client begins with a common misconception, namely that the boss *makes her* nervous. A boss can make the job more frustrating or annoying, but he or she can't *make* you nervous. Your view of the situation, your *Beliefs,* create the anxiety. The client quickly begins to see that her anxiety involves the fear that the boss would think that she is not meeting his productivity standards, and how "horrible" that would be. Two questions come to mind here: Does the boss *really* expect more? And if he does, why *must* his expectations be met?

T. How long have you worked there, by the way?

C. Several years.

T. And how is it he hasn't found you out in those years? Pretty obtuse, isn't he? Has he given you raises during that time?

T. Yes, several good raises.

C. All right, now; how come? There he sits, spying on you, and he still hasn't found you out. It looks like you passed the probation period. Now what are you upset about? Isn't it some *demand* that you're really making on yourself?

C. I guess so.

T. Now, what's the demand that you're making on yourself?

C. I'm not as fast as the other woman, who was there for 20 years and can do about ten times the amount of work that I can do.

T. Yes. And I hear you saying, "I'm not as fast as I *should* be."

C. No, it's as *he* wants me to be. I don't want to be any faster.

T. Now, wait a minute. How do you know he wants you to be faster? Has he shown this?

C. Oh, he . . . every once in a while he pushes me a little bit.

T. But he doesn't fire you? Nor make nasty remarks?

C. No.

T. And if you remain exactly as slow as you are now, the chances are he may get ulcers, but he won't fire you. Right? So what are you worrying about his ulcers for? Why do you *have* to fulfill what he would like you to fulfill?

C. I don't have to.

T. But you think you do. You just said so.

C. Well, I don't like his . . . his thoughts about me.

T. Because, "If he thinks badly about me," what will happen?

C. He'll fire me.

T. After several years? That's very unlikely.

C. Oh, he . . . he could fire me.

T. There is no question he could, but why hasn't he? He's been prodding you now for years, and increasing your wages. Now, why do you expect that suddenly he's going to fire you?

C. Maybe he thinks he pays me too much. Maybe he thinks I'm not worth what I'm getting.

T. Maybe. But why has he kept increasing your wages? Why didn't he fire you two years ago?

C. Because I keep asking for increases, so he feels he has to give them to me.

T. Why did he *have* to?

C. Because I work for a retail chain.

T. Yes, so?

C. And I get my increases just before the busy season.

T. Right. So?

C. And he can't let me go at that time. He can't afford to. He can't break in a new girl during the busy season.

T. So? Someday he's going to fire you six months before the busy season, or after?

C. After the busy season he could fire me.

T. But why *hasn't* he? He's had several times now, *after* the busy season, when he could have easily fired you and hired another woman who by the next busy season would be broken in. Now, why hasn't he done that?

C. I guess I'm not so bad.

T. You say that with such reluctance!

It becomes clear in this section that although the boss has pushed the client to work a little faster, he is probably basically satisfied with her work. Even though she tries to knock down her ability, the client really can't explain why she gets raises and is not fired. So where does her anxiety come from?

Anxiety about performance on the job stems from a *perfectionistic value system* in which people believe that they *must* meet certain standards (their own or those of the boss) and it would be *horrible* not to. That could not only lead to loss of their jobs but also to a self-created feeling of worthlessness. The irony is that such a philosophy creates anxiety and can actually cause people to do poorly on their jobs.

Ask yourself, therefore, "How would it prove I am worthless even if I did lose my job?" It never would. At worst, it would show that you didn't do well on this job, and you had better try harder on the next one.

Ask yourself, "Why would it be *horrible* to lose this job?" It wouldn't be, unless you insist on defining it that way. It would just be annoying and frustrating.

"Why *must* I meet anyone's standards?" There never is any reason why you *must,* although there may be reasons why it would be *better* to do a good job. Therefore, if you desire to keep your job, it would be wise not to goof off or insult your superiors.

Rational answers like these can become your philosophy if you work at it. This philosophy will minimize the emotional pain of anxiety and help you to keep your present job or seek a more satisfactory one.

T. Let's assume you're right, and this other woman is a lot better than you, even though it may have taken her 20 years to get that way. There probably are other women your boss has had who are worse than you. Isn't that true?

C. But they wouldn't get the salary that I get. He already told me he thinks he's overpaying me.

T. But he's still paying you.

C. And if I had any other boss, he even told me, I might have been fired.

T. But out of the goodness of his heart, he's keeping you?

C. Yes.

T. Even when the busy season is over?

C. Right.

T. Do you think that's true?

C. He might be telling the truth.

T. Well, you can be glad that you've got such a nutty boss! Why aren't you happy, if you're really such a poor worker and he so kindly keeps you on?

C. Well, no, I just can't stand him personally, I guess.

T. Well, what can't you stand about him personally?

C. I know. See, I would like him to stay in his own office and leave me alone. I want to be all by myself and do my work and—.

T. Yes, but I would like *you* to leave you alone. If *you* started leaving you alone, it wouldn't matter where he was, how much he was spying, or what wheels were turning in his head.

C. All right. How do I leave me alone?

T. By asking yourself, "Why *must* I be better than I am?"

C. I already have.

T. Yes?

C. And I don't want to be better than I am. I'm satisfied.

T. It doesn't sound to me like you're in the least satisfied.

C. I probably feel I could be better.

T. Yes. "And because I could, I *should.*"

C. Yes.

T. That make sense?

C. Yes.

T. Why? You could do a lot of things that you don't do.

C. Well, maybe I feel that I'm not earning my salary.

T. Yes, but let's even suppose that's true.

C. I mean, I talk on the phone to my friends.

T. Which is par for the course in offices. Do you see how you are perfectionistically *demanding* a certain standard of yourself?

C. No, I don't want to be perfect. *He* expects me to be.

T. But you are *accepting* his demand for perfectionism? Because if you really were saying to yourself, "Well, my poor, kooky boss is a perfectionist. Let him be, as long as he doesn't fire me. And even if he did, I could get another job, and at worst take a little less pay," then you wouldn't have a problem. Now you are clearly accepting his perfectionistic notions, and I would wager that you also accept such standards in other areas of your life. Is that right?

C. Right. I'm pretty perfectionistic.

T. So it's *your* acceptance of it. It's not his perfectionism. His perfectionism cannot magically affect you. Now what are you telling yourself after he says, "You know, I think I pay you too much," or after he prods you?

C. I tell myself that I don't give a damn.

T. Yes, that's what you *think* you tell yourself, but obviously you're saying something much louder and stronger than that.

C. "He can't stand me."

T. Which really means, "I can't stand him, because he's spying on me and letting me know what I've always believed—that I'm not good enough!" *That's* what I hear you saying. So it isn't he—It isn't he you can't stand. You can't stand *your imperfections,* which he happens to agree with. You see? He's telling you, "You *should* be better," and you're agreeing with him.

C. I guess you're right. I think he can't stand me and I'm agreeing he's right.

T. Yes!

The client says that she doesn't want to be perfect, that it's the boss who expects perfection. If this were really true, she wouldn't be upset. Since she is upset, it is safe to guess that she really is holding onto the belief that she *must* do better, and she can't accept herself with imperfections. Therefore, she is anxious when he watches or criticizes her, because it confirms *her* feeling that she is a poor worker who *should* be better.

If you find yourself feeling anxious on the job, look for the *irrational Beliefs* we have been discussing and begin to *challenge* them on a daily basis. Look for the *demands* made upon yourself, and the *self-downing* which results when you don't meet your own perfectionistic standards.

C. You know, he can go out to lunch, eat lunch, then come back and I can still be on the same page.

T. Right.

C. And . . . here it took me all this time to type one little page, and he's eaten his lunch and he's back.

T. Right.

C. And . . . he can do so much work.

T. "Therefore," I hear you saying, "I *should* be as competent and fast as he?"

C. No. No, but I'm thinking that he probably expects me to work as fast as he does.

T. Well, let's suppose he does. Let's just suppose that. So?

C. Yes, he does.

T. Well, all right, so he does. Now, why do you *agree* with him?

C. I don't.

T. You do. You wouldn't be upset if you didn't. If you were really saying, "He expects me to work as fast as he does or much better than I do, but that's *his* silly idea. He expects me to be what I am not," you wouldn't get upset. You still wouldn't like it. You would prefer to work with somebody who didn't have these expectations. But after several years, you'd gracefully lump it, and you're not doing anything like that.

By taking the attitude, "I *must* do better because the boss expects me to," this client is creating a problem *about* a problem. Her first problem is that the boss bothers her, presumably expects too much. Her second problem is that she upsets *herself* about the first problem by believing that it is *horrible* not to have her boss's approval and by blaming herself for having it. This emotional problem blocks her seeking solutions to the annoying situation and also escalates the annoying situation into something "awful."

If you are really doing a fair day's work and your boss's demands are unreasonable, then—without anxiety and hostility—you can look at alternative solutions. These may include accepting your difficult boss while trying to get pleasure from other aspects of the job; trying to persuade the boss to change his or her attitude; or seeking a new job.

T. Why don't you quit?

C. Why don't I quit?

T. Yes. Why don't you quit this job, if he's such an unreasonable boss with unreasonable expectation? Why don't you quit?

C. Because he's not around most of the time.

T. But your conscience is around most of the time.

C. Yes, it is.

T. And wouldn't you do a similar thing with some other boss?

C. No, they wouldn't bother me so much.

T. I don't know about that. In almost any office, somebody is likely to bother you.

C. That's why I've stayed where I am.

T. Ah, because in other offices there are other pains in the neck who would bother you!

C. Yes, something else I would have to put up with. So I've put up with this.

T. But it doesn't sound to me like you're putting up with it too well.

C. It's him. It's not the job. I like my job.

T. There's almost always somebody who's a perfectionist, who expects too much. You just said it—you go to another job, somebody else will be demanding of you. The office manager, or the president, or somebody else.

C. So what do I do?

T. What do you think you do? You take a guess first. What do you think you could do about this?

C. To hell with him, and just do my work; and if he fires me, that's all right. I can use a vacation. And if he doesn't, and if he keeps me on, so I have a job, that's all.

T. Yes, except that you don't have to say, "To hell with him!" which is hostile. You just can say, "This is the way he is, a perfectionist. Lots of people are. I wish he weren't, but he is. Tough! Now, I'm going to ignore it, and I'm going to *attack my own perfectionism,* my own *agreement* with him." And as you said, "Then if he fires me, he fires me. There are other jobs. All I can do is earn a little less pay. But I don't have to stay here and give myself a royal pain." Well, on the basis of what we've been saying so far, what do you think you could do to solve some of your problems?

C. Well, pretend he's not there.

T. You mean when he's watching you?

C. Yes.

T. But he is there. Let's suppose you know he is there and the pretense doesn't work. He's there, and you can't call your friends. Now, what attitude could you take?

C. But then I have to work all the time, and I don't want to work a whole day through.

T. Yes, but what can you do? He's there and he thinks it would be better if you worked all the time; and you can't make the telephone calls to your friends, because he frequently watches you. Now, what can you do, in your own head, that you're not doing now?

C. I'm not sure.

T. Well, think for a minute. You *do* know. I've given you the answer already. What can you do about your attitude?

C. Change it.

T. In what way?

C. Well, not be a perfectionist.

T. That's right. A very good place to start—not to accept his perfectionism—.

C. Right. I can do that.

T. —and make it your own. There's one other big thing you could do: Accept reality when it's grim. When you're not getting the thing you want, when he is watching you—.

C. You can't have your cake and eat it, too.

T. That's right. You can't have your cake and get your pay envelope at the end of the week.

C. Right. In other words, I have to put up with it.

T. You normally had better put up, with any boss, with a certain amount of annoyance that you definitely won't want.

A few important points are brought out in this part of the case. The first is that in almost any job, there is someone who is demanding or unreasonable in some way. Once you learn not to upset yourself about this, you can intelligently weigh the pros and cons of a job, and then you can make a decision about leaving. Also, you will be happier, wherever you work, if you adopt a more rational philosophy. If the job is really too painful and hardly worth the pay, there is no necessity to stay. If *you* are creating much of its pain with your irrational Beliefs, work at changing these Beliefs and then see if you still feel that another job represents the best solution.

The client says that she doesn't "want to work a whole day through." If she really does want to keep the job, her attitude indicates *low frustration tolerance.* This consists of the irrational beliefs, "The job is *too* hard for poor me, and I *shouldn't* have to work that hard to keep it." This can lead to goofing on the job, and consequently inviting criticism, or being fired. Whether or not you are doing a fair day's work, *anxiety* about your performance will not help. So, first work at changing your *anxiety-creating Beliefs,* and then seek practical solutions.

In the next case, the client is hostile toward his supervisor. The following discussion about how to reduce his hostility might apply to the company president, to co-workers, or to anyone one works with. We join as the session begins.

C. There is a lot of anger caused by my job situation. I work for a supervisor who has proved to me, over the last several months, that she is just lazy, useless, and shoves everything off on me. And I've been in this position, this particular job, for three years—.

T. Right.

C. —and I know what I'm doing. Most people are aware of what I'm doing, and yet this woman is a figurehead, and that's all she is.

T. Yes.

C. Anything that comes up, I make the decision.

T. All right. So at A (Activating Event), you are working for a woman who's a figurehead. Let's assume you're really correct, and any objective person would say she's a figurehead, and that she's laying too much on you and taking credit for it. Right? Does she take credit for what you do?

C. Ah, yes, she does.

T. Yes, okay. Now, how do you feel at C (Consequence) about that? What do you feel?

C. Hostile.

T. Hostile?

C. Really hostile.

T. All right. Because at B (your Belief System), you're saying *what* to yourself about that situation?

C. "She's just a jerk!" And, "I feel that she shouldn't be that way!"

T. Right.

C. "That she doesn't have to do that, be that lazy!"

T. Yes.

C. And—"I just hate that!"

T. So I hear you saying, one, "She is lazy!"

C. She *is* lazy.

T. Let's assume she is. And two, "She *shouldn't* be lazy! And because she allows herself to be what she shouldn't allow herself to be—lazy—she's a *jerk!*"

C. I have no respect for her at all, and it's difficult for me to work for someone that I have no respect for.

T. Right.

C. Who I think is just totally useless.

T. But your lack of respect comes from "She *shouldn't* be lazy, she's a *jerk!*" Right?

C. Right.

T. All right, why *shouldn't* she be lazy? I want evidence for the proposition that she shouldn't be lazy.

C. I think she has a lot of energy that she's just wasting.

T. Yes. Let's assume that.

C. And she just doesn't care what's happening; she just takes it easy.

T. But I hear you saying, "Because she's capable of not being lazy, therefore she *shouldn't* be." Is that right?

C. That's right.

T. But does that *follow?*

C. Oh, I don't know.

The client, like many workers, says he is very angry because of the way another person (his supervisor) behaves. In other words, "What someone does *causes* me to have certain emotions." Is this true? If 100 men were working at the same job with the same supervisor, would they all feel equally angry? Probably not, because they would look at the supervisor's behavior in different ways. The *Beliefs* about the situation would be different.

Some might be happy that she is "lazy," because otherwise she might be watching what they do, criticizing them (as was true in the last case), and creating other types of problems. The client, in this case, just takes for granted that because he feels the supervisor is *capable* of not being lazy, therefore she *shouldn't* be lazy. Is this a rational idea?

T. Suppose she's capable, for example, of exercising every day, and running around the block and making herself healthier, and she doesn't do it.

C. Mmm-hmm.

T. *Must* she do what she's capable of doing?

C. No.

T. But isn't that what you're saying? Because she *could* not be lazy, she *should* not be lazy?

C. Yes, that's . . . that's it.

T. But does that follow?

C. No, I guess it doesn't. But what do you do? Do you just sit back and say, "Well, she's a lazy person, and I have to work for her, and that's where it's at. And if it causes me problems, it's my problem?"

T. No, we could say that it's her problem, that she's lazy, and that she's causing you objective difficulties. But her laziness doesn't *cause* your anger. Do you want to quit this job?

C. No, that's what's frustrating. I feel that I am in a position where it's either put up with it or shut up; and I'm looking for an alternative.

T. But I think the alternative that you're looking for is to change the supervisor and not be frustrated.

C. Right. Right!

T. But let's just assume, for the moment, that she's going to continue being frustrating—that she's still lazy, acts in a jerky manner, and doesn't change. Let's just assume that.

C. Mmm-hmm.

T. Now, how can you *live* with the frustration and not *upset yourself,* make yourself angry, about it?

C. Just accept that that's what she does. That's how she is, and that's okay with me.

T. No, it's *not* okay with you. It's not okay!

C. Right. That's a different view!

T. You see, the rest of the job—especially what they pay you at the end of the week—is okay with you, isn't it?

C. It is now.

T. So if they keep giving you enough money, and if you like other aspects of the job—.

C. Mmm-hmm.

T. Because she isn't the *only* aspect of the job. So why couldn't you gracefully lump her and her laziness?

C. Well, that's what I've been trying to do.

T. But you'd better get rid of "She *shouldn't* be lazy!"

The client's anger does not change the supervisor's behavior, and it creates a pain in the gut for him. It is a self-defeating emotion that minimizes pleasure and is in direct opposition to his achieving personal happiness. Minimizing the anger and changing it to annoyance will make him feel less upset over the reality problem and more able to work toward practical solutions.

When you are really angry at another person, you become obsessed with and frequently think about this person. You also are more likely to take foolish actions rather than effective actions.

The basic philosophy of anger consists of the following irrational ideas: "The way you behave is *horrible* and I *can't stand* it! You *must not* behave that way. You are a *total jerk,* a *rotten person,* for behaving that way!"

Taking the client in this case as our illustration, where is the evidence that the supervisor's behavior is really *horrible,* rather than annoying and frustrating? Although her behavior is annoying, it is something that the client can *stand.* To say the supervisor *must* not be lazy directly opposes reality. This *command* smacks of grandiosity and really means, "What I don't like *must* not exist!" Well, it *does* exist, and that is a problem. Upsetting oneself about it creates a problem on top of the problem. The last irrational idea, the client's saying that the supervisor is a total jerk, is discussed in the next part of this case.

T. Why is she a jerk for acting jerkily?

C. Because . . . well, she is not a jerk. She just *acts* like a jerk.

T. Aha! But do you really *believe* that? When you're angry at her, don't you believe she's a *total* jerk?

C. Oh, sure.

T. But *is* she?

C. Yes, she really is.

T. No, no. She isn't. I'll show you why she isn't.

C. Why isn't she?

T. Well, does she do everything in life jerkily?

C. Yes!

T. Now, think! Think again. Let's assume that at the office she does many things jerkily. But you're saying that she does *everything* jerkily, which I doubt she does.

C. No, she goes and gets through the mail properly.

T. See? All right, so she does one thing nonjerkily. And then she goes home from the office. Now, does she do everything jerkily at home?

C. I wouldn't want to know.

T. But let's even assume the worst. Let's just suppose that she did everything at home jerkily, which would be very, very rare.

C. Mmm-hmm.

T. Suppose that she ate jerkily, drank jerkily, slept jerkily, and did everything at work jerkily. Let's just assume that. If she were really a total jerk, she would be condemned in the future to always act the same jerky way. That's what *a jerk* would do. She'd have a soul of jerkiness, and would be doomed *always* to behave badly. But is it likely that we can predict that in the future she would always continue to do everything jerkily?

C. It is unlikely. She just—simply because she can't do that.

T. That's right. She isn't that talented—to be jerky all the time.

C. Right.

T. And then also, let's now even assume the very worst: that for the rest of her life, she never did a nonjerky thing. Let's just assume that. Would she be *damnable?*

C. No. I guess she wouldn't be.

T. But aren't you really damning her when you're angry?

C. Oh, yes.

T. You see? So even if we could prove that she's the one human in all creation who has a soul of jerkiness, and would always do jerky things, there's no point in damning her. You're consigning her to hell and damnation when you are very angry at her.

Although the discussion is somewhat humorous at points, the message is quite clear. Downing a person for his or her acts is not logical or helpful. A human being is a complex process, and any total rating or label is really impossible. Because they're fallible humans, you'd better *expect* people to do foolish things. This does not mean that you have to like it; or that you'd better stay with a person who mainly acts annoyingly. But it does mean that you can avoid upsetting yourself with anger-creating Beliefs about anyone's behavior.

C. Are you saying, then, that there's just nothing to do about my supervisor?

T. Well, no, I'm not saying that. I'm saying that there's first of all something very important to do, and that's *in you.* And that is to really accept her—not her jerkiness. I'm not trying to say her behavior is good, and I'm not even trying to say, "Well, what difference does it make if she acts jerkily?" Because that's a lie. It *does* make a difference. It makes your life more miserable.

C. That's right!

T. She's putting more work on you. So I'm saying, "Accept her jerkiness as bad." Because it is, from your standpoint, not necessarily from hers. And it may even be bad from her point of view because she may be screwing herself. So accept *it* as bad, but *her* as having the right to act badly. Do you know why she has a right to act badly?

C. Why? Because it's her . . . her life. She can do whatever she wants.

T. That's right! And she's a fallible human.

C. Yes, a fallible human being.

T. You see? And all fallible humans have a right to be wrong! Now if you would really work on accepting that, maybe you'd be able to do other things. The first thing you might do may have dubious results—that is, somehow be nice to her, and try to diplomatically get her to change a little bit. If you were really not angry and were nice to her, despite her jerkiness, maybe you could get a few work rules changed so that you would do a little less and she would not be as annoying. That's possible. I don't know if it would work; but at least you'd increase your chances of having a more enjoyable position.

C. Mmm-hmm.

T. You're maximizing the disadvantages of your job. And because you have anger and low frustration tolerance, you're increasing your frustrations. Do you realize that?

C. That's why I wanted to talk to you about it.

T. Yes, because you're dwelling on, "Oh, my God! Look what she's doing to me! And look at the frustrations she's causing! How can things be this lousy?" By saying this to yourself, you'll feel *more* frustrated. On the other hand, if I help you accept her with all her jerkiness and help you thereby lose your anger at *her* but still feel displeased about her *behavior*—because we don't want you to *cheer* about her jerkiness!—then you still would be frustrated but not angry. You see what I mean?

C. I see. I can legitimately down her *acts* but not *her.*

T. Yes, that's what you could work on. Then maybe you'll be able to help her change, but I don't really know if you will succeed at that.

C. There are two other people there that I feel manipulate and use her—use the fact that she's just useless—to manipulate her into whatever they want to get from her.

T. You see! They're manipulating her, and they're getting *more* of what they want. While you're enraged and getting *less* of what you want. Isn't that true?

C. Yes.

T. But one of the reasons they're able to manipulate her is because they're not wasting too much time and energy on being angry at her.

C. That's true.

T. You see? And that just proves my point: that if you were less angry, if you made yourself less furious and just felt displeased at her behavior, you probably would become a better manipulator.

C. So I am to figure out a way to manipulate her?

T First get rid of your anger. Don't try to do it while you're angry, because then you're going to manipulate very badly!

C. Yes.

T. But first you work on *you,* in your head; and really go over mentally what we just said. Then later you can work on manipulating her, if you wish—when you're no longer angry. While you're hostile, I don't think you're going to do it very well.

C. No, I wouldn't. I don't think so either.

If you plan to leave a job, anger will help make your remaining time there miserable. If, as is the case with our client, you feel there are enough advantages to keep you at the current job, the anger will block you from making effective changes in the reality situation and can lead to your being fired.

"Manipulate" means to get others to behave more according to your liking. Most people can best be manipulated when you act nicely and unblamingly toward them. So examine your goals, and if they include being happy in your job situation and trying to get other people to behave more reasonably toward you, then you had best get rid of your hostility.

Aside from changing your basic anger-creating philosophy, you can ask yourself why people act in an annoying fashion. Generally, their goal is not deliberately to do you in, and often they are not happy about their own behavior.

You can also practice blocking your anger by acting nicely toward people you don't like, if you do not altogether choose to avoid contact. Acting nicely and being tactful (especially to a supervisor) often will foster some return of that behavior.

No matter where you work, you will come in contact with annoyances and frustrations. So make an effort to get rid of your angry, ineffective responses, and you will be happier wherever you are. When someone does something that is very annoying, just before you make yourself enraged, you will often think, "How can he/she do that to me?" The answer is: easily! Fallible humans—which we all are—will do many annoying things and make many errors—*because it is our nature to do so.*

We have found that many people tend to confuse *anger* with *assertion.* Assertion is going after what you want and saying "no" to things you don't want, but *without* the demanding and blaming that are included in anger. Assertion is based upon rational ideas: "I *prefer* certain things, and therefore I will work toward getting them by asserting myself and changing conditions whenever possible. If I don't get what I want, I will keep trying; but I won't needlessly upset myself about it by demanding that I *must* have my desires fulfilled." Assertion is not self-defeating since it allows you to work toward your goals without giving yourself a needless pain in the gut and without alienating those around you.

As we stated at the opening of this chapter, *anger* and *anxiety* are common emotional problems associated with the world of work. We hope that you will use the lessons in this chapter to help reduce your anger and anxiety, so that work will be a happier, more productive place for you and those around you.

CHAPTER 14

Summing Up: Eliminating Your Self-Created Roadblocks to Personal Happiness

Throughout this book, we have been showing how you can create your own feelings of misery and disturbance, and some of the most important things you can do to rip up your self-constructed roadblocks to personal happiness. Before we show, in our final chapter, some of the positive things you can do to achieve enjoyment and self-actualization, let us summarize some of the RET-oriented principles and practices that we have been outlining. Briefly, they may be stated as follows.

To thine own self be true. Discover, through thinking, experimenting, and risk-taking, what you personally want to do (and want *not* to do) with the one life you have and how to do (and *not* to do) exactly that.

Unless you decide to be a hermit, strive for your personal happiness in a social world. Individual and social living inextricably merge, so that the summit of your individuality and freedom involves real concern for others. Help create a malevolent universe and you, as an interactor with it, distinctly suffer too.

Working for your personal happiness *and* trying to leave the world at least a little better off when you die than when you came into it are hardly mutually exclusive goals. You can be yourself *while* and *through* helping others. This is something of an ideal goal but still an achievable one.

Your human legacy *includes* gregariousness and sociality. You inherit genes *and* culture. Gracefully acknowledge, accept, and take advantage of both.

You do not, except very moderately and sometimes not at all, control how others think, feel, and act. But you do significantly control your own reactions to others and how *you* think and feel about them. Stop insisting that you can do the impossible; that is, regulate outsiders. Stop whining that you can't do what you almost invariably can do—control yourself.

What is the greatest and most practical challenge you can accept, even second to creating a notable career, invention, or work of art? Working concertedly and consistently to achieve personal happiness! Yes, *working.*

Would you really like to get along beautifully with others, build an enjoyable and productive career, and be artistically or scientifically creative? Fine. Look to yourself and your personal happiness first, and these other achievements will much more likely follow. If they don't, you will still lead an enjoyable, meaningful existence!

Some say that life's main satisfactions come naturally, spontaneously, if you stop pushing the river and merely take things as they come, unplanfully, effortlessly. How did the great sages who said this arrive at this marvelous secret of human felicity? By substantial thought and effort!

Powerful wishes, desires, goals, purposes, and emotional attachments add to your life and make the world go 'round. Passive and detached humans may be sensible and free from much pain, but pretty damned blah. The trick is to want to strive like all get-out, but not to think you absolutely *need* what you want. Masturbation is good and delicious; but *must*urbation is evil and pernicious.

According to RET, understanding what you do to upset yourself emotionally is as simple as ABC. At A (Activating Event), you encounter some unpleasant event or situation (e.g., failure or rejection). At B (Belief System), you both rationally and irrationally, consciously or unconsciously, tell yourself something about A. At C (Consequence), you feel upset (e.g., anxious or depressed) about failing or being rejected and you act dysfunctionally (e.g., avoid trying again for what you want). The ABCs of self-understanding—simple! But finding your irrational Beliefs (iBs) is a little harder. And *surrendering them* may be a real problem!

Feelings are great—but never sacrosanct! RET helps you to acknowledge your emotions (not repress or sweep them under the rug) and to deeply experience them. When something goes wrong, it shows you how to clearly distinguish your appropriate feelings (such as pain, sorrow, regret, and annoyance) from your inappropriate feelings (such as anxiety, depression, rage, and self-pity). And it gives you precise methods of minimizing and surrendering the inappropriate and returning to the appropriate emotions. Rational never means unfeeling!

Inappropriate or disturbed feelings and self-defeating or dysfunctional behaviors are usually associated with absolutistic shoulds, musts, oughts, demands, and commands rather than with strong preferences. The three major musts that you tend to use to disturb yourself are: (1) "I *must* perform well and be loved by significant others!" (2) "Other people *must* treat me fairly and kindly!" (3) "Conditions *must* be favorable and easy!"

Your *must*urbatory thoughts have three main irrational and self-sabotaging derivatives: (1) "When things don't go as I absolutely demand that they *must,* it is awful, terrible and horrible!" (2) "Unless I get what I *must,* I *can't stand* it, *can't bear* it!" (3) "Whenever I (or you) do not perform as I (or you) *must,* I am (or you are) a *worthless, undeserving person!*"

If you had no absolutistic, dogmatic thinking and stayed only with wishes and probabilities, you could stubbornly refuse to become needlessly anxious, depressed, enraged, or self-pitying about virtually anything that happened. You would still have the problem of finding positive pleasures and joys to make yourself truly happy; but you would be one of the rare people on earth who was practically never self-flagellatingly miserable.

Are you, as psychoanalysts insist, plagued by deeply unconscious thoughts and feelings that you have repressed and must laboriously uncover before you get true insight into yourself and make significant personality changes? Most probably not. You have plenty of implicit or unaware ideas and emotions that may cause you trouble. But RET holds that you are easily able to be conscious of virtually all of them if you know how to recognize them by rational-emotive methods. RET, moreover, shows you how to quickly and effectively change your underlying thoughts and feelings when you experience them to your detriment.

RET teaches you how to go from the ABCs of your feelings of emotional disturbance to D, Disputing of your irrational Beliefs (iBs). D is really the scientific method, and RET holds that if you think scientifically about yourself, others, and the world, you will be able to appreciably increase your personal happiness.

You perform Disputing by challenging and questioning your irrational Beliefs (iBs)—by asking, for example, "What is the evidence that I *must* do well?" "Why is it *awful* to fail and be rejected?" "In what way can't I *stand* the results of doing poorly?" "Where is it written that I am a *worthless person* if I fail at an important endeavor?"

You also do active Disputing and use other cognitive methods of surrendering your irrational Beliefs (iBs) by employing several other techniques described in Chapter 4, including the use of (1) the rational Self-Help Report Form; (2) the procedure outlined in the DIBS (Disputing Irrational Beliefs) Form; (3) rational problem solving; (4) semantic precision and referenting; (5) coping statements and rational philosophies; (6) disputing attributions; (7) imagining and fantasy methods; (8) bibliotherapy and audiotherapy; (9) humor and paradoxical intention; (10) teaching RET to others.

What we call "emotion" invariably seems to include and consist of strong cognitive and behavioral, as well as feeling, components. RET, which is a comprehensive method of personality change, includes many emotive-evocative-dramatic methods that you can employ to fight against your irrational and self-destructive Belief System. As explained in Chapter 5, you can employ several emotive RET methods, such as (1) rational emotive imagery; (2) unconditional self-acceptance; (3) shame-attacking exercises; (4) self-disclosure methods; (5) role-playing and behavioral rehearsal; (6) forceful and dramatic self-statements.

RET was the first of the major cognitive behavioral therapies and has pioneered in using behavioral methods to help people change their basic self-defeating philosophies and practices. As shown in Chapter 6, some of the behavioral methods of achieving personal happiness that you may effectively employ include: (1) activity homework assignments; (2) operant conditioning and self-management procedures; (3) skill training; and (4) stimulus control.

Feelings of shyness and of inadequacy stem mainly from two pronounced and powerfully believed irrational Beliefs (iBs): (1) "I *must* do well in all important tasks, and even be outstanding at them; and it is *terrible* and I am a thoroughly *incompetent person* if I don't!" (2) "People whom I find significant *have to* approve of me and it is *horrible* and I am an unlovable, *undeserving individual* if they reject me!" If you pigheadedly refuse to believe these self-denigrating absolutes, you can unconditionally accept yourself *whether or not* you perform well and *whether or not you* are approved by others.

Feelings of guilt and shame largely originate in your demanding that you do exactly the right thing by others, that you often put them first and yourself a not-too-close second. Although you had better not needlessly harm others or commit antisocial acts, you can make yourself feel sorry and irresponsible if and when you do, but need not totally damn yourself as a human and thus sorely afflict yourself with self-damaging shame and guilt.

Feelings of depression usually are related to two main irrational Beliefs (iBs): (1) "Since I perform badly, as I *must* not, I am an *inadequate person* who will *always* act poorly. Therefore, I am a *hopeless slob,* who will practically *never* be able to get what I really want!" (2) "My life *must* not include very bad conditions and when it does, I *absolutely can't bear* it! The world then becomes an *utterly* rotten place that is not worth living in, and I might as well kill myself!" The first of these iBs leads to arrant self-downing or what we call ego anxiety; and the second to abysmal low frustration tolerance or what we call discomfort anxiety. Either or both create feelings of severe self-pity and depression. To overcome these destructive feelings, you can vehemently fight the ideas with which you create them and can convince yourself that you will *sometimes* perform badly, and that is unfortunate, but that that does not make you a hopeless slob who will *never* be able to get what you really want. And you can also strongly show yourself your life *will* at times include some bad conditions but, although you'll never *like* these conditions, you can definitely *bear* them and still be reasonably happy.

Whenever anything goes badly, you had better feel strongly irritated, annoyed, or displeased. Otherwise, you will passively accept many crummy aspects of life without trying to change them. Therefore, when you don't get what you want (or do get what you abhor), you can sensibly and even passionately tell yourself a set of rational Beliefs (rBs), such as: "I don't like what you did. How annoying! Let me see how I can induce you to change your actions." Displeasure, however, is not anger. For when you are truly angry, enraged, furious, or homicidal, you almost always add to your rational Beliefs (rBs) some highly grandiose, irrational Beliefs (iBs), such as: "Because I don't like what you did, you *should* not, *must* not do it! How horrible! I *can't tolerate* you and your behavior. What a thoroughgoing worm you are for displeasing a noble person like me!"

If, using RET, you will honestly admit that although others do displeasing acts—remember Murphy's famous law, "Everything that can possibly go wrong will!"—and you alone choose to, or choose not to, anger yourself *about* their doings, you will be able to surrender your irrational anger-creating Beliefs and return to feeling merely displeased by others' behavior, determined to try to help them change it, and rarely terribly upset and enraged about it.

Most psychological sex problems are linked with ignorance and irrationality. When you are sexually disturbed, you may define sex in a needlessly restrictive or limited way (deify penile-vaginal intercourse) and thereby seriously interfere with your and your partner's satisfactions. Or, instead of desiring sexual pleasure, you may absolutistically demand it—demand it quickly and easily, without effort, and command that you (or your partner) perform it wonderfully well. If you are so afflicted, admit your sexual ignorance and expand your knowledge of what "good" sex really can be. Give up your unrealistic and perfectionistic demands and look for sex pleasuring rather than erotic measuring. Get your ego out of your head and your genitals and get your entire body and mind into sex. You will see things—and feel things—much more enjoyably!

In regard to work problems, you will find that you tend to afflict yourself with the same kind of grandiose and idealistic *musts* that you are addicted to in other aspects of your life: namely, that you *must* have near-perfect accomplishments, you *need* the courtesy and consideration of your coworkers, and you *have to* work under conditions that give you exactly what you want for nothing—and at a fabulous rate of pay! If any or all of these are your irrational Beliefs (iBs), lots of luck! Either you will see them and strongly fight them—or you will neurotically suffer. The choice is yours, as it always is. Pamper and feed your irrational Beliefs until they massively proliferate and take a pervasive stranglehold on your life, or guide yourself to personal happiness by working—yes, strongly working—to think, feel, and act against them. As we have been consistently saying throughout this book—the choice is yours!

CHAPTER 15

Upward and Onward to Self-Actualizing and Joy

Now that you have come this far, have presumably heeded our words of rational-emotive wisdom, and have started to work at ripping up your self-created roadblocks to personal happiness, what else can you do to make yourself actively and positively happy? A great deal! Naturally, since you are a unique individual who is biologically and socially different from all other humans, we had better not be too presumptive and try to tell you what you can most enjoy and how to go about achieving pinnacles of pleasure. In most ways, this is for you, and no one but you, to discover. We, your RET guides, think we pretty much know what *we* like—and what *we* don't. But *your* best satisfactions and *your* best avoidances? Who are *we* to say?

Rather than completely cop out on these important queries, however, let us try to give you some salient guidelines on how you may efficiently ferret out and actively engender some of the vital pleasures that may well apply to you. We won't even mildly attempt to say *what* your personal pros and cons of happy living are. But *how* you may go about finding them, we will!

Uncovering your idiosyncratic likes and dislikes largely involves asking yourself—and as honestly as possible answering—several key questions. Here are some relevant queries you can ask yourself:

"What might *I like?"*

You certainly know some of the things you already like and dislike. But what *else* might you prefer? Have you really asked yourself this question recently? If not, why not?

In the Appendix, we have provided a list of some of the major areas in which people often find highly satisfying pursuits. Do any of these areas interest you? If so, which major ones?

In the Appendix, we also list some of the main subheadings under each of the major headings, and we could, of course, list many more under each major interest. Look these over. Are any of them your particular thing? Underline them. Find out more about some of them. Experiment with those you think you might enjoy.

You are, as we noted at the beginning of this chapter, uniquely you. As yourself, ask what *you* might find zestful. The problem here is to discover what you *uniquely* like and dislike. For no matter what other people enjoy, or what percentage of them enjoy it, you are never *obligated* to have similar feelings. In RET terms, there is no reason why you *must* relish sports, the ballet, reading, or anything else, even when millions of other people do enjoy it and even when it would be *preferable* if you did, too. If you are the only one in the whole world who doesn't delight in *x* or thrill to *y,* that is okay, as long as you don't get into serious trouble by choosing not to do so. You, just because you are *you,* are fully entitled to your "odd" or "peculiar" values and disvalues. Remember that!

"What do other people enjoy?"

Does this seem a strange question to ask yourself after we have just advised you to look for your *own* idiosyncratic pleasures? No, not really. For one of the best ways to discover what you really want to do is to learn as much as you can about other people's gratifications, to think about how they might work for you, to try some of them on for size, and then to *see* how pleasing they really are. You would rarely love music, art, science, or anything else unless you had some real *information* about these interests. So, by all means, discover what pleases others in order to see whether some of these things would be good for you, too.

"What will I probably like later?"

Many pleasures of today not only pall tomorrow but produce distinct disadvantages—smoking, for example, or drinking alcohol, or running when you have problems with your feet. Other enjoyments—e.g., becoming adept at ballet or basketball—may serve your interests for awhile but be impractical in your later life. So look for enjoyments that will bring you pleasure today—but that will also probably provide a long range involvement.

"What would probably be more enjoyable than some of the things I now do?"

Your range of possible pleasures is so wide and your available time to pursue them so limited that choosing almost anything to throw yourself into often provides you with relatively limited gain. You may, for example, like checkers and find it satisfactory for hours at a time. But wouldn't chess be even *more* satisfying? Your friends may involve you in their golf pursuits. But have you thought about tennis or swimming as potentially better sports for you? Allow yourself, of course, to enjoy whatever activity happens to come your way and is easily available (such as a bridge club that just happens to meet in the building across the way from your home). But is that really what you *most* want to do with your time? Consider the likely alternatives!

"What are the costs of some of my pleasures?"

Joining a country club may be a fine interest. But can you *really* afford it? Playing golf is often a great sport. But do you truly have the *time* for it? Staying out half the night drinking may be enormous fun. But in what shape are you at work the next day? All pleasures have obvious or hidden costs of time, energy, and money. So ask yourself, in many instances, not only "Do I enjoy this pastime?" but also "Is it worth it?" If it is, fine. If not, you can almost always find other pursuits that are worth it.

"How can I experiment with possible pleasures?"

As with virtually all other aspects of living, you learn about what you like and dislike by experimentation—by trial and error. I (Irving Becker) like reading psychology books. You might try this—and hate it! I (Albert Ellis) like composing rational humorous songs. You might compose a few—and be bored to death. If you are wise, you will (as noted above) inform yourself about many possible pleasures and then experiment with at least several that you think you may personally enjoy. Some you will abhor. Some you will like for awhile. A few you will thrill to forever. But how can you discover which is which without some amount of trying? You most probably can't!

"How long shall I persist in my pleasure-hunting experiments?"

A good question!—and sometimes hard to answer. Some things— e.g., scuba diving or anal intercourse—you might try exactly once and become quite rightly convinced that they are not for you. Other things— e.g., playing bridge or oral sex—you might try 10 or 20 times, and finally come to enjoy them immensely and even become passionately addicted to them. All we can say, therefore, is that you'd better try a would-be pleasure a *reasonable* number of times before you decide that you don't, and never will, like it.

"Need I ever feel ashamed of or guilty about my enjoyments?"

No, not if you use RET effectively! Some of the things you enjoy may either be wrong for you—that is, self-defeating—or be harmful to others—that is, antisocial. If so, you had better convince yourself that these acts are mistaken or immoral and you had better do your best to stop performing them. But when you feel ashamed or guilty, you are really telling yourself, (1) "My acts are wrong or bad," and (2) "I am a rotten *person* for committing these rotten *acts!*" RET holds that your second set of Beliefs when you are ashamed or guilty are irrational and needlessly self-defeating. You can, therefore, make yourself feel like *a person who* is acting irresponsibly (to yourself and/or others) and who had better change your poor behavior. But you never need see yourself as a putrid, undeserving *human.* Without self-damnation, you are more likely to be *both* a socially responsible and a personally happy individual.

Will any of these questions guarantee you eternal and complete personal happiness? Of course not. The only near-guarantee you have is that someday you will die—and even that is not absolute (since someday we may still invent the fountain of youth). But if you follow the RET principles and practices outlined in this book; if you pigheadedly insist that you damned well won't needlessly upset yourself about anything; if you look for .and work for the highest degrees of felicity and self-actualization that you choose and embrace; if these are your preferences and determinations, a rare degree of personal happiness may well be yours.

Don't take our word for this. Do take your own!

Suggestions for Enjoyable Pursuits

Aesthetic Appreciation
Attending ballets, art galleries, concerts, mime performances, museums, plays, serious motion pictures, etc.

Clothing Activities
Designing, Dressing, Making clothes, Photographing, Researching, Shopping, etc.

Child Care
Babysitting, Bathing, Big Brother and Big Sister activities, Dressing, Nursing, Playing with children, Teaching, etc.

Collecting
Books, Bottles, Cans, Coins, Comics, Match covers, Metals, Stamps, etc.

Exercising
Calisthenics, Cross bars, Gym horses, Jogging, Punching bag, Running, Shadow boxing, Skipping rope, Weight lifting, Yoga, etc.

Fantasizing
Daydreaming, Dreaming, Imagining, Planning, Plotting, Scheming, etc.

Financial Activities
Balancing checkbooks, Bill paying, Bookkeeping, Budgeting, Playing the stock market, Taking financial courses, etc.

Food Activities
   Baking, Barbecuing, Collecting recipes, Cooking, Eating out, Preparing gourmet meals, Reading cookbooks, etc.

Games
   Anagrams, Bridge, Cards, Checkers, Chess, Crossword puzzles, Go, Jigsaw puzzles, Love and sex games, Monopoly, Scrabble, Word games, etc.

Garden Activities
   Flower arranging, Gardening, Landscaping, Mowing the lawn, Planting, Raising plants at home, Visiting the botanical gardens, etc.

Graphic Arts
   Cartooning, Collages, Drawing, Finger painting, Lettering, Lithographing, Painting, Photography, Water coloring, etc.

Handicraft Activites
   Basketmaking, Bookbinding, Crocheting, Embroidering, Jewelry making, Knitting, Leathermaking, Lacemaking, Metal work, Model making, Refurbishing furniture, Stained glass making, etc.

Helping People
   Advising, Counseling, Comforting, Cheering, Companioning, Hospital and institutional activities, Psychotherapy, Group therapy, etc.

Humorous Activities
   Cartooning, Collecting jokes, Fun-making, Jesting, Joke-making, Joke-telling, Playing practical jokes and pranks, Punning, Writing humorous songs and stories, etc.

Martial Arts
   Aikido, Guns, Fencing, Jiujitsu, Judo, Karate, Wrestling, War games, etc.

Mechanical Activities
   Carpentry, Fixing appliances, Fixing apartments and houses, Woodworking, Working on cars and boats, etc.

Outdoor Activities
   Backpacking, Bicycling, Bird watching, Climbing, Butterfly catching, Canoeing, Camping, Fishing, Hiking, Horseback riding, Hunting, Ice-skating, Kite-flying, Motoring, Picnicking, Racing cars, Skating, Skiing, Sleigh riding, Sunbathing, etc.

Performing Arts
   Acting, Ballet, Dancing, Debating, Mime, Modern dance, Singing, etc.

Pets
 Breeding, Caring for pets, Showing animals, Training animals, Assisting in an animal hospital, etc.

Political and Economic Activities
 Campaigning, Discussing, Ecological causes, Consumer groups, Political groups, Proselytizing, Political writing, etc.

Reading
 Browsing, Reading fiction, nonfiction, plays, poems, Reading aloud, Play readings, Poetry readings, etc.

Relaxing Activities
 Bathing, Chanting, Massage, Meditating, Muscle relaxation, Smoking, Soaking, etc.

Religious and Mystical Activities
 Chanting, Church going, Meditating, Praying, Reading, Preaching, Studying religion, Teaching Sunday School, etc.

Scientific Activities
 Anatomy, Anthropology, Biology, Chemistry, Herpetology, Astronomy, Medicine, Physics, Psychology, Sociology, Zoology, etc.

Sex and Love Activities
 Anal sex, Caring, Caressing, Heterosexual activities, Homosexual activities, Helping, Kissing, Loving, Making sacrifices, Oral sex, Petting, Pornography, Sexual intercourse, Saying kind and loving things, etc.

Socializing
 Bar hopping, Clubs, Dinner for two, Dinner parties, Conversation, Fraternal organizations, Giving parties, Group activities, Partying, Rap sessions, Social functions, Visiting friends, etc.

Spectatoring
 Concertgoing, Listening to music, radio, etc., Watching circuses, movies, pageants, parades, plays, sports, TV, etc.

Sports
 Badminton, Baseball, Basketball, Dancing, Football, Golf, Gymnastics, Pingpong, Pool, Running, Skating, Swimming, Tennis, Track, Water sports, etc.

Studying
 Art, Language, History, Math, Music, Science, Social science, etc.

Therapy Activities
 Group therapy, Individual therapy, Self-help groups, Therapizing others, Therapy workshops, etc.

Traveling

Foreign travel, Local trips, Reading and observing travel books and films, Sightseeing, etc.

Useful Activities and Chores

Cleaning, Cooking, Dishwashing, Home improvements, Ironing, Mowing the lawn, Shopping, Washing the car, etc.

Venting Feelings

Hitting, Picketing, Punching pillows, Protesting, Screaming, Talking, Writing, etc.

Volunteer Activities

Volunteering for charitable groups, Boy Scout and Girl Scout groups, child care groups, camps, hospitals, nonprofit organizations, political groups, etc.

Selected References

The following list of references includes selected books, articles, and other materials we consulted in writing this volume, as well as useful self-help materials. We have placed a check mark (✓) in front of items that you may wish to read in your further search for some of the elements of rational living and personal happiness. We have placed an asterisk (*) before items that may be ordered from the Institute for Rational-Emotive Therapy, 45 East 65th Street, New York, N.Y. 10021. The Institute sponsors talks, seminars, workshops, and other presentations on RET and will send a current list of publications and events upon request.

✓Adler, A. *Understanding Human Nature.* Greenwich, Conn.: Fawcett World, 1974.

✓Adler, A. *What Life Should Mean to You.* New York: Putnam 1974.

✓*Alberti, R. E., & Emmons, M. *Your Perfect Right.* San Luis Obispo, Calif.: Impact, 1982.

*Ard, B. N., Jr. *Counseling and Psychotherapy.* Palo Alto, Calif.: Science and Behavior Books, 1976.

✓*Bard, J. A. *Rational Emotive Therapy in Practice.* Champaign, Ill.: Research Press, 1980.

✓Barksdale, S. *Self-esteem.* Los Angeles, Barksdale Foundation, 1977.

*Beck, A. T. *Cognitive Therapy and the Emotional Disorders.* New York: International Universities Press, 1976.

*Beck, A. T., Rush, A. J., Shaw, B. F., & Emery, G. *Cognitive Therapy of Depression.* New York: Guilford, 1979.

Becker, I. M., & Rosenfeld, J. G. Rational-emotive Therapy: A study of initial therapy sessions of Albert Ellis. *Journal of Clinical Psychology,* 1976, 32, 872-876.

*Bedford, S. *Instant Replay.* New York; Institute for Rational Living, 1978.

Blazier, D. *Poor Me, Poor Marriage.* New York: Vantage, 1975.

✓Brandt, F. M. J. *A Rational Self-counselling Primer.* Saxmundham, Suffolk, England: Institute for Rational Therapy, 1977.

√*Burns, D.D. *Feeling good.* New York: Morrow, 1980.

*Church, V.A. Behavior, law and remedies. Dubuque, Ia.: Kendall/Hunt, 1975.

√*Danysh, J. *Stop Without Quitting.* San Francisco: International Society for General Semantics, 1974.

Diekstra, R.F.W., & Dassen, W.F.M. *Rationale Therapie.* Amsterdam: Swets and Zeitlinger, 1976.

Diekstra, R.F.W., & Dassen, W.F.M. *Inleding Tot de Rationale Therapie.* Amsterdam: Swets and Zeitlinger, 1977.

√Dyer, W. Your Erroneous Zones. New York: Avon, 1976.

√*Ellis, A. *How to Live with a "Neurotic."* New York: Crown, 1957. Rev. ed., 1975.

√*Ellis, A. *The Art and Science of Love.* New York: Lyle Stuart and Bantam Books, 1960. Rev. ed., 1965.

√*Ellis, A. *Reason and Emotion in Psychotherapy.* Secaucus, N.J.: Lyle Stuart and Citadel Books, 1962.

√*Ellis, A. *Suppressed: Seven Key Essays Publishers Dared Not Print.* Chicago: New Classics House, 1965.

√*Ellis, A. *Rational-emotive Psychotherapy.* Cassette recording. New York: Institute for Rational Living, 1970.

√*Ellis, A. *Solving Emotional Problems.* Cassette recording. New York: Institute for Rational Living, 1971.

√*Ellis, A. *Growth Through Reason.* Palo Alto, Calif.: Science and Behavior Books and Hollywood: Wilshire Books, 1971.

√*Ellis, A. *How to Stubbornly Refuse to Feel Ashamed of Anything.* New York: Institute for Rational Living, 1972.

√*Ellis, A. *How to Master Your Fear of Flying.* New York: Institute for Rational Living, 1972.

√*Ellis, A. *Executive Leadership: A Rational Approach.* New York: Citadel Books and Institute for Rational Living, 1972.

√*Ellis, A. *Humanistic Psychotherapy: The Rational-Emotive Approach.* New York: Crown and McGraw-Hill Paperbacks, 1973.

√*Ellis, A. *Disputing Irrational Beliefs (DIBS).* New York: Institute for Rational Living, 1974.

√*Ellis, A. *Rational Living in an Irrational World.* Cassette recording. New York: Institute for Rational Living, 1974.

√*Ellis, A. *Twenty-five Ways to Stop Downing Yourself.* Cassette recording. Philadelphia: American Academy of Psychotherapists, 1974.

√*Ellis, A. *Twenty-one Ways to Stop Worrying.* Cassette recording. New York; Institute for Rational Living, 1974.

√*Ellis, A. *Conquering the Dire Need for Love.* Cassette recording. New York: Institute for Rational Living, 1975.

√*Ellis, A. *Sex and the Liberated Man.* Secaucus, N.J.: Lyle Stuart, 1976.

√*Ellis, A. *Conquering Low Frustration Tolerance.* Cassette recording. New York: Institute for Rational Living, 1976.

√*Ellis, A. *A Garland of Rational Songs.* Songbook and Cassette recording. New York: Institute for Rational Living, 1977.

√*Ellis, A. *Fun as Psychotherapy.* Cassette recording. New York: Institute for Rational Living, 1977.

√*Ellis, A. *How to Live With–and Without–Anger.* New York: Reader's Digest Press, 1977.

√*Ellis, A. *I'd Like to Stop, But–. Overcoming Addictions.* Cassette recording. New York; Institute for Rational Living, 1977.

✓*Ellis, A. *The Theory and Practice of RET.* Cassette recording. New York: Institute for Rational Living, 1977.

✓*Ellis, A. *RET and Assertiveness Training.* Cassette recording. New York: Institute for Rational Living, 1977.

Ellis, A. Rational-emotive therapy. In R. Corsini, Ed. *Current Psychotherapies.* Itasca, Ill.: Peacock, 1979.

✓*Ellis, A. *The Intelligent Woman's Guide to Dating and Mating.* Secaucus, N.J.: Lyle Stuart, 1979.

*Ellis, A. *Rational-emotive Therapy and Cognitive Behavior Therapy.* New York: Springer, 1983.

Ellis, A., & Abarbanel, A. *Encyclopedia of Sexual Behavior.* New York: Aronson, 1971.

*Ellis, A., & Abrahms, E. *Dialogues on RET.* Cassette recordings. New York: Aronson, 1978.

✓*Ellis, A., & Abrahms, E. *Brief Psychotherapy in Medical and Health Practice.* New York: Springer, 1978.

✓*Ellis, A., & Grieger, R. *Handbook of Rational-emotive Therapy.* New York: Springer, 1977.

✓*Ellis, A., & Harper, R. A. *A Guide to Successful Marriage.* Hollywood: Wilshire Books, 1961.

✓*Ellis, A., & Harper, R. A. *New Guide to Rational Living.* Hollywood: Wilshire Books, 1975.

✓*Ellis, A., & Knaus, W. *Overcoming Procrastination.* New York: New American Library, 1977.

✓*Ellis, A., & Whiteley, J., Eds. *Theoretical and Empirical Foundations of Rational-Emotive Therapy.* Monterey, Calif.: Brooks/Cole, 1979.

✓*Ellis, A., Wolfe, J. L., & Moseley, S. *How to Raise an Emotionally Healthy, Happy Child.* Hollywood: Wilshire Books, 1966.

✓Epictetus. *The Works of Epictetus.* Boston: Little, Brown, 1899.

✓*Fay, A. *Making Things Better by Making Them Worse.* New York: Hawthorn, 1978.

✓Fensterheim, H., & Baer, J. *Don't Say Yes When You Want to Say No.* New York: Dell, 1975.

✓Frankl, V. *Man's Search for Meaning.* New York: Washington Square, 1966.

Freud, S. *Standard Edition of the Complete Psychological Works of Sigmund Freud.* London: Hogarth, 1965.

Friedman, M. *Rational Behavior.* Columbia, S.C.: University of South Carolina Press, 1975.

✓*Garcia, E. *Homer, the Homsely Hound Dog.* New York: Institute for Rational Living, 1978.

✓*Garcia, E. *Developing Emotional Muscle.* Atlanta: Author, 1979.

✓*Gerald, M., & Eyman, W. *Thinking Straight and Talking Sense.* New York: Institute for Rational Living, 1981.

✓Ginott, H. *Between Parent and Child.* New York: Macmillan, 1965.

✓Glasser, W. *Reality Therapy.* New York: Harper, 1965.

✓Goldfried, M. R., & Davison, G. *Clinical Behavior Therapy.* New York: Holt, Rinehart and Winston, 1976.

✓*Goodman, D., & Maultsby, M. C., Jr. *Emotional Well-being Through Rational Behavior Training.* Springfield, Ill.: Thomas, 1979.

✓*Greenburg, D., & Jacobs, M. *How to Make Yourself Miserable.* New York: Random House, 1966.

✓Greenwald, H. *Decision Therapy.* San Diego: Edits, 1977.

✓*Grieger, R., & Boyd, J. *Rational-emotive Therapy: A Skills Based Approach.* New York: Reinhold, 1980.

✓*Grieger, R., & Grieger, I. Z. *Cognition and Emotional Disturbance.* New York; Human Sciences, 1982.

✓*Grossack, M. *You Are not Alone.* Boston: Marlborough, 1974.

✓*Grossack, M. *Love, sex, and Self-Fulfillment.* New York: New American Library, 1978.

Haley, J. *Problem Solving Therapy.* San Francisco: Jossey-Bass, 1976.

✓Harper, R. A. *Psychoanalysis and Psychotherapy: 36 Systems.* Englewood Cliffs, N.J.: Prentice-Hall, 1959.

Harper, R. A. *The New Psychotherapies.* Englewood Cliffs, N.J.: Prentice-Hall, 1977.

✓*Hauck, P. *The Rational Management of Children.* New York: Libra, 1967.

✓*Hauck, P. *Overcoming Depression.* Philadelphia: Westminster, 1972.

✓*Hauck, P. *Reason in Pastoral Counseling.* Philadelphia: Westminster, 1972.

✓*Hauck, P. *Overcoming Frustration and Anger.* Philadelphia: Westminster, 1974.

✓*Hauck, P. *Overcoming Worry and Fear.* Philadelphia: Westminster, 1975.

✓*Hauck, P. *Brief Counseling With RET.* Philadelphia: Westminster, 1979.

✓*Hauck, P. *Overcoming Jealousy and Possessiveness.* Philadelphia: Westminster, 1981.

✓*Hauck, P. *How to do what You Want to Do.* Philadelphia: Westminster, 1977.

✓Herzberg, A. *Active Psychotherapy.* New York: Grune & Stratton, 1945.

✓Hite, S. *The Hite Report.* New York: Macmillan, 1976.

✓Hite, S. *The Hite Report on Male Sexuality.* New York: Knopf, 1981.

✓Horney, K. *Collected Writings.* New York; Norton, 1965.

✓*Jakubowski, P., & Lange, A. *The Assertive Option.* Champaign, Ill.: Research Press, 1980.

✓Jacobsen, E. *You Must Relax.* New York: Pocket Books, 1958.

✓*Johnson, W. *So Desperate the Fight.* New York; Institute for Rational Living, 1981.

✓Johnson, W. *People in Quandaries.* New York: Harper and Row, 1946.

✓Kelly, G. *The Psychology of Personal Constructs.* New York: Norton, 1955.

✓*Knaus, W. *Rational Emotive Education.* New York; Institute for Rational Living, 1974.

Korzybski, A. *Science and Sanity.* San Francisco: International Society for General Semantics, 1933.

✓*Kranzler, G. *You Can Change How You Feel.* Eugene, Ore. Self-published, 1974.

✓*Lange, A., & Jakubowski, A. *Responsible Assertive Behavior.* Champaign, Ill.: Research Press, 1976.

Lazarus, A. A. *Behavior Therapy and Beyond.* New York: McGraw-Hill, 1971.

✓*Lazarus, A. A. *The Practice of Multimodal Therapy.* New York: McGraw-Hill, 1981.

✓Lazarus, A. A., & Fay, A. *I Can If I Want To.* New York: Morrow, 1976.

✓*Lazarus, A. A. *Learning to Relax.* Cassette recording. New York: Institute for Rational Living, 1976.

✓Lembo, J. *Help Yourself.* Niles, Ill.: Argus, 1974.

Lembo, J. *The Counseling Process.* New York: Libra, 1976.

✓Lembo, J. *How to Cope With Your Fears and Frustrations.* New York: Libra, 1977.

✓Little, B. L. *This Will Drive You Sane.* Minneapolis, Minn.: CompCare, 1977.

✓Losoncy, L. E. *You Can Do It.: How to Encourage Yourself.* Englewood Cliffs, N.J.: Prentice-Hall, 1980.

Mahoney, M. J. *Cognition and Behavior Modification.* Cambridge, Mass.: Ballinger, 1974.

Mahoney, M. J., Ed. *Psychotherapy Process.* New York: Plenum, 1980.

✓Marcus Aurelius. *Meditations.* Boston: Little, Brown, 1899.

✓Marks, I. M. *Living With Fear.* New York: McGraw-Hill, 1978.

✓Maslow, A. H. *Toward a Psychology of Being.* Princeton, N.J.: Van Nostrand, 1962.

✓*Maultsby, M. C., Jr. *Overcoming Irrational Fears.* Cassette recordings. Chicago: Institute for Human Development, 1973.

✓*Maultsby, M. C., Jr. *Help Yourself to Happiness.* New York: Institute for Rational Living, 1975.

✓*Maultsby, M. C., Jr. *A Million Dollars for Your Hangover.* Lexington, Ky.: Rational Self-Help Books, 1979.

✓*Maultsby, M. C., Jr. & Ellis, A. *Technique For Using Rational Emotive Imagery.* New York; Institute for Rational Living, 1974.

✓*Maultsby, M. C., Jr. & Hendricks, A. *Cartoon Booklets.* Lexington, Ky.: Rational Behavior Training Center, 1974.

✓*McMullin, R., & Casey, B. *Talk Sense to Yourself.* Champaign, Ill.: Research Press, 1975.

✓McMullin, R. *Straight Talk to Parents.* Lakewood, Colo.: Counseling Research Institute, 1978.

McMullin, R., & Giles, T. R. *Cognitive-behavior Therapy: A Restructuring Approach.* New York: Grune and Stratton, 1981.

Moreno, J. L. *Theater of Spontaneity.* Beacon, N.Y.: Beacon House, 1947.

Morris, K. T., & Kanitz, J. M. *Rational-emotive Therapy.* Boston: Houghton Mifflin, 1975.

Novaco, R. W. *Anger Control.* Lexington, Mass.: Lexington Books, 1975.

O'Connell, W. E. Adlerian Action Therapy Technique. *Journal of Individual Psychology,* 1972, 28, 184-191.

✓*Paris, C., & Casey, B. *Project You.* Denver: Institute of Living Skills, 1978.

Perls, F. C. *Gestalt Therapy Verbatim.* New York: Delta, 1969.

Popper, K. R. *Objective Knowledge.* London: Oxford University Press, 1972.

✓*Powell, J. *Fully Human, Fully Alive.* Niles, Ill.: Argus, 1976.

Raimy, V. *Misunderstandings of Self.* San Francisco: Jossey-Bass, 1975.

Rogers, C. R. *On Becoming a Person.* Boston: Houghton Mifflin, 1961.

Rotter, J. B. *Social Learning and Clinical Psychology.* Englewood Cliffs, N.J.: Prentice-Hall, 1954.

✓Russell, B. *Conquest of Happiness,* New York: Bantam, 1969.

Schacter, S. *Emotion, Obesity and Crime.* New York: Academic Press, 1971.

Salter, A. *Conditioned Reflex Therapy.* New York: Creative Age, 1949.

✓Shibles, W. *Emotion.* Whitewater, Wisc.: Language Press, 1974.

✓Silverstein, L. *Consider the Alternative.* Minneapolis, Minn.: CompCare, 1977.

Singer, J. L. *Imagery and Daydream Methods of Psychotherapy and Behavior Modification.* New York: Academic Press, 1974.

Skinner, B. F. *Beyond Freedom and Dignity.* New York: Knopf, 1971.

Stampfl, T. G., & Levis, D. J. *Phobic Patients: Treatment With the Learning Approach of Implosive Therapy. Voices,* 1967, 3, 23-27.

✓Thoresen, E. *Handling Rejection.* Clearwater, Fla. Living Free Publishing, 1978.

Thorne, F. C. *Principles of Personality Counseling.* Brandon, Vt.: Journal of Clinical Psychology Press, 1950.

✓Tillich, P. *The Courage to Be.* New York: Oxford, 1953.

Tosi, D. J. *Youth: Toward Personal Growth, a Rational-Emotive Approach.* Columbus, Ohio: Merrill, 1974.

✓*Walen, S., DiGiuseppe, R., & Wessler, R. *A Practitioner's Guide to Rational-Emotive Therapy.* New York: Oxford, 1980.

✓*Waters, V. *Color Us Rational.* New York; Institute for Rational Living, 1980.

✓*Waters, V. *Rational Stories for Children.* New York: Institute for Rational Living, 1981.

Watzlawack, P., Weakland, J., & Firsch, R. *Change.* New York: Norton, 1974.

✓Watson, D.L., & Tharp, R.G. *Self-Directed Behavior.* 3rd Edition. Monterey, Calif.: Brooks/Cole, 1981.

✓Weekes, C. *Hope and Help For Your Nerves.* New York: Hawthorn, 1969.

✓*Wessler, R. *Anxiety and Tension: How to Suffer Less.* Cassette recording. New York: Institute for Rational Living, 1981.

✓*Wessler, R. *Rational-Emotive Therapy Session with a Man with Low Self-Acceptance and Assertiveness Problems.* Video cassette. New York: Institute for Rational Living, 1982.

✓*Wessler, R. *Rational-Emotive Therapy Session with a Female College Student with Social Anxiety.* Video cassette. New York: Institute for Rational Living, 1982.

✓*Wessler, R., & Wessler, R. *The Principles and Practice of Rational-Emotive Therapy.* San Francisco: Jossey-Bass, 1980.

✓*Wolfe, J.L. *Rational-Emotive Therapy and Women's Problems.* Cassette recording. New York: Institute for Rational Living, 1974.

✓*Wolfe, J.L. Rational-Emotive Therapy as an Effective Feminist Therapy. *Rational Living,* 1976, *11*(1), 2-7. Reprinted: New York: Institute for Rational Living, 1976.

✓*Wolfe, J.L., & Brand, E., Eds. *Twenty Years of Rational Therapy.* New York: Institute for Rational Living, 1977.

Wolfe, J.L., & Fodor, I.G. Modifying Assertive Behavior in Women: A Comparison of Three Approaches. *Behavior Therapy,* 1977, 8, 567-574.

Wolpe, J. *The Practice of Behavior Therapy.* New York: Pergamon, 1982.

✓*Young, H.S. *A Rational Counseling Primer.* New York: Institute for Rational Living, 1974.

✓Yurick, J.C. *If It Weren't for Stupid People . . . We'd All Be Broke!!* Maitland, Fla.: Author, 1981.

SAMPLE RATIONAL SELF HELP FORM

Institute for Rational-Emotive Therapy   45 East 65th Street, New York 10021

(A) ACTIVATING EXPERIENCES (OR EVENTS)

(B) BELIEFS ABOUT YOUR ACTIVATING EXPERIENCES

(C) CONSEQUENCES OF YOUR BELIEFS ABOUT ACTIVATING EXPERIENCES

(rB) rational Beliefs (your wants or desires)

How unfortunate that they backed out!
I don't like their behavior.
I wish they had kept their promise.
How annoying and irritating!
I'll try to get the money elsewhere, but will find this quite a hassle.

(iB) irrational Beliefs

1. *How awful for them to act that way!*
2. *I can't stand their unfairness!*
3. *They should have lent me the money!*
4. *Because they didn't do what they should, that makes them rotten people!*
5. *People will always treat me unfairly like this! How horrible!*

(A) ACTIVATING EXPERIENCES

My mother and father promised to lend me money and for no good reason refused to go through with their promise.

(deC) desirable emotional Consequences (appropriate bad feelings)

Frustration and annoyance. Sorrow and regret.
Determination to help change parents' attitudes.

(dbC) desirable behavioral Consequences (desirable behavior)

Continued attempts to persuade parents to change.
Attempts to get the money in other ways.

(ueC) undesirable emotional Consequences (inappropriate feelings)

I felt angry; I hated my parents. I felt depressed.

(ubC) undesirable behavioral Consequences (undesirable behaviors)

I screamed at my parents.
I refused to consider other ways of getting the money.
I pouted and sulked.

(D) DISPUTING OR DEBATING YOUR IRRATIONAL BELIEFS
(state this in the form of questions)

1. *What makes it awful for them to act that way?*
2. *Why can't I stand their unfairness?*
3. *What evidence exists that they should have lent me the money?*
4. *How does their unfair treatment of me make them rotten people?*
5. *How do I know people will always treat me unfairly? And must I view it as horrible if they do?*

(E) EFFECTS OF DISPUTING OR DEBATING YOUR IRRATIONAL BELIEFS

(cE) cognitive Effects of disputing (similar to rational beliefs)

1. *Nothing makes it awful, but only inconvenient for them to act that way.*
2. *I can stand their unfairness; though I'll never like it.*
3. *I can find no evidence that they should have kept their promise to me though I would have found it very nice if they did.*
4. *Their unfairness doesn't make them rotten people, but merely people who have acted rottenly to me in this respect.*
5. *People won't always treat me unfairly—though they may often do so. And if they do, tough! It won't kill me!*

(eE) emotional Effects (appropriate feelings)

I felt irritated and annoyed but not angry.
I felt very disappointed and concerned but not depressed.
I still basically loved my parents but hated some of their traits.
I felt determined to find other ways of raising the money.

(bE) behavioral Effects (desirable behaviors)

I spoke to my parents about my feelings of disappointment and irritation.
I attempted to persuade them to change.
I investigated other means of raising money.

© 1976 by the Institute for Rational Living, Inc., 45 East 65th Street, New York, N.Y. 10021

RATIONAL SELF HELP FORM

Institute for Rational-Emotive Therapy   45 East 65th Street, New York 10021

INSTRUCTIONS: Please fill out the **ueC** section (undesirable emotional Consequences) and the **ubC** section (undesirable behavioral Consequences) **first.**
Then fill out all the A-B-C-D-E's. PLEASE PRINT LEGIBLY. BE BRIEF!

A ACTIVATING EXPERIENCES (OR EVENTS)

....
....
....
....
....
....
....

B BELIEFS ABOUT YOUR ACTIVATING EXPERIENCES

rB rational Beliefs (your wants or desires)

....
....
....
....

iB Irrational Beliefs (your demands or commands)

....
....
....
....

C CONSEQUENCES OF YOUR BELIEFS ABOUT ACTIVATING EXPERIENCES

deC desirable emotional Consequences (appropriate bad feelings)

....

dbC desirable behavioral Consequences (desirable behaviors)

....

ueC undesirable emotional Consequences (inappropriate feelings)

....

ubC undesirable behavioral Consequences (undesirable behaviors)

....

D DISPUTING OR DEBATING YOUR IRRATIONAL BELIEFS
(State this in the form of questions)

....
....
....
....
....
....

E EFFECTS OF DISPUTING OR DEBATING YOUR IRRATIONAL BELIEFS

cE cognitive Effects of disputing (similar to rational beliefs)

....
....
....
....
....
....

eE emotional Effects (appropriate feelings)

....
....
....
....

bE behavioral Effects (desirable behaviors)

....
....
....
....

1. FOLLOW-UP. What new GOALS would I now like to work on? ....

....

....

....

What specific ACTIONS would I now like to take? ....

....

....

2. How soon after feeling or noting your undesirable emotional CONSEQUENCES (ueC's) or your undesirable behavorial CONSEQUENCES (ubC's) of your irrational BELIEFS (iB's) did you look for these iB's and DISPUTE them? ....

....

....

How vigorously did you dispute them? ....

....

If you didn't dispute them, why did you not do so? ....

....

3. Specific HOMEWORK ASSIGNMENT(S) given you by your therapist, your group or yourself: ....

....

....

4. What did you actually do to carry out the assignment(s)? ....

....

5. How many times have you actually worked at your homework assignments during the past week? ....

...·..

6. How many times have you actually worked at DISPUTING your irrational BELIEFS during the past week? ....

....

7. Things you would now like to discuss with your therapist or group ....

....

....

© 1976 by the Institute for Rational Living, Inc., 45 East 65th Street, New York, N.Y. 10021

How You Can Have Confidence and Power in Dealing with People

A major key to success in your business and personal life is knowing how to deal with people. In fact, studies have shown that knowing how to deal with people is 85 to 90 percent of business and professional success, and 90 to 95 percent of personal happiness.

Now here's some great news. Dealing effectively with people is a skill you can learn, just as you learned to ride a bicycle, drive an automobile, or play the piano.

Discover how you can get what you want and be the way you want to be by tapping into your hidden assets. Assets you may not even realize you have. Assets that can transform an ordinary person into an extraordinary one. Assets that can give you more confidence and personal power than you ever thought possible.

Find out how to

- Feel confident in any business or social situation
- Win others to your way of thinking
- Understand and get along with people
- Make it easy for people to like you
- Create a positive and lasting impression
- Help others feel comfortable and friendly — instantly
- Make new friends and keep them
- Find love and build relationships that work

The way you lived yesterday determined your today. But the way you live today will determine your tomorrow. Every day is a new opportunity to become the way you want to be and to have your life become what you want it to be.

Take the first step toward becoming all you're capable of being. Read Marcia Grad's book *Charisma*, which teaches a proven step-by-step plan to help anyone develop the ultimate in personal power. Then get ready for an incredible adventure that will change you and your life forever.

Available wherever books are sold or send $10.00 (CA res. $10.83) plus $2.00 S/H to Wilshire Book Co., 9731 Variel Avenue, Chatsworth, California 91311-4315

For our complete catalog, visit our Web site at www.mpowers.com.

Books by Albert Ellis, Ph.D.

SEX WITHOUT GUILT

1. New Light on Masturbation 2. Thoughts on Petting 3. On Premarital Sex 4. Adultery: Pros & Cons 5. The Justification of Sex Without Love 6. Why Americans Are So Fearful of Sex 7. Adventures with Sex Censorship 8. How Males Contribute to Female Frigidity 9. Sexual Inadequacy in the Male 10. When Are We Going to Quit Stalling About Sex Education? 11. How American Women Are Driving American Males Into Homosexuality 12. Another Look at Sexual Abnormality 13. On the Myths About Love 14. Sex Fascism 15. The Right to Sex Enjoyment   192 Pages . . . $7.00

A GUIDE TO SUCCESSFUL MARRIAGE

1. Modern Marriage: Hotbed of Neurosis 2. Factors Causing Marital Disturbance 3. Gauging Marital Compatibility 4. Problem Solving in Marriage 5. Can We Be Intelligent About Marriage? 6. Love or Infatuation? 7. To Marry or Not to Marry 8. Sexual Preparation for Marriage 9. Impotence in the Male 10. Frigidity in the Female 11. Sex "Excess" 12. Controlling Sex Impulses 13. Non-monogamous Desires 14. Communication in Marriage 15. Children 16. In-laws 17. Marital Incompatibility versus Neurosis 18. Divorce 19. Succeeding in Marriage   304 Pages . . . $10.00

HOW TO RAISE AN EMOTIONALLY HEALTHY, HAPPY CHILD

1. Neurotics Are Born As Well As Made 2. What Is a Neurotic Child? 3. Helping Children Overcome Fears and Anxieties 4. Helping Children with Problems of Achievement 5. Helping Children Overcome Hostility 6. Helping Children Become Self-Disciplined 7. Helping Children with Sex Problems 8. Helping Children with conduct Problems 9. Helping Children with Personal Behavior Problems 10. How to Live with a Neurotic Child and Like It.   256 Pages . . . $10.00

A GUIDE TO RATIONAL LIVING

1. How Far Can You Go with Self-therapy. 2. You Largely Feel the Way You Think 3. Feeling Well by Thinking Straight 4. How You Create Your Feelings 5. Thinking Yourself Out of Emotional Disturbances 6. Recognizing and Reducing Neurotic Behavior 7. Overcoming the Influences of the Past 8. Is Reason Always Reasonable? 9. Refusing to Feel Desperately Unhappy 10. Tackling Your Dire Need for Approval 11. Reducing Your Dire Fears of Failure 12. How to Start Blaming and Start Living 13. How to Feel Frustrated but not Depressed or Enraged. 14. Controlling Your Own Emotional Destiny 15. Conquering Anxiety and Panic 16. Acquiring Self-discipline 17. Rewriting Your Personal History 18. Accepting and Coping with the Grim Facts of Life 19. Overcoming Inertia and Getting Creatively Absorbed   304 Pages . . . $15.00

HOW TO LIVE WITH A NEUROTIC

1. The Possibility of Helping Troubled People 2. How to Recognize a Person with Emotional Disturbance 3. How Emotional Disturbances Originate 4. Some Basic Factors in Emotional Upsets 5. How to Help a "Neurotic" Overcome Disturbance 6. How to Live with a Person Who Remains Neurotic 7. How to Live with Yourself though You Fail to Help a "Neurotic"   160 Pages . . . $10.00

GROWTH THROUGH REASON

1. Introduction 2. The Case of the Black and Silver Masochist 3. Rational-Emotive Therapy with a Culturally Deprived Teenager 4. A Young Male Who Is Afraid of Becoming a Fixed Homosexual 5. A Young Woman with Feelings of Depression 6. A Husband and Wife Who Have Not Had Intercourse During Thirteen Years of Marriage 7. A Relapsed Client with Severe Phobic Reactions   294 Pages . . . $10.00

Available wherever books are sold or from the publisher.
Please add $2.00 shipping and handling for each book ordered.
Wilshire Book Company
9731 Variel Avenue, Chatsworth, California 91311-4315

An Unforgettable Treasure
Of Laughter and Wisdom

THE KNIGHT IN RUSTY ARMOR

2 MILLION COPIES SOLD WORLDWIDE

This story is guaranteed to captivate your imagination as it helps
you discover the secret of what is most important in life. It's a
delightful tale of a desperate knight in search of his true self.

The Knight in Rusty Armor by Robert Fisher is one of
Wilshire Book Company's most popular titles. It's available in
numerous languages and has become an international bestseller.

Join the knight as he faces a life-changing dilemma upon
discovering that he is trapped in his armor, just as we may be
trapped in *our* armor—an invisible one we put on to protect ourselves from others and from various aspects of life.

As the knight searches for a way to free himself, he receives
guidance from the wise sage Merlin the Magician, who
encourages him to embark on the most difficult crusade of his
life. The knight takes up the challenge and travels the Path of
Truth, where he meets his real self for the first time and
confronts the Universal Truths that govern his life—and ours.

The knight's journey reflects our own, filled with hope and
despair, belief and disillusionment, laughter and tears. His
insights become our insights as we follow along on his intrigu-
ing adventure of self-discovery. Anyone who has ever struggled
with the meaning of life and love will discover profound wisdom
and truth as this unique fantasy unfolds.

The Knight in Rusty Armor will expand your mind, touch
your heart, and nourish your soul.

Available wherever books are sold or send $7.00 (CA res. $7.58) plus $2.00
S/H to Wilshire Book Co., 9731 Variel Avenue, Chatsworth, California 91311-4315

THE KNIGHT IN RUSTY ARMOR MUSIC TAPE

Treat yourself to the soundtrack of the musical production of
The Knight in Rusty Armor, narrated by Robert Fisher.

Send $5.00 (CA residents $5.41) to Wilshire Book Company.

For our complete catalog, visit our Web site at www.mpowers.com.

I invite you to meet an extraordinary princess and accompany her on an enlightening journey. You will laugh with her and cry with her, learn with her and grow with her . . . and she will become a dear friend you will never forget.

Marcia Grad Powers

1 MILLION COPIES SOLD WORLDWIDE

The Princess Who Believed in Fairy Tales

"Here is a very special book that will guide you lovingly into a new way of thinking about yourself and your life so that the future will be filled with hope and love and song."

OG MANDINO
Author, *The Greatest Salesman in the World*

The Princess Who Believed in Fairy Tales by Marcia Grad is a personal growth book of the rarest kind. It's a delightful, humor-filled story you will experience so deeply that it can literally change your feelings about yourself, your relationships, and your life.

The princess's journey of self-discovery on the Path of Truth is an eye-opening, inspiring, empowering psychological and spiritual journey that symbolizes the one we all take through life as we separate illusion from reality, come to terms with our childhood dreams and pain, and discover who we really are and how life works.

If you have struggled with childhood pain, with feelings of not being good enough, with the loss of your dreams, or if you have been disappointed in your relationships, this book will prove to you that happy endings—and new beginnings—are always possible. Or, if you simply wish to get closer to your own truth, the princess will guide you.

The universal appeal of this book has resulted in its translation into numerous languages.

Excerpts from Readers' Heartfelt Letters

"*The Princess* is truly a gem! Though I've read a zillion self-help and spiritual books, I got more out of this one than from any other one I've ever read. It is just too illuminating and full of wisdom to ever be able to thank you enough. The friends and family I've given copies to have raved about it."

"*The Princess* is powerful, insightful, and beautifully written. I am seventy years old and have seldom encountered greater wisdom. I've been waiting to read this book my entire life. You are a psychologist, a guru, a saint, and an angel all wrapped up into one. I thank you with all my heart."

Available wherever books are sold or send $12.00 (CA res. $12.99) plus $2.00 S/H to Wilshire Book Co., 9731 Variel Avenue, Chatsworth, California 91311-4315

For our complete catalog, visit our Web site at www.mpowers.com.

Treat Yourself to This Fun, Inspirational Book and Discover How to
Find Happiness and Serenity . . . No Matter What Life Dishes Out

The Dragon Slayer
With a Heavy Heart

*This new book by bestselling author Marcia Powers promises to be
one of the most important you will ever read—and one of the most
entertaining, uplifting, and memorable.*

*It brings the Serenity Prayer—which for years has been the guiding
light of 12-step programs worldwide—to everyone . . . and teaches
both new and longtime devotees how to apply it most effectively to
their lives.*

Sometimes things happen we wish hadn't. Sometimes things *don't*
happen we wish *would*. In the course of living, problems arise, both
big and small. We might wish our past had been different or that *we*
could be different. We struggle through disappointments and
frustrations, losses and other painful experiences.

As hard as we may try to be strong, to have a good attitude, not to
let things get us down, we don't always succeed. We get upset. We
worry. We feel stressed. We get depressed. We get angry. We do the
best we can and wait for things to *get* better so we can *feel* better. In
the meantime, our hearts may grow heavy . . . perhaps very heavy.

That's what happened to Duke the Dragon Slayer. In fact, *his*
heart grew *so* heavy with all that was wrong, with all that was not the
way it should be, with all that was unfair, that he became desperate to
lighten it—and set forth on the Path of Serenity to find out how.

Accompany Duke on this life-changing adventure. His guides will
be your guides. His answers will be your answers. His tools will be
your tools. His success will be your success. And by the time he is
heading home, both Duke and you will know how to take life's inevitable lumps and bumps in stride—and find happiness and serenity
anytime . . . even when you really, REALLY wish some things were
different.

"A BEAUTIFUL, EXCEPTIONALLY WELL-WRITTEN STORY THAT CAN HELP
EVERYONE TO BECOME EMOTIONALLY STRONGER AND BETTER ABLE TO
COPE WITH ADVERSITY."   Albert Ellis, Ph.D.
President, Albert Ellis Institute
Author of *A Guide to Rational Living*

Available wherever books are sold or send $12.00 (CA res. $12.99) plus $2.00 S/H
to Wilshire Book Co., 9731 Variel Avenue, Chatsworth, CA 91311-4315.

For our complete catalog, visit our Web site at www.mpowers.com.